THEORIES OF DELINQUENCY

THEORIES OF DELINQUENCY

An Examination of Explanations
of Delinquent Behavior

Donald J. Shoemaker
**Virginia Polytechnic Institute
and State University**

New York   Oxford
OXFORD UNIVERSITY PRESS
1984

Copyright © 1984 by Oxford University Press, Inc.

Library of Congress Cataloging in Publication Data

Shoemaker, Donald J.
  Theories of delinquency.

  Includes index.
  1. Juvenile delinquency.   I. Title.
AV9069.S525   1984   364.3'6   83-11426
ISBN 0-19-503391-4

Printing (last digit):   9 8 7 6 5 4

Printed in the United States of America

To my mother and in memory of my father

FOREWORD

The world of science, of which social science is a part, albeit often with disclaimers, is no longer as concerned with ultimate origins or beginnings as was true in the century of Darwin, but it has not abandoned its search for causal explanations. If anything, causes have assumed the central stage in scientific inquiry, as the twentieth century abandoned belief in miracles, supernaturalism, angels, and demons, except in the most symbolic and metaphoric sense. That monosyllabic question that appears at times to be the entire vocabulary of children—Why?—guides us when it does not plague us.

Thus it is with crime, and with the junior partner of crime: the delinquent behavior of young people, which can range from the annoying, mischievous, and unruly rascality of the frequently lovable rogue to the vicious, violent, and persistent criminality of the most unlovable, and often unloved, boy or girl. If efforts to explain crime have been abundant, often cyclical, those that seek to answer the same "Why?" for juvenile delinquency are not less so. In fact, many of the major theories of crime that have been promulgated appear to be more applicable to youthful than to adult misbehavior: surely this would be the case with a theory that almost dominated American criminology for several decades, Edwin Sutherland's differential association, with its emphasis on peer group influence.

Would it not, in fact, be self-evident, inevitable, even axiomatic to some, that a criminological theory—a study of the causes, including the origins, of crime (to use the expression of the McCords)—must be reflective of an assessment of juvenile delinquency? For is not the child the father of the man, and where is one to locate the beginnings of the criminality of adults if not in their youth and childhood (or infancy, too, as the Freudians would insist, but that is something else entirely, because although these would be the roots of antisocial adults, at least for those who adhere to Freudian hermeneutics, they would not be manifestations of it).

As I look at the vast social science literature on crime and delinquency, it strikes me as more than incidental that it is richer in works that focus on juvenile delinquency than adult criminology. This would include the ecological studies of Shaw and McKay, the matched samples of the Gluecks, the largely psychological or perhaps psychosocial studies of Healy, the methodological analyses of Hirschi and Selvin, and such elegant adumbrations, speculative but not the less insightful, as Cohen's *Delinquent Boys*, Cloward and Ohlin's *Delinquency and Opportunity*, and Matza's *Delinquency and Drift*, among many others. It is surely worthy of consideration to note that this body of literature overshadows the corresponding material concerned with adult lawbreaking.

There appear to be several reasons for the concentration of empirical, descriptive, and theoretical studies concerning society's younger rather than its older mischief makers (a somewhat mild epithet for many, it should be admitted).

At the outset, youngsters are our center of hope. They are our responsibility, our children, the people that we, the adults, have created and shaped and fashioned. They are, or are supposed to be, in the words of Ralph Waldo Emerson, the nobility of the land. And in a land that recognizes no other nobility, at least in its official stance, we look to the youth. There is a cult of youth, a belief that beauty and strength are concentrated in a few years of a brief age span, and that one is over-the-hill, or at least on the road to decline, only a short time after maturity. Death at an early age, the apt phrase that describes the bleak hopelessness of some of the very young, may be said also to describe the widely shared attitudes that characterize those no longer children or adolescents. Even as people relinquish their once strongly held beliefs and illusions of pristine childhood, they continue to idolize youth—its beauty and energy and strength. Yet, something is wrong: a nation cannot worship at the temple of youth and at the same time look with fear and disdain at those they label "teenagers" while they make that word synonymous with raucous, noisy, ungovernable, and even delinquent, if not criminal.

The young are not only our future, they are our present, in a sense and to a degree that cannot be said of those who have reached maturity and yet are still in need of care and aid. All juveniles, not only delinquents, are "persons in need of supervision," to use the now terrible and damning phrase that has become part of the juvenile justice system. When they become what society cannot or will not tolerate, it seems clear on the face of it that supervision must somewhere have broken down, which means, in short, that we, the elders, have failed. Not only as parents, as teachers, as police officers, but as a community and as a society. Faced with this specter, people often turn away from the awesome reality of their own responsibility for a creation that must sometimes seem monstrous. In short, none of us wants to be Frankenstein, although some may believe that it is better than being the monster that he created.

There are other reasons for the relative richness of delinquency theory and research, and for the deep concern with youthful crime. A disproportionate part of America's crime problem can be laid at the door of the young. According to the U.S. Census of 1980, those between the ages of 15 and 19 constituted 9.4 percent of the total population, but when we turn to the FBI official statistics for arrests involving the eight crimes used to make up an index of serious criminality in the United States, this age group accounts for just about twice that number. However, the figures here are misleading, although a public that is fed this information is not always aware of this. One should certainly remove from the general population with which adolescents are compared those 9 years and younger, as well as those 75 years and over. This would bring the

15- to 19-year-olds up to about 11.3 percent of the total populace, and yet they continue to be overrepresented in arrests, not only for the index crimes, but for crimes in general. And when only violent index crimes are counted, the disproportionate representation of the youth is even more striking.

By the mid-thirties, participation in crime goes into a decline; the street criminal is about burned out. (White-collar, corporate, organized, computer, and political crimes, those most important categories, are never the domain of the adolescent.) Furthermore, while many delinquent and crime-oriented youth have relinquished the criminal life for job, family, and a life-style that is called "going straight" by the time they are in their twenties, those in that decade or the following one who are pursuing the road in and out of violence, arrests, courtroom encounters, jails, release, and prisons, in a recurrent and patterned manner, appear to have launched their lawbreaking careers in their teens (perhaps earlier).

Of course, it is entirely possible that the Uniform Crime Reports issued by the FBI do not accurately reflect youthful crime, but only youthful arrest rates, for two opposing reasons that probably do not just neatly cancel out each other. It is widely assumed that youth are more likely to be apprehended than adults committing similar crimes: they do not have the wherewithal, the experience, to escape arrest. But if arrested, by contrast, they may more frequently be diverted to community centers, and thus never appear in the statistics: in short, they may be apprehended, but not officially booked as arrested.

From an examination of the relatively high participation of youth in crime, people conclude that a successful attack on juvenile delinquency will not only reduce the predatory activities that presently plague us, but will bring benefits in the years ahead, in the form of reduced crime rates a decade or two in the future. If these are accurate figures and assumptions, it is no wonder, then, that public, journalistic, political, and criminological attention becomes focused on youth.

When criminologists have turned their attention to youth, they have discovered a rich and highly researchable field of study awaiting them. It is sometimes said—not without irony, I would hope—that the two best populations for careful examination of behavior appear to be youths and rats, for both are captive groups in which 100 percent samples and excellent controls are not difficult to come by. Porterfield launched his self-report studies with young people, for where else could he have so easily and so inexpensively located a cross section of an age cohort? Indeed, almost all self-report studies of lawbreaking activities since have concentrated on young people. Countless college professors have asked their students (anonymously, I hope) of their background in deviant activities, which in the end means their participation in acts of juvenile delinquency. Correlations of violent and other criminal activity with IQ scores, school achievement, and home background are far easier to make with young people than with older people. The massive study of Wolfgang, Figlio, and Sellin, in which an entire age cohort in a large city was followed to study brushes with the law, recidivism, and serious criminality, would have been far more difficult to carry out with older people. Youths seem to lend themselves more easily to studies that determine the effectiveness of various intervention programs or of various thera-peutic techniques; and the young can be followed in the years of their maturity to determine what occurred in their lives as a result of different factors.

Out of the concerns of society, on the one hand, and oppor-tunities for study, on the other, has come rich research, the monographs, essays, descriptions, and theories that punctuate the literature on juvenile delinquency. These works are numerous, sometimes apparently contradictory, at other times mutually complementary, and their explanatory values are not always readily seen. With this medley of material at hand, there was surely a need to sit back, recapitulate, and take a look at the vista that was jointly created by the youths themselves and the adult scholars. This is precisely what Donald Shoemaker has done, with ex-cellence, perceptivity, willingness to listen, and eagerness to be skeptical.

The author of this book has taken the theories, perspectives, orientations, and emphases that have been found in the literature on delinquency and has organized his analysis around some recurrent themes. He has sought to discover the underlying assumptions of a theory, the key terms and how the theory builders have used and defined them, the empirical testing that tends to validate or disconfirm the theory, and from this he offers a summary and assessment of his own.

Reading this book, one can only be surprised that the task that Shoemaker set out for himself was not attempted before. There is a need for this work, precisely because of the wealth of material from which it draws. That the task of sifting through, analyzing, summarizing, and critically assessing the corpus of social science was done so well is something for which we will all be grateful and long indebted to the author.

Furthermore, it appears that the work comes at an excellent moment, for two reasons: first, and most obvious, because of public agitation over crime generally, and youthful depredations more specifically; second, because a discipline that has been offered such a wealth of facts, studies, insights, perspectives, and theories should stop to catch its breath, so to speak, to look over its prized holdings, to take inventory, so that it can synthesize, retain, and discard. It is difficult to imagine any reader of this book failing to be enthusiastic about the manner in which Donald Shoemaker has accomplished this task.

Now I have said enough. Turn the page and you will be in for a scholarly treatise and a personal treat.

City University of New York   Edward Sagarin
November 1983

ACKNOWLEDGMENTS

The credit for writing a book can often be spread among a number of people who have influenced the author. In my case, several individuals have contributed, both indirectly and directly, to the publication of this book.

I first would like to thank some of my mentors who have helped shape my ideas and ideals. Foremost among these is Clifton Bryant, mentor and valued colleague, without whose efforts and encouragement I would have never embarked on an academic career. Beyond this, it was Cliff's inspiration which spawned the topic and scope of the present book.

I would also like to express appreciation to Imogene Dean, Jay Lowe, the late Raymond Payne, and especially Donald South for their valued contributions to my formal introduction to crime and delinquency as a field of inquiry. Their advice and teachings have continued to influence my professional and personal values.

Of course, over the years many students have indirectly contributed to this book, through their comments and questions in courses dealing with the subjects of crime and delinquency. More recently, LeGrande Gardner and Barbara Zaitzow have contributed many useful comments and suggestions regarding the manuscript.

Among those who have contributed directly to this book, I would like to express my deepest gratitude to Edward Sagarin, whose continual encouragement and advice have proven more invaluable than I ever imagined.

Many other colleagues have contributed useful ideas and information and sound advice for the book. Besides the anonymous reviewers, I would like to recognize the following for their willingness to help a colleague: Simon Dinitz, Paul Friday, Mike Hughes, Julian Roebuck, Richard Schuster, and especially Jim Skipper.

The editorial staff at Oxford University Press has been most helpful with the editing and technical advising, which are so important in the production of a manuscript. In particular, the work and advice of Susan Rabiner, Naomi Schneider, and Kim Lewis have been most helpful. Also, Spencer Carr, formerly of Oxford, gave vital encouragement and support to the project, from its earliest stages.

I would also like to express appreciation to the secretarial staff at Virginia Tech who worked on the numerous drafts of the book—Debbie Rhea, Sherri McGuyer, and especially Pat Baker.

Lastly, I want to acknowledge my deepest appreciation for the unwavering cooperation, confidence, and encouragement I have received throughout the entire project from my dear wife Lynda and through her our children, Kim and Holly.

Blacksburg, Virginia   D. J. S.
December 1983

CONTENTS

1 EXPLANATIONS OF DELINQUENCY   3
   The Problem of Delinquency   3
   The Issue of Causality   6
   What Is a Theory?   8
   Verification of Theories   9
   The Plan of This Book   10

2 BIOLOGICAL AND BIOSOCIAL
   EXPLANATIONS   13
   Historical Overview   13
   Generic Assumptions   13
   Somatotypes and Delinquency   15
      Specific Assumption   15
      Key Concept   15
      Discussion   15
      Evaluation   19
   Inheritance and Delinquency   20
      Specific Assumption   20
      Key Concept   20
      Discussion   20
      Evaluation   24
   Emerging Trends in Biological Explanations
   of Delinquency   25
      The Biochemical Approach   26
      Evaluation   27

Learning Disabilities and Delinquency   28
Evaluation   30
Conditionability and Delinquency   31
Evaluation   32
Summary   35

3   PSYCHOLOGICAL THEORIES   40
Historical Overview   40
Generic Assumptions   41
Intelligence and Delinquency   42
Specific Assumptions   42
Key Concept   43
Discussion   44
Evaluation   48
The Psychiatric-Psychoanalytic Approach   49
Specific Assumptions   49
Key Concepts   50
Discussion   51
Evaluation   53
General Personality Characteristics   55
Specific Assumptions   55
Key Concept   56
Discussion   56
A Note on Psychopathy   59
Evaluation   61
Summary   64

4   SOCIAL DISORGANIZATION AND ANOMIE   70
Historical Overview   70
Generic Assumptions   71
Social Disorganization   72
Specific Assumptions   72
Key Concepts   73
Discussion: The Work of Shaw and McKay   74
Evaluation   80
Anomie and Delinquency: Discontinuities in Society   86
Specific Assumptions   86
Key Concepts   87
Discussion   87

Evaluation   91
Summary   95

5   LOWER-CLASS-BASED THEORIES OF
    DELINQUENCY   100
    Historical Overview and Generic Assumptions   100
    Cohen and the Middle-Class Measuring Rod   102
        Specific Assumptions   102
        Key Concepts   102
        Discussion   103
        Evaluation   105
    Cloward and Ohlin's Theory of Differential
    Opportunity Structure   109
        Specific Assumptions   109
        Key Concepts   109
        Discussion   110
        Evaluation   114
    Miller's Theory of Lower-Class Culture and
    Delinquency   119
        Specific Assumptions   119
        Key Concepts   119
        Discussion   120
        Evaluation   122
    Summary   125

6   INTERPERSONAL AND SITUATIONAL
    EXPLANATIONS   132
    Historical Overview   132
    Generic Assumptions   133
    Differential Association   134
        Specific Assumptions   134
        Key Concepts   135
        Discussion   136
        Evaluation   139
    Drift and Delinquency   143
        Specific Assumptions   143
        Key Concepts   143
        Discussion   144
        Evaluation   146
    Summary   148

7   CONTROL THEORIES   152
     Historical Overview   152
     Generic Assumptions   153
     Personal Controls   155
        Psychoanalysis Revisited   155
        Containment Theory   155
        Specific Assumptions   156
        Key Concepts   156
        Discussion   156
        Evaluation   158
     Social Controls—The Social Bond   161
        Specific Assumptions   161
        Key Concept   161
        Discussion   161
        Evaluation   162
           Religion and Delinquency   163
           Family Factors   167
           Broken Homes   168
           Family Relationships   170
           School Experiences and Delinquency   172
           Other Considerations   173
     Summary   175

8   LABELING THEORY   180
     Historical Overview   180
     Generic Assumptions   181
     Key Concepts   182
     Discussion   183
     Evaluation   185
        Labeling and Self-Concept   186
        Labeling and Delinquent Behavior   191
     Summary   194

9   THE RADICAL THEORY OF
     DELINQUENCY   199
     Historical Overview   199
     Basic Assumptions   201
     Key Concepts   202
     Discussion   202

Evaluation   205
Summary   211

10 FEMALE DELINQUENCY   218
    Historical Overview   218
    Basic Biological and Psychological Approaches   219
    Sex Roles and Delinquency   222
    Women's Emancipation   225
    Evaluation   227
    Summary   233

11 MIDDLE-CLASS DELINQUENCY   238
    Historical Overview   238
    Youth Culture and Middle-Class Delinquency   240
    Male Anxiety and the Middle-Class Delinquent   244
    Diffusion of Lower-Class Culture   245
    Status Inconsistency and Social Mobility   246
    Evaluation   248
    Summary   252

12 DELINQUENCY THEORY: ANALYSIS AND
    SYNTHESIS   255
    Individualistic Explanations: Biological and
    Psychological   255
    Social Disorganization and Anomie   257
    Subcultural Explanations   258
    Interpersonal and Situational Explanations   259
    Control Theories   260
    Societal Reaction: The Labeling Approach   261
    Inequality and Oppression as Causes of Delinquency:
    Conflict and Radical Theory   263
    Where Do We Stand? A Synthesis   264
       Synthesis of Theories: An Example   266

    AUTHOR INDEX   271
    SUBJECT INDEX   278

THEORIES OF DELINQUENCY

1

EXPLANATIONS OF DELINQUENCY

THE PROBLEM OF DELINQUENCY

Practically no day passes without the appearance of some news item carrying a story of a crime committed by youth. From shoplifting to murder, the accounts continue to appear. A quick glance at national crime statistics indicates that youngsters under 18 are disproportionately involved in major crimes of theft and violence. Criminal behavior of juveniles involves all types of activity, and it is committed by youth from all backgrounds. In some activities, such as illegal drug use, it is believed that over half of our nation's young people are involved (Siegel and Senna, 1981).

The problem of juvenile crime has existed for hundreds of years. Indeed, as Wiley Sanders indicates, juvenile offenders have been noted in much of the written records of human history (1970). Numerous editorials, commission reports, and governmental statistics reveal that juvenile crime, including that of youth gangs, not only existed but was a source of concern to the citizens of Europe and America in the eighteenth and nineteenth centuries. Even early Anglo-Saxon laws contained provisions for the punishment of child offenders (Sanders, 1970).

In essence, adults have always been concerned about the miscreant behavior of their youth. Perhaps this worry and attention derive from the perception that a nation's future rests on the development of its youth. Perhaps the concern over youthful deviance stems from the thought (however accurate) that today's delinquent is tomorrow's criminal, if nothing is done to change the antisocial behavior of the youth. Be that as it may, when youngsters are known to have been involved in criminal activity, people become concerned. Why did they do it? What should we do with them? These are the questions adults ask, and the demand for answers seems to become stronger with each new generation of adults.

Proposals for preventing and diminishing delinquency, as well as controlling and punishing the young perpetrators, have assumed so many different forms that any casual reader of the literature can be excused for being totally confused and bewildered. But essentially the question of causation is paramount. In the Middle Ages, and into the nineteenth century, children and adults were lumped together as one group, and whatever explained the misbehavior of older criminals was equally applicable to younger ones. Such was the case with demonology, and it was equally true of the first systematic criminology of the modern era, known as the classical position (Inciardi, 1978; Vold, 1979; Empey, 1982).

Demonology assumes that criminal and delinquent behavior is caused by demonic possession. While this view of criminality can be traced to primitive societies, it still maintains some popularity today among laypersons. A recent popular example of demon possession of a child is presented in the novel *The Exorcist.*

The classical school in criminology argues that people, adults and children, act according to free will, rationally exercised, in the pursuit of happiness and the minimization of pain. According to some of the early proponents of this thought, such as Cesare Beccaria, and his English utilitarian follower, Jeremy Bentham, all persons, including children, are thought to weigh the costs and benefits of their proposed actions before they embark on them, and all persons, it is assumed, possess the ability to do so.

Although the American legal system is based on the notions of free will and individual responsibility, it has been recognized for some time that not all individuals have the same ability to reason and weigh the outcome of their behavior; witness, for example, the mentally ill and children (including adolescents). For this reason, juveniles are thought to be less responsible than adults for their behavior, and an entire system of juvenile justice, from separate court proceedings to separate confinement facilities, has been established for them over the past 150 years. Of course, this separate system of handling juvenile offenders does not always result in protective and treatment-oriented practices (Murphy, 1974; Wooden, 1976). In addition, juvenile court procedures are assuming many of the characteristics of adult courts in response to Supreme Court decisions since the 1960s. Whatever changes may have been introduced, the juvenile is still considered by many to be less responsible than the adult, and thus in need of different procedures for adjudication and different policies that emphasize prevention and treatment over punishment.

Along with the assumption that young delinquents need special treatment, the idea has developed that *explanations* of crime among juveniles must be applied specifically to experiences common to youth. Particularly associated with this thought is what came to be known as the positive school of criminology initiated in the latter half of the nineteenth century (Radzinowicz, 1966). Although some thinkers equate the positive school with nineteenth-century studies of the criminal personality, the name positive can be applied to any theory that systematically and, in varying degrees, empirically analyzes the causes of crime and delinquency and concludes that personal or social and environmental factors *determine* criminal behavior. As such, many modern theories of delinquency may be called *positivistic*.

Contributions to an understanding of crime and delinquency from a positivist approach have come from a variety of disciplines, most notably biology, psychology, and sociology. While not all positivist theories distinguish juveniles from adults, many do. Some specify several stages of development, from infancy to old age, with accompanying explanations of crime and deviance for each growth period (the psychoanalytic approach, for example). Others focus on pressures, uniquely from an adolescent point of view (such as the middle-class measuring rod theory proposed by Albert Cohen, which is discussed in Chapter 5).

It is the many and varied theories of delinquency, particularly those stemming from the positivist tradition, that create much of the confusion concerning the causes of delinquency. The object of this book is to present the major theories of delinquency to the reader in a manner that is systematic and comparative. Before discussing more fully what will be included in this book, however, a few comments concerning the concepts of causality and theory are in order.

THE ISSUE OF CAUSALITY

The positive school is associated with determinism, that is, the idea that criminal behavior is determined, or caused, by something (Radzinowicz, 1966). It is the identification of that "thing," or set of things, that has elevated the question of causation to a central position in the analysis of crime and delinquency.

A strict interpretation of causality would argue that one phenomenon (the cause) always precedes the result, or the effect, and that the effect never occurs without the previous existence of the cause (MacIver, 1942). For example, broken homes would be considered a cause of delinquency if broken homes always led to delinquency and if all delinquents came from broken homes. In actuality, such an interpretation of causality would eliminate the "causal" explanations of a variety of phenomena, both natural and social. This view of causation is particularly inappropriate for the development of concepts and theories in the social sciences because of the existence of multiple causes in human behavior (MacIver, 1942; Hirschi and Selvin, 1978; Gibbons, 1981).

In the development of causal explanations of delinquency, the usual procedure is to identify contributory factors, or variables, that are *associated* with delinquency. In identifying these factors, however, some attention must be paid to a minimal set of criteria for the development of causal explanations: (1) there must be an association or connection between the contributory or causal variable and delinquency; (2) the connection must be temporally established such that the causal factor is known to occur before the effect, that is, delinquency; and (3) the original connection between delinquency and the causal variable must not disappear when the influences of other variables, causally located prior to the causal variable, are considered (Hirschi and Selvin, 1978).

Sometimes, correlational data are interpreted in deterministic terms. For example, broken homes are often described as a cause of delinquency because broken homes and delinquency are correlated with one another (that is, delinquents often come from broken homes). The temporal order of this association must be established, however, before causation can be determined. If all we knew was that broken homes and delinquency were correlated, we might just as easily reason that *delinquency* causes broken homes (through parental conflicts over what to do with a troublesome child) or that coming from a broken home causes delinquency (perhaps because trouble and conflict or lack of supervision in the home create problems for a child, which are manifested in the form of illegal behavior).

Even when it has been established that two variables are not only connected, but that one variable precedes another in a time sequence, the preceding variable may not be causal. It could be that a third variable, preceding both of the others, is the real causal agent. When this occurs, it is assumed that the originally identified association between two variables is *spurious*, that is, misleading or false. For example, if a relationship has been established between delinquency and poor grades in school, the relationship may not be a causal one. Perhaps conflicts in the home are contributing to both poor school performance and delinquent behavior. If family conflicts were then introduced into the analysis, the original association between grades and delinquency would disappear, and we would then be able to call that relationship spurious.

In reading the following chapters of this book, the student should be aware of these points. The theories to be discussed are attempts to explain delinquency. While no one theory is able to provide *the* causal answer, some appear to be stronger than others in consideration of the criteria just discussed.

WHAT IS A THEORY?

The word "theory" means many things to different people. To the layperson, a theory often suggests a wild speculation, or set of speculations, an unproved or perhaps false assumption, or even a fact concerning an event or a type of behavior, based on little, if any, actual data. To some scientists, or philosophers of science, a theory consists of a set of descriptions or classification schemes concerning a particular phenomenon (some would call such schemes "taxonomies"; Zetterberg, 1963). To others, a theory is a systematic collection of concepts and statements purporting to explain events or behavior (Timasheff, 1957).

Other students feel that theories should not only be able to explain phenomena on an abstract level but also that theories should be applicable to practical, everyday situations. In other words, a significant feature of a theory is its ability to explain things for the layperson who may wish to use the theory in an applied setting (Glaser and Strauss, 1967).

Whatever the definition, the social scientist sees a theory, in one way or another, as an attempt to make sense out of observations. It is in this general sense that the word "theory" will be used in this work. Thus, a view of delinquency will be recognized as a theory if it attempts to explain or understand delinquency, regardless of the level of its causal assumptions and irrespective of the sophistication of its concepts and propositions. It is tempting to adopt a strict interpretation of theory, but to do so would eliminate some useful and interesting approaches to an understanding of delinquency. At one time or another, each of the explanations presented in this book has been referred to as a theory, and it is for this context that the term has been chosen.[1]

VERIFICATION OF THEORIES

The utility of any theory lies in its validity. Can it be verified? Is it true? Will it predict what will be found in groups not yet observed and studied? Theories are analyzed and verified in a variety of ways. Most often, they are verified by gathering data designed to test the validity of their concepts and propositions. This way of testing a theory may be referred to as the empirical, or inductive, method. A goal of scientific disciplines is to continually test their theories and refine their concepts. To ignore a theoretical explanation of delinquency, or any other type of behavior, because it is unsophisticated or untested would be denying the validity of the scientific process and foreclosing, perhaps prematurely, what might eventually become a meaningful interpretation of delinquency.

Included in the empirical method of evaluating theories of delinquency is the implementation of a theory's assumptions in prevention or treatment programs. A major concern in this approach to the evaluation of a theory is the gap that can develop among particular questions concerning what the theory proposes, how a practitioner interprets the theory, and how the major elements of the theory are implemented. While these problems occur in the testing of theories in all disciplines, they are pronounced in the social sciences. The outcomes of practical tests of a theory can be highly affected by the practitioner's understanding of the theory as well as the practitioner's commitment to its success (or failure). What are the chances of a theory being designated successful in reducing delinquency if the practitioner does not believe in the validity of the theory in the first place? Such issues as these make it impractical to evaluate theories of behavior on the basis of their ability to effect changes in behavior in a purposeful manner.

Another method of testing theories is to examine their logical consistency and conceptual clarity. Regardless of whether the theory coincides with empirically gathered data, its logical and conceptual properties may be so faulty or unclear as to render the theory practically useless. For example, it may be true that the proportion of babies born each year in a country is highly correlated with the migratory patterns of storks. Would it be logical, however, to propose from that association that storks bring babies? Some theories are worded so abstractly or with such conceptual unclarity that it is difficult to test them empirically. For instance, theories which argue that behavior is influenced by cultural norms and values are difficult to test with experimental or survey data because the central concepts of the theories are so far removed from day-to-day behavior that it is hard to connect behavior specifically with the concepts. Similarly, psychoanalytical theories which stress unconscious motives for behavior are difficult to test because such motivations are outside the scope of normal observation. These kinds of theories are better evaluated primarily according to their internal logic and consistency rather than their empirical accuracy.

THE PLAN OF THIS BOOK

The purpose of this book is to present the student with a systematic discussion of the dominant explanations of delinquency. It is not the intention of the author to develop a new theory of delinquency but, instead, to explain the existing theories in a consistent, organized manner. It is hoped that this procedure will enable the reader not only to obtain an understanding of each theory, but also to be able to compare and contrast these explanations.

It is recognized from the beginning that no single theory will ever be able to explain all types of delinquency. The theories presented are assessed according to their general empirical and logical adequacy. In some cases, such as with theories of lower-class and middle-class delinquency, the evaluation is based on the ability of the theory to explain the specific form of delinquency addressed. The more usual procedure, however, is to discuss each theory in relationship to delinquent behavior in general.

The format of the book is the same in most chapters. First, a brief historical overview of the theory, or set of theories, is presented. Next, the basic assumptions of these theories are examined. These items are followed by discussions of specific theories within the general set, including specific assumptions, key concepts, a general discussion, and an evaluation. Each chapter concludes with a summary and comparative overview. Exceptions to this format occur in the chapters on female and middle-class delinquency.

This book is not intended to "sell" anyone on the merits of any particular theory, although comparative evaluations will point to the apparent efficacy of one theory over another. Despite the support received from scholarly training or the concentration of experts favoring particular causes of delinquency, students must make up their own minds on explanatory approaches but should reach conclusions based on information and not ignorance, with an open mind and not a rigid one, and free from precommitments and prejudices. If the contents of this book help students in formulating a considered and thoughtful opinion concerning the etiology of delinquency, its purpose will have been fulfilled.

NOTE

1. Only in one instance, the discussion of labeling, can it be argued that it is not a theory under consideration (because there is no causal explanation), but a perspective. This problem is considered later.

REFERENCES

Empey, Lamar T., 1982, American Delinquency, second edition. Homewood, Ill.: Dorsey.

Gibbons, Don C., 1981, Delinquent Behavior, third edition. Englewood Cliffs, N.J.: Prentice-Hall.

Glaser, Barney G. and Anselm L. Strauss, 1967, The Discovery of Grounded Theory. Chicago: Aldine.

Hirschi, Travis and Hanan C. Selvin, 1978, "False Criteria of Causality." Pp. 219–232 in Leonard D. Savitz and Norman Johnston (eds.), Crime in Society. New York: Wiley.

Inciardi, James A., 1978, Reflections on Crime. New York: Holt, Rinehart and Winston.

MacIver, R. M., 1942, Social Causation. New York: Ginn and Company.

Murphy, Patrick T., 1974, Our Kindly Parent—The State. New York: Viking.

Radzinowicz, Leon, 1966, Ideology and Crime. New York: Columbia University Press.

Sanders, Wiley B. (ed.), 1970, Juvenile Offenders for a Thousand Years. Chapel Hill, N.C.: University of North Carolina Press.

Siegel, Larry J. and Joseph J. Senna, 1981, Juvenile Delinquency. New York: West.

Timasheff, Nicholas S., 1957, Sociological Theory, revised edition. New York: Random House.

Vold, George B., 1979, Theoretical Criminology, second edition, prepared by Thomas J. Bernard. New York: Oxford University Press.

Wooden, Kenneth, 1976, Weeping in the Playtime of Others. New York: McGraw-Hill.

Zetterberg, Hans L., 1963, On Theory and Verification in Sociology, revised edition. Totowa, N.J.: Bedminster Press.

2

BIOLOGICAL AND BIOSOCIAL EXPLANATIONS

HISTORICAL OVERVIEW

An essential component of the biological approach to delinquency is that such behavior is caused by some mechanism *internal* to the individual. Biological theories of crime and delinquency (criminality) have been proposed for hundreds of years (Fink, 1938). However, the works of early theorists varied considerably on just exactly what this internal mechanism, or set of mechanisms, might be. Furthermore, many of the early attempts, like those of the eighteenth and nineteenth centuries, made little distinction between biological and psychological characteristics, assuming in general that the criminal's mind is affected by biological composition. Since nearly all of these theorists had been trained as physicians, it is logical that they would focus on the physical properties of the body as the topic of research.

GENERIC ASSUMPTIONS

Besides positing that delinquency is a product of internal, physical properties, modern biological theories usually assume that these properties at least predispose one to criminality. The predispositions, however, are said to interact with environmental factors which can affect the influence of biology on behavior. Prior to the twentieth century, many assumed that biological factors did more than predispose one to crime—they directly caused the behavior. A general diagram of the relationship between biological factors and delinquent behavior should incorporate these two explanatory views (Jeffery, 1979). The assumptions may be depicted as shown in Figure 1.

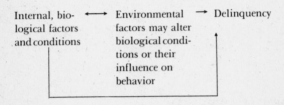

FIGURE 1

It should be noted that the predisposition connection between biology and delinquency is a reciprocal one. That is, environmental factors (which can be of a wide variety, such as family and peer associations, school performance, and social class membership) may both be shaped by and influence biological factors. It is the result of this reciprocal influence that contributes to delinquency. The direct causation position, however, bypasses environmental situations and suggests that a biological phenomenon, such as a brain tumor or some kind of chemical imbalance, can directly lead to delinquency.

Although numerous biological explanations of crime have been offered in the past (Fink, 1938; von Hentig, 1948), many of these theories made no theoretically substantive distinctions between adult and juvenile offenders. The subjects of this chapter are some of the more dominant biological explanations of *delinquency*, with minimal attention paid to explanations of both crime and delinquency. The specific topics to be discussed are somatotypes and delinquency, the issue of inheritance and delinquency, and emerging trends in biosocial explanations of delinquency.

SOMATOTYPES AND DELINQUENCY

Specific Assumption

A *somatotype* is the overall shape of the body, in consideration of the relative development of the various parts of the body in comparison with each other. An important feature of somatotype explanations of delinquency is that one's character and behavior can be correlated with the shape and structure of the body. One of the foremost supporters of this view, William Sheldon, maintains that the relationship between behavior and one's personality, or character, and physical features, including body shape, can be traced back approximately 2500 years to the works of Hippocrates (1944).

Key Concept

Somatotype or Body Type   Numerous body characteristics are included in the analysis of somatotypes, such as arm and leg length, head size, muscle development, and bone structure. Implicit in the concept is that the shape of the body is a reflection of constitutional makeup, that it is strongly influenced by factors present at birth, and that, nutrition notwithstanding, the basic shape, or body type, remains constant.

Discussion

Somatotype theories can be traced to a very influential body of research—the work of the late-nineteenth-century physician and psychiatrist Cesare Lombroso. Even though Lombroso did not analytically separate delinquents from adult criminals, his views are considered "classic" and are thus worthy of some attention at this point. Essentially, Lombroso viewed much criminality as a type of degeneracy. Specifically, he referred to some criminals as "atavists" or throwbacks to an earlier form of human life on the evolutionary scale (Lombroso, 1911). Furthermore, Lombroso maintained that a large portion of criminal behavior was inborn, although he entertained exceptions to this view in the twilight of his career (Lombroso, 1911; Lombroso-Ferrero, 1911).

Although Lombroso did not believe in body type in the manner in which it was developed by Sheldon and others, he did contend that criminals had definite *physical* characteristics that distinguished them from the law-abiding population. The criminal man was supposedly characterized by such features as a large jaw, high cheekbones, handle-shaped ears, and even tattoos (Lombroso, 1911). Obviously, tattoos are not inborn, but were included in the Lombrosoian list because they are physical.

The research conducted by Lombroso and his followers was painstaking but hardly persuasive, because control groups—that is, people selected for comparisons—were rarely used and direct connections between physical features and criminality were never established. While a thorough examination of physical characteristics in relation to criminality questioned several of Lombroso's claims that criminals have distinct physical appearances, it did not diminish and lay to rest the biological orientation to explaining crime (Goring, 1913), and research on this topic continued well into the twentieth century (Fink, 1938; Hooton, 1939).

The first attempt to relate body traits systematically with delinquency came from the work of William Sheldon (1949). Borrowing largely from an earlier attempt to correlate body physiques with general personality and behavior traits (Kretschmer, 1921), Sheldon maintained that elements of three basic body types could be found in all people: (1) *endomorphic*, or soft, round, and fat; (2) *mesomorphic*, or muscular and hard; and (3) *ectomorphic*, or thin, frail, and weak. According to Sheldon, one could not be characterized as totally one or the other of these types, but *relatively* so, on a scale of 1 to 7. Thus, a person might be predominantly mesomorphic, but still possess some endomorphic or ectomorphic traits. His somatotype might thus be 2-6-3. Furthermore, a few people possess no dominant physical shape characteristics and are described as having a mixed or midrange somatotype.

Sheldon viewed body types as inborn. Moreover, the importance of body types in the explanation of behavior lay in the strong association between physique and temperament, or personality. Endomorphy is associated with a viscerotonic temperament, characterized by extroversion and love of comfort. Mesomorphy is related to assertive, aggressive behavior, a somatotonic temperament. Ectomorphs are described as sensitive, shy, and introverted, referred to as a cerebrotonic temperament (Sheldon, 1949; Vold, 1979).

Sheldon applied his somatotype theory in a study of 200 young males who had been referred to a specialized rehabilitation home for boys in Boston (Hayden Goodwill Inn). Using subjective assessments of body-typing, that is, the observation of photographs, Sheldon concluded that the mean somatotype for the "delinquent" sample was 3.5–5.6–2.7, "decidedly mesomorphic" (1949:726–729). Furthermore, this mesomorphic nature of delinquents was held in contrast to a more even distribution of body types that was found among 4000 college students.

William Sheldon's study was shortly followed by a massive exploration of delinquency by a husband and wife team at Harvard, Sheldon and Eleanor Glueck (1950). Among dozens of other factors, the Gluecks examined the relationship between body type and delinquency in 500 institutionalized, "persistent" delinquents and a matched control sample of 500 "unquestionable nondelinquents." Measuring body types through examinations of photographs, the Gluecks concluded that over 60 percent of the delinquents were mesomorphic, compared with about 31 percent of the nondelinquents. On the other hand, only 14 percent of the delinquents were ectomorphic, whereas nearly 40 percent of the nondelinquents were so cast.

Further investigation of somatotypes and delinquency, conducted by the Gluecks (1956), revealed that mesomorphy is highly associated with such characteristics as high levels of inadequacy, of "not being taken care of," and of emotional instability. However, whether the mesomorphic body structure determines these characteristics, or whether the personality traits are generated from environmental factors, including being considered "delinquent," or a combination of environmental and constitutional factors, was not determined by the Gluecks. Their conclusion was that delinquency is caused by a combination of environmental, biological, and psychological factors. From their exhaustive research, they concluded that there is no such thing as a "delinquent personality," among mesomorphs or any other body type. Mesomorphs, for example, may be more delinquent than others because their physical and psychological traits "equip them well for a delinquent role under the pressure of unfavorable sociocultural conditions. . ." (Glueck and Glueck, 1956: 270).

A third attempt to relate somatotypes to delinquency was proposed as a more definitive approach to the subject by trying to eliminate the problems involved with the research of Sheldon and the Gluecks (Cortès and Gatti, 1972). The method of somatotyping in this study was based on comparative measurements of skinfolds, bone structure, muscle development, and body weight and height rather than from observations of photographs. In addition, assessments of temperament were based on self-report inventories, as opposed to subjective opinions of observers. The definition of delinquency in the Cortès and Gatti study, however, was based on the *official* records of institutions or court appearances, which limit the applicability of their findings.

Using these measurements and definitions, Cortès and Gatti found that over half of the 100 delinquents possessed a mesomorphic body type, compared with 19 percent of the 100 nondelinquents. On the other hand, 14 percent of the delinquents were endomorphic, while 37 percent of the nondelinquents were endomorphic.

Cortès and Gatti attempted to provide information on *why* delinquents are predominantly mesomorphic. In this regard, they reported that there is a statistical association between high achievement motivation and mesomorphy, both for delinquent and nondelinquent youth. In addition, delinquents, as a group, have higher achievement motivation than nondelinquents. The association between achievement motivation and mesomorphy, however, is greater for nondelinquents than delinquents, which suggests that other factors, both biological and environmental, are operating in conjunction with achievement orientations to produce delinquency. The explanation of the relationship between body type and delinquency, therefore, remains unsolved. The causal connection has not been established.

Evaluation

What began as an attempt to detail the constitutional, physical, and perhaps hereditary prerequisites to delinquency has developed into a complex biopsychosocial explanation of delinquent behavior. Over the past 50 to 70 years, during which the somatotype explanations of delinquency have been researched, measurements have become more sophisticated and the biological connection has become less distinct, less powerful, and less imbued with moral and evolutionary characteristics. Nonetheless, the specific physiological connection between body type and behavior is missing. Furthermore, since mesomorphic, aggressive males may be expected to predominate in several competitive fields, such as business and athletics (Cortès and Gatti, 1972), the explanation of the association between physique and delinquent behavior cannot be based solely on internal properties, even if these factors could be identified. To be sure, the importance of both environmental and physical variables in the explanation of delinquency is often readily acknowledged. The specific contribution of biological processes to delinquent behavior, however, can more readily be assessed when *biological* properties are detailed. To say that delinquency is in part caused by biologically "expressive factors" or that the proximate cause of delinquency is some kind of "negative imbalance within the individual" is interesting, but hardly lends itself to empirical testing.

Although officially acknowledged delinquents appear to be disproportionately mesomorphic, a logical, biological interpretation of this relationship has not been established, and thus the theoretical significance of somatotypes as an explanation of delinquency remains questionable.

INHERITANCE AND DELINQUENCY

Specific Assumptions

The assumption of a link between inheritance and delinquency claims that behavior in general is determined by factors that are not only present at birth, but are transmitted, biologically, from parent to child. In some ways this position is a more general statement of the somatotype explanation of delinquency. While it is posited that something inborn is causing delinquency, the specific agent is variously interpreted and only loosely identified. Rarely are such items as male-female contributions isolated and more rarely still are the specific mechanisms explained concerning how inherited factors determine behavior.

The general inheritance explanation also assumes that delinquency is a wrong that must be caused by a bad or negative source, thus ignoring the possibility that a good cultural trait might result in both good and bad consequences. In general, therefore, the inherited factor, or factors, that underlies delinquency is considered abnormal or aberrant.

Key Concept

Concordance Rate   Concordance rates refer to the agreement in behavioral outcomes among pairs of individuals—for example, twins or siblings. These rates are significant because they are a major consideration in the analysis of inheritance through studies of twins and other relatives. The behavioral outcome is considered concordant if *both* members of the pair exhibit it—that is, if both members of a set of twins have delinquent records or both are free from such records. When one is delinquent and the other is not, the pair is discordant.

Discussion

The issue of heredity versus environment, nature versus nurture, as the primary cause of behavior has occupied the attention of social and behavioral theorists for hundreds of years. It is not surprising that this debate has also been waged in the literature on crime and delinquency. During the latter part of the nineteenth century and early twentieth century, the nature-nurture debate with respect to criminality was being vigorously waged, mostly in favor of heredity. Besides Lombroso's claims of having discovered the "born criminal," numerous other investigators were trying to establish not only that there was a biological cause of criminality, but that whatever the biological explanation might be, it was inherited (Fink, 1938).

One of the most popularized of these studies was Richard Dugdale's late-nineteenth-century analysis of the Jukes in New York (Dugdale, 1888). The lineage of this family included a large number of criminals, prostitutes, and paupers, thus establishing, in Dugdale's mind, that pauperism, illegitimacy, crime, and heredity were all related and fixed in nature.

There were other attempts to establish a hereditary connection with crime using this "family tree" method, most notably the work of H. H. Goddard, who attempted to establish a connection between heredity, *feeblemindedness*, and crime (Goddard, 1912; 1914). These family tree investigations, however, are extremely weak in terms of scientific proof and logic. For example, transmission of criminal, or delinquent, traits may just as easily be explained through processes of social learning and societal reaction rather than biological and genetic processes. Dugdale stated in his study, for instance, that the Juke family had, over several generations, established an infamous reputation in their community. It does not stretch one's imagination much to envision the difficulty a "Juke" boy might have, at the turn of the century, in convincing local residents that he was a bright, "good," promising child with a respectable future.

To sort out more accurately the separate effects of heredity and environment on criminality, studies of twins began to emerge early in the twentieth century. The logic behind these studies is that hereditary influences on behavior can be accurately determined by comparing concordance rates of behavior among monozygotic (one-egg, identical, or MZ) twins, dizygotic (two-egg, fraternal, or DZ) twins, and siblings. If heredity influences behavior more than environment, concordance rates should be higher among identical twins than fraternal twins or siblings.

Numerous studies of criminality among twins have appeared since the 1930s and they have generally, although not invariably, reached the conclusion that higher rates of concordance are found among identical twins than fraternal twins or siblings (Cortès and Gatti, 1972; Christiansen, 1977a; Reid, 1979; Vold, 1979).

When patterns of delinquency are separated from adult criminality, however, other conclusions are often reached. Aaron Rosanoff and colleagues (1934), for example, examined official rates of crime, delinquency, and behavioral problems among 340 pairs of same-sex twins. The twins were classified as "probably monozygotic" or "probably dizygotic." The uncertainty in classification is based on the authors' recognition that look-alike or identical twins are not always MZ, although twins resembling each other very little are likely to be DZ. In fact, they indicate that "physical, intellectual, and temperamental" inequalities among monozygotic twins are the rule rather than the exception (Rosanoff et al., 1934:930).

With these uncertain classifications in mind, the authors generally concluded that adult criminality is mostly inherited but that juvenile delinquency, particularly female delinquency, is largely attributable to environmental factors (the number of female twin pairs included in the study of delinquency, however, was nine, a number too small to yield reliable conclusions).

Such conclusions should be viewed cautiously at this point. With respect to *delinquency*, too few studies have been conducted to reveal a pattern. Data from Japan, for instance, indicate that concordance rates of delinquency are higher for MZ twins than for DZ twins, although the information is not very detailed (Christiansen, 1977a).

Studies of twins and criminality have numerous flaws, which present difficulties in the interpretation of results. The criticisms of this research include: (1) the use of a small number of twin pairs, which prevents adequate statistical comparisons; (2) the difficulty in accurately determining whether twins are one-egg or two-egg (although efforts in this area are improving); (3) the exclusive use of official definitions of crime and delinquency; (4) the inadequate control of environmental factors, particularly since these may affect identical twins and twins reared apart (Reid, 1979; Sutherland and Cressey, 1978). To this list should be added the element of doubt concerning the representativeness of the twins studied. In the Rosanoff study, for example, *all* of the twin pairs had at least one officially identified crime, delinquency, or behavior problem case. This fact suggests that the researchers first checked the official files on crime and delinquency to locate the twins rather than locating the twins first and then checking the files, which is a more valid way of investigating criminality *among* twins.

Recent research, particularly in Scandinavia, is beginning to address most of the criticisms of previous studies, thus providing more valid results (Christiansen, 1977a; 1977b). Unfortunately for the purposes of this book, none of these more recent studies deals separately with juvenile delinquency; thus the application of their results to the issue of heredity and delinquency is tentative.

A good example of the type of research currently being conducted on twins and criminality is provided by Odd Dalgard and Einar Kringlen (1978). These workers checked the names of all twins born in Norway between 1921 and 1930 with the national criminal record in Norway as of December 31, 1966. The procedure yielded a total of 205 pairs of twins, 134 of which could be included in this study. The results of the comparison indicated that concordance rates for widely sanctioned criminal acts, such as violence, theft, and sexual assault, were higher among 31 pairs of MZ twins than among 54 pairs of DZ twins, although the differences were not statistically significant. The measurement of zygosity in this study was more sophisticated than in most other investigations in that it was based on blood and serum tests, prompting Dalgard and Kringlen to contend that their "zygosity diagnosis" was "almost 100 percent correct" (1978:296).

Dalgard and Kringlen's research also went a step further than previous studies in attempting to control environmental factors. Interviews with the twins elicited information concerning their life histories and experiences, going back to childhood. These interviews allowed the researchers to assess the extent to which the twins felt close to one another or were treated alike during their childhood. The results demonstrated that the MZ twin pairs felt they had been reared as a unit, dressed and treated alike as children, and experienced closeness and common identity as children much more than the DZ twins. When these environmental factors were considered in the analysis, Dalgard and Kringlen observed that the relationship between twin status and recorded criminality was virtually eliminated.

Evaluation

Investigations that attempt to cipher out the unique effects of heredity versus environment on criminality, or behavior in general, are bound to yield conflicting results and conclusions. By now, it is clear that both types of factors influence behavior in a very complex manner. Environmental factors are now thought to exert an influence on behavior before birth, making the determination of hereditary influences even more difficult (Shah and Roth, 1974). Nonetheless, the issue is still important in the view of many scholars and research continues to be conducted.

In a comparative sense current research on the hereditary influences on criminality is more objective and generally superior to past investigations. As with other areas of biological research, moralistic assumptions tend to be absent from current studies, and conclusions tend to be more tentative. If anything, sweeping statements are beginning to appear *against* the hereditary position, such as the conclusion of the Dalgard and Kringlen study discussed above: *"the significance of hereditary factors in registered crime is non-existent"* (1978:302; italics are in the original).

Although current research on criminality among twins is addressing most of the criticisms of prior studies, several shortcomings still remain. First, the definition of *criminal* or *delinquent* is still based on official records. This situation not only poses the problem of generalizability, but it also raises the question of validity, since concordance of official criminal records may reflect similarities of societal reactions as well as similarities of behavior.

Second, more careful assessments of environmental influences on criminality are beginning to develop, including studies of criminality among adoptees and among twins reared apart (Christiansen, 1977a; 1977b; Hutchings and Mednick, 1977). For example, a study of criminality among male adoptees in Denmark indicated that the percentage of adoptees with a criminal record increased with an increase in the percentage of biological fathers who also had a criminal record (Hutchings and Mednick, 1977). This relationship persisted despite the social class of the adoptees' adopted fathers and despite the record of criminality of the adoptive fathers. In no instance, however, did the criminal concordance rate between adoptees and their fathers reach 50 percent.

Most important, there remains the total absence of a specific, biological explanation of just *what* is being inherited to produce crime or delinquency. Until such an explanation is developed, the utility of this whole line of research will be little more than that of somatotype research. That is, the delineation of "hereditary" effects on crime and delinquency will only provide a clue to the existence of a biological contribution. The determination of what the biological factor or factors may be or of how it (or they) operates to produce crime or delinquency will have to come from other lines of inquiry.

EMERGING TRENDS IN BIOLOGICAL EXPLANATIONS OF DELINQUENCY

In the last several decades, many developments have occurred that can influence the investigation of biological factors in criminality (Shah and Roth, 1974; Mednick and Christiansen, 1977). Many of these developments, such as research on the XYY chromosomal configuration, do not relate to juvenile delinquency. Three topics that have specifically been related to delinquency are biochemical imbalances, learning disabilities, and conditionability factors.

Each of these topics is now separately discussed and evaluated. Major assumptions and key concepts are incorporated into the general discussion of each explanation.

The Biochemical Approach

Research on the connection between endocrinological, and other physiological characteristics, and criminality has been conducted for many decades (Schlapp and Smith, 1928; Shah and Roth, 1974). This line of inquiry has been applied specifically to juvenile delinquency, with respect to the adverse consequences of chemical processes in the body. This perspective on delinquency has been termed the "biochemical" or "orthomolecular medicine" approach (Hippchen, 1978; Hoffer, 1978).

A major assumption of the biochemical position is that internal chemical deficiencies, or imbalances, affect thinking patterns and motor control—the brain, in general. These imbalances can lead directly to criminal or delinquent behavior, or indirectly to such behavior through lessened abilities to learn and obey social rules. These *altered brain patterns* may derive from various sources, including brain damage caused by cancer or traumatic injury. An important source of "antisocial" behavior in children, however, is nutritional deficiency or low blood sugar, that is, hypoglycemia (Hippchen, 1978).

Of course, proponents of this theory of delinquency recognize environmental factors as playing some role in the etiology of delinquent behavior, even, perhaps, to the extent of influencing dietary habits and nutritional intake. Their argument is that biochemical processes have been neglected over the last several decades, in favor of unproductive social and psychological theories of delinquency. If delinquency is to be more fully understood, and thus more effectively controlled, then much more needs to be understood about the operation of biochemical reactions on behavior, either independent of, or in conjunction with, environmental factors (Hippchen, 1978; Kelly, 1979; Schauss, 1981).

Evaluation

Much of the evidence offered in support of this approach to delinquency is either anecdotal or indirect. Two articles on the subject, for example, provide great detail concerning the presumed effects of vitamin deficiencies and other chemical imbalances on mental illness and antisocial behavior, without any supporting evidence whatsoever (Bonnet and Pfeiffer, 1978; Wunderlich, 1978). There is little question that vitamin-deficient diets are related to certain diseases. Some maintain that such deficiencies lead to perceptual distortions, which may in turn lead to antisocial behavior; and there *is* some evidence that most officially identified criminals and many "hyperactive" children have vitamin deficiencies, particularly among the B-complex vitamins (Hippchen, 1978).

Systematic research on this topic, however, is lacking. Moreover, that research which has been reported is indirect and inconclusive. Ellis Ware (1978), for example, presents evidence that indicates that the perceptual and emotional characteristics of institutionalized delinquents can be significantly improved by the consumption of nicotinic and ascorbic acids—vitamin therapy, as it were. This type of evidence, while impressive, provides only indirect support for a connection between nutritional deficiencies and delinquency. It tells us something about the operations of chemicals on the behavior of officially identified delinquents. It says little, however, about how vitamin or other biochemical deficiencies operate to produce delinquency, or that they in fact do lead to such behavior.

It may also be true that hypoglycemic or other chemical or nutritional disorders are related to episodic criminal or delinquent behavior, particularly of a drunken or violent nature (Shah and Roth, 1974; Philpott, 1978; Yaryura-Tobias, 1978). Research evidence to support a direct, consistent link between such disorders and general delinquency, however, is not available.

To summarize, the biochemical approach to delinquency is buttressed by a mound of evidence that supports a connection between nutritional intake or chemical properties and emotional states and behavior. Nonetheless, direct, consistent evidence of a specific connection between biochemical properties and the development of delinquency, either with or without the mediation of environmental factors, has not been supplied. In addition, it would appear that the true value of this approach would be in the connection between biochemical imbalances and other conditions that might be more directly related to delinquency, such as school problems and interpersonal difficulties. As such, this approach would be useful in the understanding of learning disabilities and their connection with delinquency.

Learning Disabilities and Delinquency

The term "learning disability" is a fairly new one, having been coined in the early 1960s (Murray, 1976). Although the concept embodies many diverse elements, and some subjectivity in measurement, it is generally considered to be a disorder or deficiency involving speech, hearing, reading, writing, or arithmetic (Murray, 1976).

While several forms of learning disbaility are thought to exist, the most common types are *dyslexia, aphasia,* and *hyperkinesis.* Dyslexia involves problems in reading, specifically the inability to interpret written symbols. Aphasia includes both visual and auditory deficiencies, which can sometimes lead to speech difficulties. Hyperkinesis is often equated with hyperactivity and comes the closest to overlapping with biochemical deficiencies. It generally refers to "abnormally excessive muscular movement," which can involve both small muscles, such as in the eye, and large muscles, such as leg muscles (Murray, 1976).

The specific cause of learning disabilities is unknown. Conventional wisdom, however, appears to place the greatest confidence in eventually finding an organic or neurological basis for these disorders (Murray, 1976; Cott, 1978; Kelly, 1979). To illustrate this point, many such children are labeled as having "minimal brain dysfunction" or as being "brain injured." Or, these children are considered learning disabled when it looks *as if* there is an organic basis for their learning problems because they are otherwise intelligent and docile. In addition, the presumed biological basis of learning disabilities is illustrated by Charles Murray's contention that hyperkinesis and hyperactivity, though behaviorally similar, are not the same thing because "the hyperkinetic child is thought to have problems which will eventually be traceable to neurological origins" (Murray, 1976:14).

The organic, biological link to learning disabilities is a presumption, albeit a dominant one. Research, however, suggests the possibility of *environmental* factors, particularly family and home conditions, in the etiology (Shah and Roth, 1974). That is, learning disabilities may be connected with deficiencies in early learning settings which leave a child less able to cope with the traditional academic exercises stressed in school.

Whether or not learning disabilities are organically based, there are two theoretical rationales linking such disorders to delinquency. One explanation is that learning disabilities produce poor academic achievement and thus negative attitudes toward the juvenile from relatives, peers, and school officials. The poor grades and negative attitudes, in turn, result in the child's associations with others who are also failing in, and disenchanted with, school, truancy, additional school-related problems, and delinquency (Murray, 1976; Cott, 1978; Holzman, 1979).

A second theoretical link stresses that learning disabilities create physical and personal problems, and thus personality characteristics, that can make children susceptible to delinquency. Such children are thought to be impulsive and unable to learn from experience, characteristics which can lead to disruptions in organized settings, such as schools, general rule violations, and, of course, delinquency. In short, children with learning disabilities are thought to have a breakdown in the usual sensory-thought processes that enable other children to understand societal punishment-reward systems attached to behavior. Thus, the general effectiveness of sanctions on behavior is lessened (Murray, 1976; Morrison, 1978; Satterfield, 1978).

Evaluation

The first theoretical link between learning disability and delinquency basically constitutes a social-psychological explanation. The organic cause of delinquency, the learning disability, is a precondition, and probably only one of many preconditions. The more proximate cause of delinquency is the combination of school failure, social rejection, and association with "bad" companions.

The second theoretical rationale linking learning disabilities with delinquency is more biologically based than the first. The suggestion that learning disabilities affect cognitive development and processes of understanding, which, in turn, render one less appreciative of social rules and sanctions, represents a combination of biological and psychological concepts in the explanation of delinquency. This type of collaborative conceptualization is related to one's ability to learn and appreciate social rules.

The connection between learning disabilities and delinquency, however, must first be clearly established before any plausible theoretical link can be thoroughly developed. This connection has *not* been established to date. Although some researchers maintain that over 90 percent of delinquents have some type of learning disability, these kinds of assertions are based on subjective and uncritical assessments (Murray, 1976).

Very often, the evidence cited to support a link between learning disabilities and delinquency is circumstantial and anecdotal, based on the general opinions and experiences of teachers and clinicians (Murray, 1976; Cott, 1978). Attempts to compare rates of learning disabilities (though still not consistently defined) among delinquent and nondelinquent samples, for the most part, find higher rates of learning disability among the delinquent samples (Slavin, 1978; Holzman, 1979). But further investigation indicates that the disabled juveniles commit the same amount and types of delinquency as other youngsters (Keilitz et al., 1982). In addition, a careful assessment of these quantitative studies reveals that the number of delinquents labeled as learning disabled ranges from 22 to over 90 percent (Murray, 1976). Inconsistent methodology and statistical procedures, contradictory results, small sample sizes, narrow definitions of delinquency, and, of course, variable measurements of learning disability associated with these studies, all lead to the conclusion that a causal connection between learning disability and delinquency has not been established.

To summarize, the theoretical links between learning disabilities and delinquency are plausible. The basic evidence in support of a statistical connection between delinquency and learning disability is suggestive, but not persuasive at this point. However, the significant contribution of learning disabilities in the understanding of delinquency seems to lie with its connection to other determinants, such as school failure and social rejection, rather than through its representation of a direct, organic link to delinquency.

Conditionability and Delinquency

One link between learning disabilities and delinquency is the presumed effect that the former may have on attention spans and associations between behavior and sanctions—in other words, the *conditionability* of people. The subject of conditioning and delinquency, of course, can be approached from a variety of social and psychological perspectives. The connection between *organic* or *physiological* factors and conditionability has been the subject of much theoretical and research interest, particularly with respect to crime and delinquency. The general relationship between conditionability and criminality is most often associated with the work of Hans J. Eysenck (1977). To summarize a rather complex theoretical scheme, Eysenck argues that personality influences behavior. Personality, on the other hand, is largely determined by physiological, perhaps even inherited, characteristics. Of central concern in this explanation of criminality is an understanding of two key personality traits, extroversion (outgoingness) and introversion (shyness). An extroverted personality is sometimes associated with psychopathy, which, in turn, is associated (not equated) with criminality (Eysenck, 1977).

The concept of psychopathy is central to Eysenck's theory, and the term "psychopath" has been widely defined in the literature. Eysenck views the psychopathic personality as including an orientation on the present rather than the future, an inability to develop emotional attachments with others, severe unreliability, and uncontrollable impulsiveness. Essentially, a psychopath is unable to appreciate the feelings of others or to become tractable. These traits, in turn, make one susceptible to criminality (Eysenck, 1977).

The *biological* component of Eysenck's theory lies in the assumption that defects in the *autonomic nervous system* (ANS), the control center for emotions in the body, are responsible for the extroversion and intractability of criminals and delinquents. Specifically, he maintains that extroverts have low *inhibitory* control and behavior operates without constraint. Furthermore, they need greater amounts of stimulation than others in order to be aroused. The lack of inhibitory controls and the greater need for stimulation reduce conditionability, which in turn increases the chances of criminality (Eysenck, 1977; Eysenck and Eysenck, 1978).

While Eysenck's theory is applied to both adult criminals and juvenile delinquents, others have adopted many of his basic assumptions and applied them specifically to juveniles. Sarnoff Mednick (1977), for example, suggests that fear is a great inhibitor of behavior and thus necessary for the development of conformity among juveniles. The fear response in humans is controlled by the ANS. Normally, the ANS recovers quickly from the experience of punishment, thus facilitating inhibitory control of behavior. The child who possesses an ANS that is slow to recover from punishment is unlikely to develop strong inhibitory controls and is thus a likely candidate for delinquency.

Evaluation

The evidence concerning a connection between the ANS, extroversion, and criminality is suggestive, but not commanding. For instance, Eysenck cites data that indicate that samples of over 1800 prisoners are significantly more extroverted than a sample of over 1800 nonprisoners (Eysenck, 1977). In addition, Eysenck and Eysenck (1978) provide evidence that samples of over 2000 criminals and delinquents are more extroverted than samples of over 2000 controls. Furthermore, this relationship is most pronounced among adolescents and young adults.

In his longitudinal studies of people (that is, the same people followed over a period of time), Mednick (1977) indicates that those who experienced "serious disagreements with the law" have slower "electrodermal recovery" (a measure of ANS) than the controls. In addition, Mednick cites evidence that psychopathic prisoners have slower electrodermal recovery rates than less psychopathic but "maximum-security prisoners," and that prisoners in general have much slower recovery rates than a sample of college students.

Other studies suggest that officially identified delinquents have slower electroencephalographic (EEG) readings and fewer conditional responses than nondelinquents, even when the response measurements preceded the recorded delinquencies (Loeb and Mednick, 1977; Mednick et al., 1981), and that more repetitive delinquent reformatory inmates have slower skin conductance rates than less repetitive inmates (Siddle et al., 1977).

Not all of the evidence, however, is in support of the basic assumptions behind this theory (Hoghughi and Forrest, 1970; Eysenck, 1977; Eysenck and Eysenck, 1978). A review of several studies of persistent juvenile property offenders in England and Wales, for example, indicated that most often the delinquents were either no different or more *introverted* than comparison groups of boys (Hoghughi and Forrest, 1970). In addition, the relationships appear to be stronger for some types of criminality than for others. Eysenck maintains, for example, that the relationship between characteristics of the ANS and criminality is particularly strong with the psychopathic offender, juvenile or adult. A considerable body of literature is emerging that documents physiological response differences, associated with the ANS, between psychopaths and others. Moreover, these results appear in

studies using different definitions of psychopathy (Hare and
Schalling, 1978; Reid, 1978). Thus, Eysenck may be correct, but
these reservations should be duly noted in the overall assessment
of his theory.

The research that does support an association between the ANS
and criminality should be interpreted cautiously at this point.
Sample sizes are often small, numbering less than 10 cases in
some studies. In addition, the representativeness of the samples,
both of offenders and nonoffenders, is unclear. Virtually all of the
studies utilize officially identified samples of delinquents or
criminals, although not always incarcerated offenders. Not only
does this procedure limit the scope of the testing of the theory, but
it also raises the question of which came first, the delinquency or
the physiological response characteristics. Since the ANS is supposed to govern emotions and reflexes, it is plausible to assume
that official identification of one as delinquent or criminal,
whether or not incarceration occurs, may alter reflexes and conditioned responses, in contrast to the assumption that slow reflexes
and low conditioned response rates lead to the delinquent behavior in the first place. One way to resolve this difficulty would
be to conduct longitudinal studies, as is now being done (Mednick,
1977). At this time, however, the temporal order of the relationship between ANS characteristics and criminality remains open
to debate.

Even if consistent evidence is produced which indicates that
defects in the ANS precede and lead to delinquency, there would
still remain the question of environmental influence superseding
physiological influence. Eysenck has considered this prospect,
with respect to child-rearing practices in the family, and found it
wanting (Eysenck, 1977). In truth, however, Eysenck's consideration of environmental factors is brief and incomplete. Mednick
and co-workers (1977) contend that electrodermal recovery rates
are "highly related to criminality only in the lower-middle and
middle classes" (p. 23), thus suggesting the importance of environmental factors in the etiology of lower-class criminality.

In summary, the theoretical connection between delinquency
and differences in personality and ANS characteristics is plausible.

However, research evidence relative to the theory is suggestive but not overwhelming. This line of inquiry is promising, but firm conclusions cannot yet be reached, particularly regarding the interplay between the ANS and environmental factors in the explanation of delinquency.

SUMMARY

The biological approach to delinquency has undergone several changes in this century. First, modern biological theories seldom display the evolutionary themes so common in the eighteenth and nineteenth centuries. Delinquents are no longer seen as evolutionary throwbacks or degenerates. The modern view characterizes biological factors as predisposing certain individuals toward criminality rather than determining crime and delinquency. Second, modern theories are much more interdisciplinary than in the past. Personality factors and environmental conditions are often considered, if not formally included, in the propositions of the theories and in research designed to test them. Seldom are claims made that solely profess biological explanations of delinquency over all other possible explanations, as was common at the turn of the century. Third, research on the biological contributions to delinquency is more sophisticated than in the past. Control groups are more often used, longitudinal designs are beginning to emerge, and definitions of key variables are being revised and refined.

As these conceptual and methodological changes develop, the overall explanatory power of biological factors appears to diminish. This is not to say that modern theory and research reduce the biological aspects of delinquency to a level of unimportance. Instead, this conclusion is meant to emphasize the relative decline in the overall importance attributed to the biological roots of delinquency, particularly in view of recent theory and research. At the same time, many of the biological explanations that are now emerging are plausible and worthy of continued investigation, particularly those theories which address the biological influences on cognitive development and learning capabilities. It should be anticipated that these aspects of the biological bases of delinquency will be more fully developed in the future and will contribute to a better understanding of delinquent behavior. It should also be anticipated, however, that the importance of biological factors in the explanation of delinquency will increasingly be focused on the connections between these conditions and the more proximate, environmental bases of delinquency rather than on their direct relationship to the antisocial behavior of juveniles.

REFERENCES

Bonnet, Phillip and Carl C. Pfeiffer, 1978, "Biochemical Diagnosis of Delinquent Behavior." Pp. 183–205 in Leonard J. Hippchen (ed.), Ecologic-Biochemical Approaches to Treatment of Delinquents and Criminals. New York: Van Nostrand Reinhold.

Christiansen, Karl O., 1977a, "A Review of Studies of Criminality among Twins." Pp. 45–88 in Sarnoff A. Mednick and Karl O. Christiansen (eds.), Biosocial Bases of Criminal Behavior. New York: Gardner Press.

———, 1977b, "A Preliminary Study of Criminality among Twins." Pp. 89–108 in Sarnoff A. Mednick and Karl O. Christiansen (eds.), q.v.

Cortès, Juan B. with Florence M. Gatti, 1972, Delinquency and Crime. New York: Seminar Press.

Cott, Allan, 1978, "The Etiology of Learning Disabilities, Drug Abuse and Juvenile Delinquency." Pp. 61–74 in Leonard J. Hippchen (ed.), q.v.

Dalgard, Odd Steffen and Einar Kringlen, 1978, "Criminal Behavior in Twins." Pp. 292–307 in Leonard D. Savitz and Norman Johnston (eds.), Crime in Society. New York: Wiley.

Dugdale, Richard L., 1888. The Jukes: A Study in Crime, Pauperism, Disease and Heredity, fourth edition. New York: Putnam.

Eysenck, H. J., 1977, Crime and Personality, third edition. London: Rutledge and Kegan Paul.

Eysenck, H. J. and S. B. G. Eysenck, 1978, "Psychopathy, Personality, and Genetics." Pp. 197–223 in R. D. Hare and D. Schalling (eds.), Psychopathic Behavior. New York: Wiley.

Fink, Arthur E., 1938, Causes of Crime. New York: A. S. Barnes.

Glueck, Sheldon and Eleanor Glueck, 1950, Unraveling Juvenile Delinquency. New York: Commonwealth Fund.

———, 1956, Physique and Delinquency. New York: Harper and Brothers.

Goddard, Henry H., 1912, The Kallikak Family. New York: Macmillan.

———, 1914, Feeble-Mindedness. New York: Macmillan.

Goring, Charles B., 1913, The English Convict. Reprinted, Montclair, N.J.: Patterson Smith Reprint, 1972.

Hare, R. D. and D. Schalling (eds.), 1978, Psychopathic Behavior. New York: Wiley.

Hippchen, Leonard J., 1978, "The Need for a New Approach to the Delinquent-Criminal Problem." Pp. 3–19 in Leonard J. Hippchen (ed.), q.v.

Hoffer, Abram, 1978, "Some Theoretical Principles Basic to Orthomolecular Psychiatric Treatment." Pp. 31–55 in Leonard J. Hippchen (ed.), q.v.

Hoghughi, M. S. and A. R. Forrest, 1970, "Eysenck's Theory of Criminality: An Examination with Approved School Boys." British Journal of Criminology 10:240–254.

Holzman, Harold R., 1979, "Learning Disabilities and Juvenile Delinquency: Biological and Sociological Theories." Pp. 77–86 in C. R. Jeffrey (ed.), Biology and Crime. Beverly Hills, Calif.: SAGE.

Hooton, Earnest A., 1939, Crime and the Man. Cambridge: Harvard University Press.

Hutchings, Barry and Sarnoff A. Mednick, 1977, "Criminality in Adoptees and Their Adoptive and Biological Parents: A Pilot Study." Pp. 127–141 in Sarnoff A. Mednick and Karl O. Christiansen (eds.), q.v.

Jeffery, C. R. (ed.), 1979, Biology and Crime. Beverly Hills, Calif.: SAGE.

Keilitz, Ingo, Barbara A. Zaremba, and Paul K. Broder, 1982, "Learning Disabilities and Juvenile Delinquency." Pp. 95–104 in Leonard D. Savitz and Norman Johnston (eds.), Contemporary Criminology. New York: Wiley.

Kelly, Henry E., 1979, "Biosociology and Crime." Pp. 87–99 in C. R. Jeffrey (ed.), q.v.

Kretschmer, Ernst, 1921, Physique and Character, second edition, translated by W. J. H. Sprott. Reprinted, New York: Cooper Square Publishers, 1936.

Loeb, Janice and Sarnoff A. Mednick, 1977, "A Prospective Study of Predictors of Criminality: 3 Electrodormal Response Patterns." Pp. 245–254 in Sarnoff A. Mednick and Karl O. Christiansen (eds.), q.v.

Lombroso, Cesare, 1911, Crime, translated by Henry P. Horton. Reprinted, Montclair, N.J.: Patterson Smith Reprint, 1968.

Lombroso-Ferrero, Gina, 1911, Criminal Man. New York: Putnam.

Mednick, Sarnoff A., 1977, "A Bio-Social Theory of the Learning of Law-Abiding Behavior." Pp. 1–8 in Sarnoff A. Mednick and Karl O. Christiansen (eds.), q.v.

Mednick, Sarnoff A. and Karl O. Christiansen (eds.), 1977, Biosocial Bases of Criminal Behavior. New York: Gardner Press.

Mednick, Sarnoff A., Lis Kirkegaard-Sorensen, Barry Hutchings, Joachim Knop, Raben Rosenberg, and Fini Schulsinger, 1977, "An Example of Bio-social Interaction Research: The Interplay of Socioenvironmental and Individual Factors in the Etiology of Criminal Behavior." Pp. 9–23 in Sarnoff A. Mednick and Karl O. Christiansen (eds.), q.v.

Mednick, Sarnoff A., Jan Voluvka, William F. Gabrielli, Jr., and Turan M. Itil, 1981, "EEG as a Predictor of Antisocial Behavior." Criminology 19:219–229.

Morrison, Helen L., 1978, "The Asocial Child: A Destiny of Sociopath?" Pp. 22–65 in William H. Reid (ed.), The Psychopath. New York: Brunner/Mazel.

Murray, Charles A., 1976, The Link Between Learning Disabilities and Juvenile Delinquency. Washington, D.C.: U.S. Department of Justice.

Philpott, William H., 1978, "Ecological Aspects of Antisocial Behavior." Pp. 116–137 in Leonard J. Hippchen (ed.), q.v.

Reid, Sue Titus, 1979, Crime and Criminology, second edition. New York: Holt, Rinehart and Winston.

Reid, William H., 1978, The Psychopath. New York: Brunner/Mazel.

Rosanoff, Aaron J., Leva M. Handy, and Isabel Avis Rosanoff, 1934, "Criminality and Delinquency in Twins." Journal of Criminal Law and Criminology 24:923–934.

Satterfield, James H., 1978, "The Hyperactive Child Syndrome: A Precursor of Adult Psychopathy?" Pp. 329–346 in R. D. Hare and D. Schalling (eds.), Psychopathic Behavior. New York: Wiley.

Schauss, Alexander, 1981, Diet, Crime and Delinquency, revised edition. Berkeley, Calif.: Parker House.

Schlapp, Max G. and Edward H. Smith, 1928, The New Criminology. New York: Boni and Liveright.

Shah, Saleem A. and Loren H. Roth, 1974, "Biological and Psychophysiological Factors in Criminality." Pp. 101–173 in Daniel Glaser (ed.), Handbook of Criminology. Chicago: Rand McNally.

Sheldon, William H., 1944, "Constitutional Factors in Personality." Pp. 526–549 in J. McV. Hunt (ed.), Personality and the Behavior Disorders, Volume 1. New York: Ronald Press.

——, 1949, Varieties of Delinquent Youth. New York: Harper and Brothers.

Siddle, David A. T., Sarnoff A. Mednick, A. R. Nicol, and Roger H. Foggitt, 1977, "Skin Conductance Recovery in Anti-social Adolescents." Pp. 213–216 in Sarnoff A. Mednick and Karl O. Christiansen (eds.), q.v.

Slavin, Sidney H., 1978, "Information Processing Defects in Delinquents."
    Pp. 75–104 in Leonard J. Hippchen (ed.), q.v.

Sutherland, Edwin H., 1951, "Critique of Sheldon's Varieties of Delin-
    quent Youth." American Sociological Review 16:10–13.

Sutherland, Edwin H. and Donald R. Cressey, 1978, Criminology, tenth
    edition. New York: Lippincott.

Vold, George, 1979, Theoretical Criminology, second edition, prepared
    by Thomas J. Bernard. New York: Oxford University Press.

von Hentig, Hans, 1948, The Criminal and His Victim. New Haven:
    Yale University Press.

Ware, M. Ellis, 1978, "Some Effects of Nicotinic and Ascorbic Acids on
    the Behavior of Institutionalized Juvenile Delinquents." Pp. 153–
    178 in Leonard J. Hippchen (ed.), q.v.

Wunderlich, Roy C., 1978, "Neuroallergy as a Contributing Factor to
    Social Misfits: Diagnosis and Treatment." Pp. 229–253 in Leonard J.
    Hippchen (ed.), q.v.

Yaryura-Tobias, Jose A., 1978, "Biological Research on Violent Behavior."
    Pp. 138–152 in Leonard J. Hippchen (ed.), q.v.

3

PSYCHOLOGICAL THEORIES

HISTORICAL OVERVIEW

Many scholars, policymakers, and laypersons have argued that there are individual differences in intelligence, personality, or other factors that not only separate delinquents from all other youths but that are, directly or indirectly, the causes of their delinquency. These can be summarized as psychological theories, and while it is possible that some of these factors are hereditary or inborn, and hence can be thought of as biological, this is not necessarily the case.

Perhaps the earliest attempt to isolate the psychological or mental aspects of criminal behavior was the development of the concept of insanity, particularly moral insanity (Fink, 1938). It was typically suggested that criminals and delinquents were deficient in basic moral sentiments and that, furthermore, this condition was inherited. The assumption that the lack of basic moral sentiments was an inherited trait contributed to the fusion of biological and psychological properties in the explanation of criminality.

With the introduction of intelligence tests around the turn of the twentieth century, students of crime and delinquency began to concentrate on the specific mental aspects of aberrant behavior, although, again, earlier analyses of the intellectual capacities of criminals and delinquents assumed that intelligence was inherited and thus, essentially, a biological component of behavior.

Toward the end of the nineteenth century, Sigmund Freud and others began to write of the internal workings of the mind and personality configurations, and how these components of the human condition affected behavior, including criminality. Collectively, this position is often referred to as the psychiatric-psychoanalytic approach, although it is generally recognized that psychoanalysis is a form of psychiatry, which is focused on the treatment of human behavioral problems. With the establishment of the juvenile court concept in 1899, the influence of the psychiatric position relative to delinquency became prominent. Delinquents were viewed as behaving under the influence of a disease, a condition which would become worse if it were not treated. In accordance with this philosophy, psychiatrically influenced child-guidance clinics were established during the first third of the twentieth century, often as extensions of the juvenile court (Krisberg and Austin, 1978).

GENERIC ASSUMPTIONS

Throughout the twentieth century, the psychological approach to delinquency developed and, at times, flourished. Some of the more prominent variations of this overall approach included concepts of mental deficiency, psychiatric disturbances, and general personality configurations. Generically they shared some common, basic assumptions: (1) The basic cause of delinquency lies *within* the individual's patterns and developments. Delinquent behavior, in other words, is a manifestation of internal, underlying disturbances. (2) Whatever the specific psychological disturbance which might exist in any particular delinquent behavior pattern, it most probably began to develop not later than early childhood and has become a fairly characteristic feature of the individual. (3) While allowance is given for the potential modifying effects of external, environmental factors, it is the individual who has the problem and it is thus on the individual that one must focus if the problem is to be resolved and the consequent delinquent behavior is to be changed.

The causation chain that links psychological theories to delinquency may be depicted as shown in Figure 2.

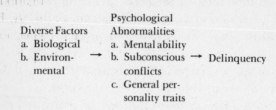

FIGURE 2

Thus, the proximate cause of delinquency, and the appropriate focus of concern, is the psychological abnormality, not the factors which produced it. The psychological abnormalities may be considered as responses to biological or environmental conditions. Delinquency, in turn, may be seen as a response to psychological problems. It is recognized that both the psychological conditions and the delinquent behavior may affect the antecedent biological and environmental factors, thus generating new psychological and behavioral adjustments. From this perspective, however, the focus remains on the psychological conditions and their effect on delinquency.

INTELLIGENCE AND DELINQUENCY

Specific Assumptions

At the turn of the century, a number of investigators concluded that a general lack of intelligence was an important contributing factor to crime, delinquency, and a host of assorted social ills. A basic assumption of these earlier investigations was that lack of intelligence directly led to criminal behavior by rendering one less capable of appreciating the immorality of behavior or the complexity of a particular situation. Second, it was assumed that those of low intelligence were less able to control their emotions and desires, and were thus more likely to engage in criminality, not because they particularly wanted to, but because they could rarely keep their behavior in check. Later investigations have assumed that intelligence affects delinquency *indirectly*, because it affects other factors which have a more direct connection with delinquency.

Key Concept

Intelligence   In the literature connecting intelligence with delinquency, the key concept is *intelligence*. Besides the issue of whether intelligence is innately or environmentally determined, which goes beyond the scope of this book, there remains the crucial question of how to measure the concept.

Many of the earlier investigations of criminality utilized definitions of intelligence that were based on logic; that is, low intelligence was often associated with placement in institutions for those of low intelligence (the feebleminded) or with some similar "official" judgment. Typically, these judgments were based on commonsense observations, association and memory tests, or just plain guesswork (Fink, 1938).

At the turn of the century, Alfred Binet, and later Theodore S. Terman, devised intelligence tests (IQ tests), which have come to be used, in modified versions, in most intelligence tests today. IQ tests have themselves become the center of much controversy and debate in terms of their validity (Jensen, 1969; Richardson and Spears, 1972; Senna, 1973; Whimbey and Whimbey, 1975; Block and Dworkin, 1976; Jensen 1980; Eysenck and Kamin, 1981), but, again, these issues lie on the periphery of the present discussion. The main point to be made for now is that the dominant measurement of intelligence today is that which an IQ test measures and that the validity of these tests is still being examined.

Discussion

With the introduction of IQ tests as the basic measure of intelligence, the investigation between intelligence and criminality began to flourish. This interest in the intellectual characteristics of criminals and delinquents was spearheaded by H. H. Goddard, an administrator of the New Jersey School for the Feeble-Minded. In 1912, Goddard published an examination of the Kallikak family, a member of whom had been sent to the school. This family had two lines of progeny, one emanating from a "feebleminded" barmaid and the other from a "respectable girl of good family." The former line "produced" an assorted array of illegitimate children, prostitutes, alcoholics, criminals, and other deviants. The latter lineage consisted of a variety of governors, senators, doctors, and "good" people.

Two years later, Goddard (1914) published a study on the intellectual capacities of inmates in 16 reformatories. He found the percentage of "defectives" or feebleminded inmates to range from 28 to 89 percent, with an estimated average of 50 percent. The results of these studies led Goddard to conclude that criminal behavior was largely attributable to weak intelligence.

Although Goddard's study of the Kallikak family employed a subjective definition of feeblemindedness, the later investigation identified feeblemindedness on the basis of the IQ distributions among those in institutions for the feebleminded. These distributions yielded an IQ of 75 or less, or a mental age of 12 or below, as the cutoff points for classifying one as feebleminded.

The initial wave of research which followed Goddard's earlier studies reported that feebleminded prisoners constituted from about 25 to 90 percent of prison populations (Fink, 1938). The validity of this research, however, came into question when the U.S. Army began to administer IQ tests to Army draftees during World War I. These tests indicated that roughly one-third of the draftee population was feebleminded, according to the definition of feeblemindedness then in use (Zeleny, 1933). Clearly, this was an unsettling proposition for most people to accept. Accordingly, the definition of feeblemindedness was revised downward to an IQ of 50, or a mental age of 8 or below, to conform to more trustworthy proportions. This readjustment cast doubt on the earlier work of Goddard and others which had so often linked low intelligence and feeblemindedness with delinquency.

Subsequent investigations, armed with the revised guidelines for feeblemindedness, and using direct comparisons between criminals and delinquents and other population subgroups, have generally failed to establish any clear, consistent connection between IQ and criminality (Zeleny, 1933; Tulchin, 1939; Sutherland and Cressey, 1978; Vold, 1979). Some studies, for example, have found criminals to be of higher intelligence than Army draftees (Murchison, 1926).

Besides numerous methodological problems, such as sampling design and definitions of criminality, the inconsistent findings of these latter studies tended to focus attention on causative factors other than intelligence. For several decades, therefore, scant attention was paid to the intelligence of delinquents and criminals. Recently, however, several investigators have begun to include intellectual functioning in their theories of criminality, and nearly all of these formulations have been addressed to delinquency. Roy Austin (1975), for example, suggests that intelligence is a major factor in the development of interpersonal maturity levels.

In a discussion of delinquency rate measurement, Robert Gordon (1976) examines delinquency *prevalence* rates, in contrast to delinquency incidence rates. Prevalence rate is a measurement of the proportion of a given age cohort, or specific age category of people, that have committed delinquent acts by a certain age in life. Gordon proceeds to analyze existing delinquency prevalence figures, based on official accounts, and concludes that nonwhite juvenile males have uniformly higher arrest rates and court appearance rates than white males or females, regardless of any specific geographical location, rural or urban.

Gordon proposes that differences in IQ may provide the greatest explanation of the persistent differences that he sometimes documents and sometimes assumes. Differences in IQ distributions in specific populations are offered as the basic explanation for differences in delinquency rates between these same populations for the following reasons: (1) the IQ distribution in a population is constant across time and geographical location; (2) IQ is directly associated with delinquency among whites (which, Gordon suggests, also explains the consistently higher official delinquency rates among lower-class, as opposed to middle-class, whites); (3) low IQ could be responsible for the higher crime and delinquency concordance rates among monozygotic twins compared to dizygotic twins; (4) low IQ might explain the results of one study wherein a higher rate of criminality was found among adoptees of unknown parentage; (5) IQ differences in general between racial groups are in the same direction and of similar magnitude as the differences between these racial groups in terms of delinquency (when differences in IQ between blacks and whites are controlled, delinquency prevalence rates between blacks and whites disappear); (6) there is a relatively high rate of delinquency in middle-class black neighborhoods (which some would challenge; Gordon, 1976:256-265).

Although Gordon raises the issue of innate ability as a basic component of IQ, he eventually appears to be implicating IQ in the causation of delinquency because *low IQ* is presumed to inhibit the socialization process of children. Not only are low-IQ children less likely to comprehend the world in which they are forced to live (particularly those whose IQ score falls between 50 and 90), but they will more likely be raised by parents whose IQ is also low. Thus, the ability of these parents to socialize their children appropriately is diminished. It should be noted that many of Gordon's assertions, especially the idea that low-IQ parents are poor socializers, are conjectural. As Edward Sagarin states:

> We have no empirical proof—or disproof—that low-IQ parents are ineffective socializing agents. We do not have evidence that low-IQ delinquents have low-IQ parents or that high-IQ delinquents (yes, there are such) have high-IQ parents. . . . We do not know whether high-IQ children or children of high-IQ parents have greater oppor-

tunities to escape official recognition as delinquents. The entire argument suffers from a lack of parsimony: Occam's razor has never been so dull as in the hands of Gordon. (Sagarin, 1980:17)

In another article, Travis Hirschi and Michael Hindelang (1977) analyze earlier studies of the relationship between intelligence and delinquency and conclude that the available evidence does support a connection between the two variables.

As far as official rates of delinquency are concerned, Hirschi and Hindelang conclude from their secondary analysis that IQ predicts delinquency as well as do race and social class and better than other variables, such as family status, which has traditionally been linked with delinquency.

With respect to self-report or unofficial delinquency, the relationship with intelligence is evident, but not as strong as the relationship between intelligence and official records. Hirschi and Hindelang offer two suggestions for this discrepancy: (1) those with low IQs may be the least able or the least willing to respond meaningfully to a self-report questionnaire but still be the most delinquent youth in a sample and (2) IQ is a better predictor of multiple offense delinquents (as officially recorded) rather than delinquency in general. Since self-report surveys typically reveal less serious and less repetitive instances of delinquency (see Elliott and Ageton, 1980), this measure of delinquency may be less sensitive to the effects of IQ than official indices. It is also possible to postulate that adolescents with high IQs have the cunning to conceal their delinquent acts on a self-report questionnaire. This possibility would also reduce the connection between IQ and delinquency.

Hirschi and Hindelang conclude that after the initial popularity of IQ as a cause of criminality, subsequent research failed to support the existence of a consistent relationship between the two variables. At the same time, sociological theories began to dominate the literature on delinquency, and these theories, *ostensibly*, have ignored IQ as a causal factor. In actuality, Hirschi and Hindelang argue that recent research has established a consistent eight-point IQ difference between delinquents (presumably official delinquents) and nondelinquents, a difference they argue is too large to be ignored. Furthermore, they argue that many sociological theories *implicitly* recognize the importance of IQ on delinquency, but for different reasons, especially those theories which focus on class-based strains and conflicts.

Hirschi and Hindelang do not attribute any direct effects of IQ on delinquency. Instead, like Gordon, they suggest an indirect effect, especially the school system and the juvenile's ability to function well in that arena of competition.[1] Juveniles with low IQs do poorly in school, become discouraged and develop a negative attitude toward school work, and search elsewhere for acceptance and activity. More and more, "acceptable" alternatives such as work become unavailable to these youth, leaving unacceptable choices, such as delinquency, as more likely. This is a far cry from Gordon's race and heredity theories, and it allows for a host of intervening factors connecting the influence of low IQ to delinquency.

Evaluation

The history of research on the relationship between IQ and delinquency shows an uneven pattern. The original studies claimed to demonstrate a consistently strong inverse relationship between the two variables, such that those with low IQs had higher rates of delinquency. With the introduction of more reliable measures of IQ, the strength of the association between IQ and delinquency was reduced to insignificance. This conclusion was reinforced by the introduction of self-report studies of delinquency, which have consistently yielded lower levels of association with IQ than official measures of delinquency. More recently, analyses have begun to resurrect the importance of IQ in the explanation of delinquency, although the bulk and persuasiveness of these arguments rest with official measures of delinquency.

In a field with as few absolutes as the subject of juvenile delinquency, sweeping conclusions either for or against the validity of a theoretical position, such as the inverse relationship between IQ and delinquency, should be greeted with caution. It is probably true that many students of delinquency have "thrown the baby out with the bathwater," so to speak, with respect to the influence of IQ on delinquency. The issue has frequently assumed racial, even moral, overtones and has thus been shrouded with emotional judgments. This situation has tended to obscure the factual elements of the studies that have been conducted.

The relatively moderate conclusions reached by more recent analyses must be carefully weighed for two reasons: (1) they are largely based on official measures of delinquency, which might reflect the tendency of those with low intellect to be caught more often than others; and (2) they are based on a number of assumptions concerning IQ that are still unresolved. Two of these assumptions are that IQ scores are constant over time and experience, and that IQ scores are culturally unbiased measures of native intellect. Although Gordon tends to deny that these factors influence the results, which indicate a low IQ-high delinquency correlation, and Hirschi and Hindelang acknowledge the existence of doubt, they all nevertheless brush the issues aside and determine that the case is settled. Suffice it to say that the validity and reliability of IQ scores are still in question, and any attempt to deal with the connection between IQ and delinquency must account for these questions.

THE PSYCHIATRIC-PSYCHOANALYTIC APPROACH

Specific Assumptions

The field of psychiatry is quite broad, encompassing several different orientations and approaches to an understanding of human personalities. One of these psychiatric perspectives is referred to as the psychoanalytic perspective. Although derived from a single source, the seminal teachings of Sigmund Freud, it has developed different orientations, which can lead to different causal explanations of delinquency (Feldman, 1969).[2]

The psychoanalytic approach received wide support in the

delinquency literature and in treatment programs for several decades; although in the 1970s it appeared to be losing adherents, it survived, particularly in modified neo-Freudian form. The basic assumptions of the psychoanalytic approach to delinquency include the following points: (1) each person (presumably, other than the severely retarded) grows and develops in stages, particularly in stages which focus on sexual development; (2) in some cases, and for a variety of specific reasons, abnormalities occur that create conflict within a person's developing personality, usually at an early age (preadolescence); (3) these conflicts arise generally from the interplay between instinctual drives and societal restraints; (4) the conflicts, and the specific reasons for their development, become painful to the individual's awareness and are pushed into the realm of the unconscious; and (5) attempts to handle the painful conflicts are developed within the personality in the form of defense mechanisms, and these mechanisms can lead to abnormal personality patterns, of which delinquency is one behavioral manifestation.

Key Concepts

Unconscious The concept of the unconscious is essential to psychoanalysis. By the unconscious, Freud referred to that which was repressed but ultimately capable of becoming conscious, although not always in ordinary ways (S. Freud, 1927).

Id, Ego, Superego According to Freud, all people have three personality components, called the id, ego, and superego. Essentially, the id refers to the basic instinctual drives and motivations of humans, the "passionate" aspect of the human psyche. An element of the id is the libido, the constellation of sexual drives and energies. The ego assumes the role of regulating the id's potentially damaging impulses. The ego represents "reason and sanity" within the personality. The superego is the individual's inner restraints, derived from societal norms and the fear of sanctions. It is equated with the human *conscience*, the sense of guilt for perceived or contemplated transgressions (S. Freud, 1920; 1927; 1930; A. Freud, 1935).

Oedipus Complex   Among several conflicts that develop during the process of sexual growth, one of the most significant, according to Freud, is the Oedipus complex. The term refers to the one-sided rivalry a son feels with his father for the attention of his mother, which develops in the second or third year of life. For Freud, the resolution of the oedipal conflict determined the development of the socially restraining superego (S. Freud, 1927); failure to resolve this conflict could, however, lead to serious personality and behavioral disorders. While many of these ideas were known and utilized in psychiatry before Freud, the terminology and the influence of the psychoanalytic approach in the delinquency literature are attributable largely to the work of Freud and twentieth-century psychoanalytic studies.

Discussion

Two conclusions can be drawn from the foregoing discussion: (1) that delinquency is *symptomatic* of underlying conflicts (often unconscious) and emotional stress, and (2) that these conflicts and stresses can be compared to a *disease*, which, if untreated, will become progressively worse. These two conclusions regarding delinquency are predominant in the psychoanalytic literature.

Franz Alexander and William Healy (1935) offer an example of the symbolic nature of delinquency when they conclude in a particular case that the real motivation behind a juvenile's repeated thefts was a repressed sexual desire for his mother. To these psychiatrists, the conflicts over a forbidden sexual object were so painful that stealing, as a "lesser crime," took the place of the forbidden sexual desires. In another instance, August Aichhorn (1925) relates the account of a 17-year-old who repeatedly stole denatured alcohol from his father's carpenter shop and urinated into the empty bottles, presumably to cover up the thefts. Aichhorn concluded from his analysis of the case that the urination was probably a symbolic way of striking back at a father whom the boy perceived as a rival for the affections of a young step-mother. Another psychoanalyst, Kate Friedlander (1947), relates the history of a 7-year-old antisocial boy who was constantly involved in fights with other children, cruelty to animals, exhibitionism in front of adults, property destruction, and truancy. After an extensive analysis of the boy's life and his family relationships, Friedlander concluded that the antisocial behavior was a reaction to an unconscious oedipal conflict with the boy's father and to an imperfect superego.

The conception of delinquency as the outward manifestation of a disease is advocated by many proponents of psychoanalysis. William Healy and Augusta Bronner (1936), for example, compare delinquency and tuberculosis. Just as fever may be a symptom of TB, delinquency is a symptom of psychological conflicts and illnesses. Similarly, Aichhorn (1925) argues that *delinquency* is the disease and the "dissocial" behavior of a delinquent is the outward sign of the disease. To complete this analogy, Aichhorn argues that there are two kinds of delinquency, latent and manifest. Latent delinquency refers to potential delinquency, the situation Aichhorn refers to as a disease. Manifest delinquency refers to "overt bad behavior" (1925:41).

Explicit in the distinction between latent and manifest delinquency is a recognition of the connection between predisposing, underlying conditions and environmental stimuli needed to transform the potential behavior problems into actual ones (see also Alexander and Healy, 1935; Friedlander, 1947).

An example of the interplay between internal and environmental factors in the psychoanalytic approach to delinquency is provided by Richard Jenkins' analysis of three behavioral-personality types identified by Lester Hewitt and Jenkins (1947). In a study of 500 juveniles referred to the Michigan Child Guidance Institute, they identified the following problem behaviors: (1) overinhibited, shy, seclusive; (2) unsocialized aggressive and assaultive; and (3) socialized delinquent gang. The last two are clearly delinquent behavior patterns, according to the authors, while the first is more of a neurotic behavior pattern.

Although some psychoanalytic proponents make a clear distinction between delinquent and neurotic behavior (Friedlander, 1947), the two terms have often been used interchangeably in the literature.

Jenkins describes these three behavior patterns in terms of their psychoanalytically derived personalities. The overinhibited behavior pattern is referred to as a Type I personality and is characterized as having an excessive shell of inhibition (superego). The Type II personality corresponds to the unsocialized aggressive behavior pattern and is characterized by the relative lack of inhibitions, or an underdeveloped superego. The Type III personality is associated with the socialized gang delinquent or "pseudo-social" person and is characterized by a dual superego configuration. In this individual there is a normal superego with respect to fellow gang members but an inadequate superego in regard to others. Out-group members may thus be victimized by this person who feels no sense of guilt or restraint toward the victim (Hewitt and Jenkins, 1947). Thus, the personality configuration of the gang delinquent depends on the setting in which behavior occurs.

Although many psychoanalytic explanations of delinquency recognize environmental factors in the etiology of delinquency, the focus of attention is on the internal psychological conflicts that the factors influence.

Evaluation

One of the most critical drawbacks of psychoanalytic theory is the difficulty encountered in attempts to measure key concepts and to test basic assumptions and specific hypotheses. Concepts such as "superego," "id," "unconscious conficts," among others, are, by their very nature, incapable of being directly observed. Their existence and influence must be inferred rather than observed through overt means. The inference of "hidden" motives is often made from subjective techniques, such as dream analysis, hypnosis, and Rorschach tests. Since these techniques are largely subjective, they are susceptible to great variations in interpretation (Hakeem, 1957–58; Waldo and Dinitz, 1967). The field of psychotherapy thus becomes based more on art than on science.

In lieu of using objective measurements of concepts, psychoanalysts often use analogies to illustrate a point, such as a connection between various parts of the personality. Freud, for example, compared the connection between the id and the ego to that of the relationship between a horse and its rider. The horse (id) is stronger, but the rider (ego) is more intelligent and able to control and guide the potentially dangerous impulses of the horse. Sometimes, however, the horse is able to assume command over the rider, just as the id is sometimes able to overcome the ego (S. Freud, 1927). In another example, Aichhorn likened the relationship between the superego and the ego to a radio. The superego is the societal broadcast (radio), while the ego is the receiver and interpreter of social messages (Aichhorn, 1925).

All of these concepts are to be interpreted as metaphors. While metaphors can be very enlightening, they can also be misleading, particularly when they are interpreted literally rather than as figures of speech, and when not supported with empirical evidence. Most of the literature documenting a connection between psychoanalytic concepts and delinquency is based on detailed examinations of a few case histories. A disturbing element in these analyses is that they start from a presumed consequence—delinquency—and proceed to develop an elaborate explanation of why the event occurred, or what the behavior really meant, by using essentially anecdotal evidence. In short, the connection between unconscious conflicts and repressed experiences and delinquency is tautological or circular; that is, the effect (delinquency) is taken *as evidence* of the presumed cause (unconscious personality conflicts).

Besides the use of anecdotal and analogous evidence and tautological explanations of delinquency, the psychoanalytic approach has been criticized for its strong emphasis on early childhood experiences rather than current situations in the explanation of behavior (Parsons, 1947; Cohen, 1966; Clinard and Meier, 1979). A basic tenet of the sociological position is that people act in accordance with their perceived role expectations (Goffman, 1961;

Inkeles, 1964). Roles are attached to the positions and situations people occupy, and these positions can vary widely. Of course, some sociologists, for example Talcott Parsons (1947), find psychoanalytic concepts to be somewhat useful in the explanation of human behavior, such as aggression. Also, Albert Cohen (1955) incorporates psychoanalytic terms into a largely sociological explanation of delinquency (see Chapter 5).

Even though psychoanalysis emphasizes early childhood influences, it does not fail to recognize the effects of environmental factors on personality and behavior. The major focus of attention in psychoanalysis, however, is on the internal mechanisms of the mind as these are influenced and developed early in life. As such, this theory is most aptly applied to small numbers of delinquents who truly do have personality problems. To the extent that these factors are stressed, the utility of the psychoanalytic position for an understanding of delinquency in general can be questioned.

GENERAL PERSONALITY CHARACTERISTICS

Specific Assumptions

In many ways, the assumptions of the general personality approach to delinquency are similar to those of psychoanalysis. Typically proponents of the personality trait approach assume that delinquency is a manifestation of underlying conflicts within the individual's psychological framework. Unconscious drives and motives and analogous imageries, however, are not part of the general personality perspective, in contrast to the psychoanalytic approach.

Second, and also similar to psychoanalysis, it is assumed that the genesis of one's personality is in childhood, although some of the proponents of this approach recognize the influence of ongoing life experiences in the development of personality characteristics.

A third assumption of the general personality perspective is that a specific trait, or a coherent set of traits, characterizes a person's general outlook on life and consequently his or her overall behavior.

Finally, it is assumed that a "negative" consequence, such as delinquency, must be preceded by a "negative" cause. Those personality traits that are characteristic of delinquents, therefore, are considered aberrant. This assumption is also similar to that of psychoanalysis, although the specific nature of the "disease" is not always explained. Instead, it is assumed that negative or abnormal personality traits act in a general way to produce delinquency.

Key Concept

Core Personality The general personality trait approach to delinquency is rather straightforward. There are few entangled pathways that must all converge to produce delinquency. One is delinquent because of who he is—a delinquent "kind of person" (Cohen, 1966). This perspective is focused on the general concept of the *core personality;* that is, the delinquent, like others, is seen as possessing a dominant, overriding set of values and attitudes that guide his behavior. As will be demonstrated below, dependence on the existence of a core personality among delinquents has often caused problems of interpretation and understanding. Nevertheless, the concept remains a vital component of this approach and should be so recognized.

Discussion

The predominant view within the general personality perspective is that delinquents are disturbed, but very seldom psychotic. Sheldon and Eleanor Glueck, for example, concluded from their comparison of 500 delinquents and a matched sample of nondelinquents that less than 1 percent of the delinquents could be characterized as psychotic, although 1.6 percent of the nondelinquents were thus classified (Glueck and Glueck, 1950). In another controlled study, William Healy and Augusta Bronner (1936) compared the psychological characteristics of 105 delinquents (who had been referred to child guidance clinics) and 105 sibling nondelinquents. Their conclusion was that less than 7 percent of the delinquents were mildly psychotic, as compared with none of the controls.

The Healy and Bronner study is also known for the conclusion that 91 percent of the delinquents were unhappy and discontented with their lives or emotionally disturbed. In contrast, only 13 percent of the control siblings were so characterized (1936). In terms of personality characteristics, the delinquents were variously described as jealous, feeling personally inadequate, and guilt ridden. While this study has been used to demonstrate a strong link between personality characteristics and delinquency, there are some methodological problems that tend to cast doubt on its validity: (1) the personality differences between the delinquents and the nondelinquents were noted by a clinical staff of psychiatrists and psychologists; (2) the staff had much greater opportunity to observe and analyze the delinquents because they were clients (or patients) at the clinic; (3) the staff of the clinics knew the identity of the delinquents and the nondelinquents (Sutherland and Cressey, 1978). In short, the striking personality differences between the delinquents and nondelinquents could have been as much a result of the expectations (even though unintended) of the psychiatrically trained observers as a result of basic personality differences between the two groups.

Beyond the establishment of quantitative differences in personality characteristics between delinquents and nondelinquents, research in this area has attempted to specify those personality traits that particularly distinguish delinquents. There have been several reviews of these efforts and they generally demonstrate inconsistencies and difficulties in identifying a coherent "personality type" among delinquents. Walter Bromberg (1953), for example, listed 14 identifiable personality traits of delinquents including aggressiveness, emotional instability, immaturity, egocentricity, lack of ethics or inhibitions, suggestibility, and passivity. Not only is this list rather long, but it includes some patently contradictory traits, such as aggressiveness and passiveness. Although it may be true that contradictory personality traits are present in different delinquents, a general theory of delinquency based on that fact would have little predictive power.

Another review of the personality trait literature covered 113 comparisons of delinquents (and criminals) and nondelinquents using 30 personality tests (Schuessler and Cressey, 1950). In only 42 percent of the comparisons were any significant differences found. Furthermore, there was no evidence that any particular personality inventory or trait best identified delinquents or criminals.

The Schuessler and Cressey review was updated by Gordon Waldo and Simon Dinitz (1967). In addition, the Waldo-Dinitz review assessed the research according to its methodological characteristics, such as sample size, the use of control groups, and the consideration of other variables which might also influence criminality. In contrast to the earlier review, Waldo and Dinitz concluded that 81 percent of the post-1950 studies differentiated delinquents (criminals) from nondelinquents. They further noted that the differences between their conclusion and that of Schuessler and Cressey lay mainly in the greater sophistication of personality tests developed between 1950 and 1967. In particular, Waldo and Dinitz singled out "objective tests" as better discriminators between offenders and nonoffenders than performance tests or projective tests.

The objective personality test that Waldo and Dinitz selected as the most reliable was the Minnesota Multiphasic Personality Inventory (MMPI). The results of the use of the MMPI in distinguishing delinquents and other offenders from nonoffenders are rather impressive, particularly for the psychopathic deviation (Pd) subscale. Of the 29 reviewed instances in which the Pd scale of the MMPI was used, it significantly discriminated offenders from nonoffenders in 28 cases (Waldo and Dinitz, 1967). The developers of the inventory, Starke Hathaway and Elio Monachesi, and others have applied it to thousands of juvenile delinquents and nondelinquents with consistent discriminatory results, again mostly with the Pd subscale (Hathaway and Monachesi, 1963).

Another personality explanation of delinquency has recently become quite popular, especially in California. The common name for this explanation is "interpersonal maturity" (Sullivan et al., 1957). According to the proponents of this explanation, it is possible for people to attain a maturity in social or interpersonal skills in the form of seven progressive stages or levels of development, each one being associated with a "core personality."

Although no specific names were originally given to these personality levels, later modifications and discussions of the theory began to isolate specific descriptive components, in the form of subtypes, of those personality levels within which most officially defined delinquents were located, Levels 2 to 4. In these classifications, those in maturity Level 2 are seen as asocial, aggressive, and power oriented, those in Level 3 are most often identified as conformist to the rules of delinquent groups, and those in Level 4 are typically called neurotic (Warren, 1970; Palmer, 1974). Since these three maturity levels represent close to 90 percent of officially identified delinquents (Warren, 1970; Palmer 1974), it may be surmised that the personality of the delinquent is not only "immature," but simultaneously aggressive, passive, and neurotic.

A Note on Psychopathy

Perhaps no other criminological term exerts more interest and fascination from the public than "psychopath." The term developed in the latter part of the nineteenth century to refer to aggressive criminals who acted impulsively with no apparent reason or goal (Fink, 1938). Since that time, it has been used widely in the mass media, often referring to murders such as those depicted in Alfred Hitchcock's *Psycho*. Clinically, however, the term has referred to a veritable host of attitudinal and behavioral characteristics. Over 200 terms have been used to describe people and to link them as a result of these descriptions with psychopathy, and of these it can be said that 55 are generally agreed on as describing the psychopathic personality (Sutherland and Cressey, 1978). Furthermore, several synonyms have appeared in the literature and in clinical manuals, particularly "sociopath" and "antisocial personality," which add to the confusion.

While it seems that such a wide range of attributes cannot produce a meaningful entity, there are some particularly recurring themes that provide a limited degree of intuitive understanding of the concept. Themes such as impulsiveness, inability to relate to others, inability to learn or profit from experiences, lack of guilt or remorse for harmful behavior, insensitivity for pain of others (and even relative insensitivity to pain experienced by oneself), and repeated transgressions are often used in scholarly treatises on the subject (McCord and McCord, 1956; Robins, 1966; Cleckley, 1976; Eysenck, 1977). The American Psychiatric Association's Diagnostic and Statistical Manual of Mental Disorders (1968) utilizes these characteristics, and a few others, such as irresponsibility, in its clinical definition of the antisocial personality, or sociopath.

Some investigators wish to arrange psychopathy on a scale (Robins, 1966; Cleckley, 1976). Robins, for example, selected 19 life circumstances as the symptomatic criteria for identifying sociopathy, including the use of aliases, a "wild" adolescence, suicide attempts, and financial dependency. Arbitrarily, Robins decided that anyone whose behavior fit any 5 of the 19 symptoms would be under *consideration* as a sociopath. Other criteria, unspecified, were thus apparently utilized in arriving at a final conclusion that one had the "disease" of sociopathy.

Whether students of psychopathy regard the concept as an illness, almost all *associate* it with criminality. There is disagreement, however, over whether psychopathy or sociopathy pertains to juveniles as well as adults. On the one hand, Lewis Yablonsky (1970) argues that core members of violent gangs are so psychopathic and emotionally disturbed that they cannot even form primary groups. He thus refers to these types of gangs as "near groups." In addition, Hans and Sybil Eysenck (1978) are somewhat emphatic on the point that psychopathy is inversely related to age (that is, psychopathy is reduced as one gets older), although they cite some literature that is unable to find psychopathic personality differences among adolescents.

On the other hand, Robins (1966) is equally convinced that sociopathy is an adult disease and that juveniles can only be considered potentially sociopathic. The behavior that might be regarded as sociopathic in an adult is only symptomatic of sociopathy among juveniles. Moreover, the clinical definition of sociopathy or the antisocial personality seems to associate the condition with adulthood. Those children who are impulsive, self-centered, and apparently guiltless are often referred to as having a "tension-discharge disorder" or an "impulse-ridden personality" (Hare, 1970:5), as opposed to a sociopathic personality.

Evaluation

The nature of the personality explanations of delinquency allows for more direct testing of assumptions than is true of psychoanalytic theories. Indeed, the literature on this topic is much more quantified and empirical than the psychoanalytic literature. Thus, the validity of the assumptions and concepts can be more confidently assessed. This evaluation focuses on two major concerns relative to the validity of personality theories: (1) the problem of *personality* classification and (2) the documented relationship of personality patterns to delinquency.

The idea that people have a dominating, "core" personality can sometimes lead to forced judgments and, ultimately, to misclassification. For example, several attempts have been made to test the validity of the I-level explanation of delinquency, and a recurring problem has been interjudge agreement on just what a person's personality is (Butler and Adams, 1966; Jesness, 1971; Beker and Heyman, 1972). Inventories or paper and pencil tests are quite unlikely to capture the core identity of people. It is difficult, even with in-depth interviews, to measure the variability of thought, mood, and behavior which people experience and express as they go through their daily lives.

The problem in adequately measuring and classifying one's personality is indicated in the numerous personality types and subscales that have been related to delinquency, some of which are contradictory. With so many dimensions and attributes assigned to the *criminal* and *delinquent* personality, much less to human personality in general, it is hard to imagine that any one characteristic or coherent set of attributes can accurately summarize a person's feelings and relationships with others. Perhaps misclassifications, or incomplete classifications, are the reasons for changes in the personality types of delinquents (Butler and Adams, 1966; Beker and Heyman, 1972). Of course, changes in personality can occur because of treatment interventions. Indeed, such change is at the heart of most treatment programs. But noted changes in personality classifications do occur in the absence of specific treatment. Robins' longitudinal examination of sociopathy (1966) noted that 39 percent of those diagnosed as sociopathic improved or "remitted" (changed, presumably) with age and with no apparent organized treatment, other than perhaps the help and guidance of ministers, friends, and relatives. Large rates of change, with no programmatic treatment, were also noted for those diagnosed as psychotic and alcoholic. Clearly, such changes in personality cannot be supportive of a permanent core personality concept. Nor does such evidence provide trust in the accuracy of original diagnoses.

Even if core personalities existed and could be accurately identified, the relationship between personality differences and delinquency is far from conclusive. The demonstration of personality or emotional differences between delinquents and nondelinquents by Healy and Bronner has already been critiqued and found methodologically questionable. The two literature reviews mentioned earlier reached somewhat different conclusions regarding the relationship between personality and delinquency. The review that was more favorable to the significance of personality differences among delinquents (Waldo and Dinitz, 1967), however, was supportive only of personality differences measured by objective tests. Furthermore, Waldo and Dinitz note that the control study of the Gluecks (mentioned earlier) concluded that delinquents were more assertive, hostile, defiant, suspicious, and less cooperative than nondelinquents, using the Rorschach test as a measure. But they did *not* note that the Gluecks also found that nondelinquents were more neurotic than delinquents and that, overall, nearly half of the delinquents had "no conspicuous pathology," as compared with nearly 56 percent of the nondelinquents (Glueck and Glueck, 1950).

The two specific examples of personality explanations discussed earlier, MMPI and interpersonal maturity or I-level, have also been questioned regarding their connection with delinquency. Differences between delinquents and nondelinquents on the Pd subscale of the MMPI, for example, are often *statistically* significant, but numerically small. The scoring procedure of the inventory is such that a difference in responses to 4 items out of 50 between delinquents and nondelinquents would give statistically significant results. Considering the wording of the items ("I like school"; "My sex life is satisfactory"), such small differences in responses are hardly indicative of basic personality differences (Waldo and Dinitz, 1967; Vold, 1979). Furthermore, since the Pd subscale was originally developed from "asocial" young patients, many of whom were delinquent, and since one of the items on the subscale is "I have never been in trouble with the law" (Hathaway and Monachesi, 1963; Waldo and Dinitz, 1967), it is not surprising that investigators, using this subscale, have often found significant differences between delinquents and nondelinquents. Some have noted, moreover, that much of the relationship that exists between delinquency and MMPI scores can be attributed to exaggerated responses, if such manipulations are not controlled (Rathus and Siegel, 1980). Finally, the MMPI comparisons often yield greater differences among various delinquent populations than between delinquents and nondelinquents (Waldo and Dinitz, 1967).

The interpersonal maturity explanation of delinquency has attracted a great deal of attention in treatment programs (Jesness, 1971; Palmer, 1974). Its relationship to delinquency, however, has not been established, nor has it even been tested systematically (Gibbons, 1970; Beker and Heyman, 1972).

Damaging to this theory is the difficulty in connecting I-level classifications with either traditional psychiatric concepts or with similar personality conceptualizations (Butler and Adams, 1966). In fact, an attempt to assess the construct validity of "interpersonal maturity" characteristics among institutionalized male delinquents in California failed to confirm "maturity" as an important characteristic of the I-level classification of delinquents. While there was a slight positive association between maturity level and I-level classification (as predicted), its importance was minuscule and ranked far below other variables, such as verbal aptitude, reasoning ability, and concern over right and wrong (Austin, 1975).

Along with all these shortcomings is the problem of cause and effect. The vast majority of delinquency research informed by personality theories and concepts has been conducted with *officially* defined delinquents, mostly those who have been referred to court or institutionalized. Consequently, it is possible that whatever personality differences have been detected in these studies between delinquents and nondelinquents may stem from the effects of identifying juveniles as delinquents. This issue has never been thoroughly resolved and it will be discussed in more detail in Chapter 8 when the labeling perspective is examined.

The overall assessment of personality theories is that their validity is not very strong. Although personality differences between delinquents and nondelinquents have been noted, these differences are often numerically small, inconsistent in meaning, and possibly influenced by the effects of labeling juveniles as delinquents. Vold's assessment of the Gluecks' research on personality and delinquency represents a good overall comment:

> In theory-making based on personality traits, the fact that the delinquent often is, or may be, as attractive and as socially acceptable a sort of person as the non-delinquent must be recognized and explained. (Vold, 1979:142)

SUMMARY

The traditional view that delinquents, and criminals in general, are produced from degenerate stock is no longer evident in modern psychological theories. IQ theories have been modified to include indirect influences through socialization and school experiences. While the emphasis on individual differences between delinquents and nondelinquents remains strong in these theories, there is an increasing recognition that personality and behavior are complex phenomena.

Nonetheless, the search for a unique set of personal, psychological antecedents of delinquency continues and remains unfulfilled. The psychoanalytic approach, once so popular in the literature and so influential in juvenile courts and institutional settings, has tended to give way to newer personality images of the delinquent. The contributions of Freud, his students, and subsequent generations of psychoanalysts will not be lost in the search for the psychological roots of delinquency. We will probably always be mindful of the possibility of underlying, "hidden" motives of behavior. Newer conceptions of the delinquent personality, however, have focused more on the objective, cognizant meanings of behavior. But these conceptions have lacked convincing evidence, particularly when it is argued that a core personality exists which is formed early and dominates one's behavior through most of life.

At the same time, few would suggest that juveniles, and adults for that matter, do not have personalities, as well as values and outlooks that can influence social relationships. These constructs are probably variable and malleable, and contingent on social roles and experiences. They are to be located on a continuum, not dichotomized (Gough, 1960). Indeed, many of the theories to be discussed in subsequent chapters assume, at least implicitly, that attitudes, personalities, and the like play some role in the translation of external events into individual behavior. The emphasis in these other theories, however, is on the external, social antecedents to delinquency.

Despite the shortcomings of psychological theories of delinquency, they cannot be completely discarded. Even if sociologists provide evidence that environmental factors offer the best explanations of delinquency, they would still eventually be forced to account for the translation of these influences into behavior, whether this occurs through reasoning abilities, subconscious motives, or personality characteristics.

NOTES

1. The most detailed examination to date of this proposition was provided by John Conger and Wilbur Miller's longitudinal analysis of IQ, personality, and official delinquency in Denver (1966). Their analysis, however, indicated that the relationship that exists among IQ, school performance, and delinquency characteristics is neither linear nor simple. IQ, for example, was found to clearly differentiate future delinquents from nondelinquents (basically through social adaptation, school performance, and so forth) in kindergarten through third grade. In grades 4 to 6, however, the importance of IQ as a direct or indirect predictor of future delinquency diminished in favor of social class status. In grades 7 to 9 both IQ and social class status combined to explain observed delinquent behavior.

2. It would be impossible to discuss all of the published psychoanalytic studies of delinquency. Some of the more notable analyses which are not cited elsewhere in this chapter include Lindner (1944), Redl and Wineman (1951), Abrahamsen (1952), and Halleck (1967, especially chapters 9 and 10).

REFERENCES

Abrahamsen, David, 1952, Who Are the Guilty? New York: Rinehart.

Aichhorn, August, 1925, Wayward Youth. Reprinted, New York: Viking, 1965.

Alexander, Franz and William Healy, 1935, Roots of Crime. Reprinted, Montclair, N.J.: Patterson Smith Reprint, 1969.

Austin, Roy L., 1975, "Construct Validity of I-Level Classification." Criminal Justice and Behavior 2:113–129.

Beker, Jerome and Doris S. Heyman, 1972, "A Critical Appraisal of the California Differential Treatment Typology of Adolescent Offenders." Criminology 10:3–59.

Block, N. J. and Gerald Dworkin (eds.), 1976, The IQ Controversy. New York: Pantheon.

Bromberg, Walter, 1953, "American Achievements in Criminology." Journal of Criminal Law, Criminology and Police Science 47:166–176.

Butler, Edgar W. and Stuart N. Adams, 1966, "Typologies of Delinquent Girls: Some Alternative Approaches." Social Forces 44:401–407.

Cleckley, Hervey, 1976, The Mask of Sanity, fifth edition. St. Louis: Mosby.

Clinard, Marshall B. and Robert F. Meier, 1979, The Sociology of Deviant Behavior, fifth edition. New York: Holt, Rinehart and Winston.

Cohen, Albert K., 1955, Delinquent Boys. New York: Free Press.

———, 1966, Deviance and Control. Englewood Cliffs, N.J.: Prentice-Hall.

Conger, John Janeway and Wilbur C. Miller, 1966, Personality, Social Class and Delinquency. New York: Wiley.

Diagnostic and Statistical Manual of Mental Disorders, 1968, second edition. Washington, D.C.: American Psychiatric Association.

Elliott, Delbert S. and Suzanne S. Ageton, 1980, "Reconciling Race and Class Differences in Self-Reported and Official Estimates of Delinquency." American Sociological Review 45:95–110.

Eysenck, H. J., 1977, Crime and Personality, second edition. London: Routledge and Kegan Paul.

Eysenck, H. J. and S. B. G. Eysenck, 1978, "Psychopathy, Personality, and Genetics." Pp. 197–223 in R. D. Hare and R. Schalling (eds.), Psychopathic Behavior. New York: Wiley.

Eysenck, H. J. and Leon Kamin, 1981, The Intelligence Controversy. New York: Wiley.

Feldman, David, 1969, "Psychoanalysis and Crime." Pp. 433–442 in Donald R. Cressey and David A. Ward (eds.), Delinquency, Crime and Social Process. New York: Harper & Row.

Fink, Arthur E., 1938, Causes of Crime. New York: A. S. Barnes.

Freud, Anna, 1935, Psycho-Analysis for Teachers and Parents. New York: Emerson Books.

Freud, Sigmund, 1920, A General Introduction to Psycho-Analysis, translated by Joan Riviere. New York: Liveright, 1935.

———, 1927, The Ego and the Id, translated by Joan Riviere. London: Hogarth, 1949.

———, 1930, Civilization and Its Discontents, edited and translated by James Strachey. New York: Norton, 1961.

Friedlander, Kate, 1947, The Psycho-Analytical Approach to Juvenile Delinquency. London: Routledge and Kegan Paul.

Gibbons, Don C., 1970, "Differential Treatment of Delinquents and Interpersonal Maturity Levels Theory: A Critique." Social Science Review 44:22–33.

Glueck, Sheldon and Eleanor Glueck, 1950, Unraveling Juvenile Delinquency. Cambridge: Harvard University Press.

Goddard, H. H., 1912, The Kallikak Family. New York: Macmillan.

———, 1914, Feeble-Mindedness. New York: Macmillan.

Goffman, Erving, 1961, Asylums. Garden City, N.Y.: Doubleday/Anchor.

Gordon, Robert A., 1976, "Prevalence: The Rare Datum in Delinquency Measurement and Its Implications for the Theory of Delinquency."

Pp. 201-284 in Malcolm Klein (ed.), The Juvenile Justice System. Beverly Hills, Calif.: SAGE.

Gough, Harrison, G., 1960, "Theory and Measurement of Socialization." Journal of Consulting Psychology 24:23-30.

Hakeem, Michael, 1957-58, "A Critique of the Psychiatric Approach to the Prevention of Juvenile Delinquency." Social Problems 5:194-205.

Halleck, Seymour L., 1967, Psychiatry and the Dilemmas of Crime. New York: Harper and Row.

Hare, Robert D., 1970, Psychopathy. New York: Wiley.

Hathaway, Starke R. and Elio D. Monachesi, 1963, Adolescent Personality and Behavior. Minneapolis: University of Minnesota Press.

Healy, William and Augusta F. Bronner, 1936, New Light on Delinquency and Its Treatment. New Haven: Yale University Press.

Hewitt, Lester E. and Richard L. Jenkins, 1947, Fundamental Patterns of Maladjustment. Springfield, Ill.: State of Illinois.

Hirschi, Travis and Michael J. Hindelang, 1977, "Intelligence and Delinquency: A Revisionist Review." American Sociological Review 42:571-587.

Inkeles, Alex, 1964, What Is Sociology? Englewood Cliffs, N.J.: Prentice-Hall.

Jensen, A. R., 1969, "How Much Can We Boost IQ and Scholastic Achievement?" Harvard Educational Review 39:1-123.

———, 1980, Bias in Mental Testing. New York: Free Press.

Jesness, Carl F., 1971, "The Preston Typology Study: An Experiment with Differential Treatment in an Institution." Journal of Research in Crime and Delinquency 8:38-52.

Krisberg, Barry and James Austin (eds.), 1978, The Children of Ishmael. Palo Alto, Calif.: Mayfield.

Lindner, Robert, 1944, Rebel Without a Cause. New York: Grove Press.

McCord, William and Joan McCord, 1956, Psychopathy and Delinquency. New York: Grune and Stratton.

Murchison, Carl, 1926, Criminal Intelligence. Worcester, Mass.: Clark University Press.

Palmer, Ted, 1974, "The Youth Authority's Community Treatment Project." Federal Probation 38:3-14.

Parsons, Talcott, 1947, "Certain Primary Sources and Patterns of Aggression in the Social Structure of the Western World." Pp. 298-322 in Talcott Parsons (ed.), Essays in Sociological Theory, revised edition. New York: Free Press, 1954.

Rathus, Spencer A. and Larry J. Siegel, 1980, "Crime and Personality Revisited: Effects of MMPI Response Sets in Self-Report Studies." Criminology 18:245-251.

Redl, Fritz and David Wineman, 1951, Children Who Hate. Glencoe, Ill.: Free Press.

Richardson, Ken and David Spears (eds.), 1972, Race and Intelligence. Baltimore: Penguin.

Robins, Lee N., 1966, Deviant Children Grown Up. Baltimore: Williams and Wilkins.

Sagarin, Edward, 1980, "Taboo Subjects and Taboo Viewpoints in Criminology." Pp. 7–21 in Edward Sagarin (ed.), Taboos in Criminology. Beverly Hills, Calif.: SAGE.

Schuessler, Karl and Donald R. Cressey, 1950, "Personality Characteristics of Criminals." American Journal of Sociology 55:476–484.

Senna, Carl (ed.), 1973, The Fallacy of IQ. New York: Third Press.

Sullivan, Clyde, Marguerite Q. Grant, and J. Douglas Grant, 1957, "The Development of Interpersonal Maturity: Applications to Delinquency." Psychiatry 20:373–385.

Sutherland, Edwin H. and Donald R. Cressey, 1978, Criminology, tenth edition. New York: Lippincott.

Tulchin, Simon H., 1939, Intelligence and Crime. Chicago: University of Chicago Press.

Vold, George B., 1979, Theoretical Criminology, second edition, prepared by Thomas J. Bernard. New York: Oxford University Press.

Waldo, Gordon and Simon Dinitz, 1967, "Personality Attributes of the Criminal: An Analysis of Research Studies, 1950–65." Journal of Research in Crime and Delinquency 4:185–202.

Warren, Marguerite Q., 1970, "The Case for Differential Treatment of Delinquents." Pp. 419–428 in Harwin L. Voss (ed.), Society, Delinquency, and Delinquent Behavior. Boston: Little, Brown.

Whimbey, Arthur, with Linda Shaw Whimbey, 1975, Intelligence Can Be Taught. New York: Dutton.

Yablonsky, Lewis, 1970, The Violent Gang, revised edition. Baltimore: Penguin.

Zeleny, L. D., 1933, "Feeble-Mindedness and Criminal Conduct." American Journal of Sociology 38:564–576.

4

SOCIAL DISORGANIZATION
AND ANOMIE

HISTORICAL OVERVIEW

The suggestion that delinquency is caused by environmental factors has a long history. Urban studies in the nineteenth century, particularly in Europe, regularly demonstrated correlations between delinquency (and crime) and such factors as population density, age and sex composition, poverty, and education. Morris (1958) maintains that the three dominant nineteenth-century hypotheses concerning crime causation were poverty, ignorance, and population density. Largely because of the academic and public popularity of individualistic explanations of delinquency, this earlier interest in environmental research became eclipsed for several years (Voss and Petersen, 1971).

A distinguishing feature of the earlier, European environmental analyses of criminality, particularly by A. M. Guerry and Adolphe Quetelet, was the extensive use of maps and charts to demonstrate the quantitative distribution of crime and delinquency. The use of such research methods has prompted some to name this approach the "Cartographic School" (Sutherland and Cressey, 1978).

While the results of research conducted within the Cartographic School supported environmental explanations of criminality, there was no underlying theory that guided the interpretation of these results. Often the findings were used to indicate the lack of morality in certain parts of a city or region of a country, or among members of certain population categories. The late-nineteenth-century theoretical development of the concept of "anomie" by the Frenchman Emile Durkheim and the Marxist theory of class-based behavior patterns, plus the later work in America of Clifford Shaw and Henry McKay, contributed to the merger of fact with theory in this area of delinquency research.

Thus, the theoretical constructs that underlie social disorganization and anomie as explanations of delinquency extended from prior methodological, but essentially atheoretical, environmental-ecological studies of criminality. At the same time, these explanations represent the earliest modern sociological and social psychological explanations of crime and delinquency. The concepts, hypotheses, and research generated from these theories have influenced the analysis of delinquency and crime for most of this century.

GENERIC ASSUMPTIONS

As explanations of delinquency, social disorganization and anomie share a common set of assumptions. First, delinquency is assumed to be *primarily* caused by social factors. Both explanations consider personal or situational influences in delinquency, but the dominant factor is social. Second, the structure and institutions of society are assumed to be in disarray or disorganization. Just specifically what component of society is thought to be in a state of disorganization is one of the factors that distinguishes the two explanations. Third, the uncertainty and confusion that accompany social disorganization and anomie are said, in this approach, to leave one vulnerable or susceptible to delinquent behavior. In essence, it is assumed that social factors control delinquency and, when these factors become unstable, juveniles are rendered less able to resist deviant temptations. Fourth, implied is that the erosion of stability in social structure is most pronounced among the lower classes, an assumption made because these theories were developed to explain a disproportionate rate of delinquency (and crime) among the working and lower classes. This excess of criminality among the lower classes of society was partly the result of using police and court records as the measure of delinquency. Nonetheless, both explanations assume that criminality is inversely related to social class, although, *in the abstract,* this assumption is not necessary for either theory.

These assumptions are diagrammed in Figure 3.

| Disruption and instability in social structures and institutions | → | Uncertainty and confusion concerning appropriate behavior and the connection between present conforming behavior and future rewards | → | Weakened effectiveness of social structures and institutions as controls of delinquent behavior | → | Delinquency |

FIGURE 3

It is apparent from the preceding discussion that social disorganization and anomie are partly *social control* theories of delinquency. That is, it is assumed that delinquency results, in part, from a lack of significant attachment to social institutions, such as the family and school. The thrust of these explanations, however, is on the social factors that produce weakened controls on delinquency. The specific processes and dimensions of weakened controls in relationship to delinquency will be discussed in Chapter 7.

SOCIAL DISORGANIZATION

Specific Assumptions

The foremost assumption of social disorganization as an explanation of delinquency is that delinquency is primarily the result of a breakdown of institutional, community-based controls. The individuals who live in such situations are not necessarily themselves personally disoriented; instead, they are viewed as responding "naturally" to disorganized environmental conditions. A second assumption of this approach to delinquency is that the disorganization of community-based institutions is often caused by rapid industrialization, urbanization, and immigration processes, which occur primarily in *urban* areas. Third, it is assumed that the effectiveness of social institutions and the desirability of residential and business locations correspond closely to natural, ecological principles, which are influenced by the concepts of competition and dominance. Largely because of this assumption, the social disorganization explanation of delinquency is associated with the term "ecological approach." A fourth assumption is that socially disorganized areas lead to the development of criminal values and traditions, which replace conventional ones, and that this process is self-perpetuating.

The causal chain depicting the assumptions of social disorganization in relationship to delinquency is presented in Figure 4.

Rapid changes in industrialization or urbanization or increased immigration → Decline in the effectiveness of institutional and informal social control forces in communities or neighborhoods—that is, social disorganization, which often occurs in gradient or concentric zones as a city grows and expands →

Development of delinquency areas, as exemplified by high rates of delinquency, and the existence of delinquent traditions and values in specific geographical areas or neighborhoods

FIGURE 4

Key Concepts

Social Disorganization   This term is variously defined throughout the literature, but in relationship to delinquency, it typically refers to either: (1) a breakdown in conventional institutional controls, as well as informal social control forces, within a community or neighborhood (cf. Thomas and Znaniecki, 1927) or (2) the inability of organizations, groups, or individuals in a community or neighborhood to solve common problems collectively.

Growth Zones   As formulated by Burgess (1967), this concept refers to concentric zones that represent distinctive characteristics and that are thought to appear in successive stages as the result of growth and expansion in a city.

Ecological Approach   This term refers to the systematic analysis of delinquency *rates* as these are distributed geographically within a city or locality. The distribution of rates is often mapped, or spotted, and correlated with other community characteristics, and the results are used to describe patterns of delinquency in a statistical fashion.

Delinquency Area   A geographical unit (often approximately a square mile) that has a higher than average rate of delinquency is referred to as a delinquency area. It is also presumed that delinquency areas are characterized by traditions and values that support or even encourage criminality.

Discussion: The Work of Shaw and McKay

While the mapping of crime, delinquency, and other "social ills" has been in existence for over a hundred years, the connection between social disorganization and delinquency is associated with the work of Clifford Shaw and Henry McKay, two sociologists connected with the University of Chicago and the Illinois Institute for Social Research during the early to mid-twentieth century.

Starting with *Delinquency Areas* (Shaw et al., 1929), Shaw, and later McKay, produced a number of books and reports that described the distribution of delinquency rates in Chicago and that also discussed the processes which delinquent values and traditions developed and continued. The bulk of this work culminated in a detailed investigation of delinquency rates in Chicago covering a period of over 30 years, as well as descriptions of the distribution of rates in 20 other American cities (Shaw and McKay, 1942). This work has also been revised and updated to include data through the mid-1960s (Shaw and McKay, 1969).

The work of Shaw and McKay was decidedly influenced by the principles of human ecology enunciated by Robert Park and his associates at the University of Chicago during the early part of the twentieth century (Park, 1936; 1967). For example, they utilized the depiction of urban growth outlined by Burgess (1967). This analysis of urban growth identified five concentric zones characterizing growth in American cities in the 1920s, particularly in Chicago. Zone I was called the central business district or the "Loop" and was located at the center of the city. Zone II was termed the zone of transition, the oldest section of the city, and the one being "invaded" by business and industrial expansion. The residential attractiveness of this zone had declined and it had become inhabited by recent migrants and the poor. Zone III was referred to as the zone of working-class homes, usually those in skilled and semi-skilled occupations. Zone IV was the location of single-family homes and more elegant apartments. Zone V was called the commuter's zone, consisting of suburbs and satellite cities surrounding the central city.

Of course, this depiction of urban growth is not complete. Even where the pattern does appear to be accurate, the specific dimensions of the zones can be influenced by numerous conditions, such as historical landmarks and natural barriers. The point is, however, that this analysis of urban growth was used by Shaw and McKay not only to describe the distribution of delinquency, but also to explain why delinquency was distributed in urban areas as it was. For their purposes, each zone in Chicago was assumed to be 2 miles in width.

The culminating work of Shaw and McKay presented detailed discussions of delinquency rates in Chicago over three time periods: 1900–1906, 1917–1923, and 1927–1933. "Delinquency" in these analyses was first measured by the number of young males, under a specified age, depending on time period and location, who were petitioned to juvenile court, whether or not their case was actually heard by a judge. Delinquency rate was the percentage of 10- to 16-year-old boys in an area or zone who had been petitioned to court in the mid-year of the time series under investigation (Shaw and McKay, 1969). Thus, delinquency was measured in terms of official criteria and in terms of where delinquents *lived* rather than where the offense was committed.

The results of Shaw and McKay's investigations revealed that rates of delinquency decreased as one moved from the zones located at or near the central business district outward to the commuter's zone, as Figure 5 demonstrates. This pattern was replicated for all three time series under investigation. Although changes in areas or neighborhoods occurred during the three time periods, 75 percent of the neighborhoods with the highest delinquency rate in 1900–1906 were among the highest delinquency areas in 1927–1933, with a total correlation of .61 between the two time periods.

In addition to the distributions charted for court petitions, Shaw and McKay measured the distribution of rates of males committed to correctional institutions and the rate of males who appeared in police records for the various time periods between 1900 and 1935. The results were essentially the same as for the earlier analyses of juvenile court petition rates. That is, the highest rates were found in the center of the city, near the central business district, and the rates decreased regularly by zone as one moved farther out from the center of the city. Furthermore, the correlations between the three separate measures of delinquency and the various time periods ranged from .81 to .97.

Despite skepticism as to the applicability of the concentric zone theory to other cities, research conducted in American cities, such as Philadelphia, Boston, Cleveland, and Richmond, Virginia, also concluded that official rates of delinquency decreased from the center of the city outward to the suburbs (Shaw and McKay, 1969). Follow-up studies in Chicago during the 1950s and 1960s, for both male *and* female delinquents, also confirmed the conclusions of the earlier studies in Chicago, although these later analyses did not compare delinquency rates by concentric zones.

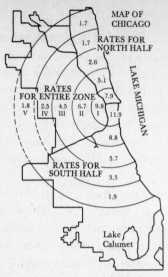

A. Zone rates of male juvenile delinquents, 1927-33 series

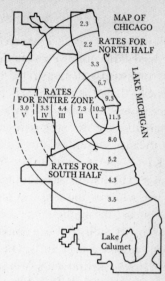

B. Zone rates of male juvenile delinquents, 1917-23 series

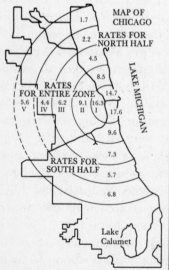

C. Zone rates of male juvenile delinquents, 1900-1906 series

CRITICAL RATIOS OF SELECTED ZONE RATES
Juvenile Court Series (Individuals)

Zones	Difference	Standard Error of the Difference	Critical Ratio
A. 1927-33			
1 and 4	7.3	.301	24.2
1 and 5	8.0	.302	26.5
2 and 4	4.2	.142	29.6
2 and 5	4.9	.142	34.5
B. 1917-23			
1 and 4	7.0	.293	23.9
1 and 5	7.3	.314	23.2
2 and 4	4.0	.162	24.7
2 and 5	4.3	.196	21.9
C. 1900-1906			
1 and 4	11.9	.371	32.1
1 and 5	10.7	.467	22.9
2 and 4	4.7	.241	19.5
2 and 5	3.5	.371	9.4

FIGURE 5   Zone maps for three juvenile court series.

(Source: Clifford R. Shaw and Henry D. McKay, *Juvenile Delinquency and Urban Areas*. Revised edition. Chicago: The University of Chicago Press, 1969. Copyright, 1942, 1969, The University of Chicago Press.)

Thus, the ecological research by Shaw, McKay, and others conducted in a number of American cities over a period of 60 years has consistently demonstrated one basic fact concerning delinquency—that official rates of delinquency *decline* with movement away from the inner city. By itself, this finding, apart from its remarkable consistency, is interesting, but hardly theoretically significant. A number of related findings reported by Shaw and McKay, however, point to the theory of social disorganization as a basic explanation of delinquency.

First, when delinquency rates were observed according to square mile areas, the highest rate areas were usually located near or adjacent to industrial or commercial sites, such as the Chicago stock yards and steel mills. On the other hand, those areas with low rates of delinquency were primarily residential neighborhoods (Shaw and McKay, 1969).

Second, the persistence of high delinquency rates in Chicago neighborhoods or areas from 1900–1933 occurred despite the predominance of several *different* ethnic and racial categories of people. At the turn of the century, the predominant populations in high delinquency areas were of northern European background, such as German, Irish, and English-Scotch. By 1920, the ethnic composition had changed to eastern and southern European nationalities, such as Polish and Italian. By the 1930s, the increased presence of blacks was beginning to appear (Shaw and McKay, 1969). Since certain areas were characterized by high delinquency rates regardless of ethnic or racial predominance, Shaw and McKay concluded that delinquency was more a product of economic conditions and locality-based traditions and values than ethnic culture. This view was reinforced by the observation that delinquency rates among blacks and the members of various nationality groups varied considerably throughout the city and in accordance with the general geographic distribution of overall delinquency rates.

Third, delinquency rates by areas were highly correlated with the rates and severity of other "community problems." Included in this list of additional problems were rates of school truancy (which they apparently had separated from delinquency), young adult (17 to 20 years of age) criminality, infant mortality, tuberculosis, and mental disorders (Shaw and McKay, 1969; see also Farris and Dunham, 1939).

Fourth, delinquency rates were also correlated with a number of economic characteristics, thought by Shaw and McKay to be indicators of stability or growth, or their opposites. For example, delinquency rates were generally associated with population decline, although the relationship was not consistent. In addition, delinquency was positively associated with the percentage of families on relief and rates of financial dependency. Finally, delinquency rates were inversely related to median monthly rental values and percentage of home ownership, although in the case of the latter the relationship was not consistent.

All of these relationships concerning rates of delinquency did not *prove* delinquency causation to Shaw and McKay. What the relationship did was to point to an underlying or overriding condition that led directly to delinquency. Just what to call this factor, and how best to describe it, presented Shaw and McKay with some difficulty. Their earlier analyses, their supporters (see Burgess, 1942), and later their reviewers (Voss and Petersen, 1971; Finestone, 1976), all seem to have agreed on one term to describe the set of conditions evident in Shaw and McKay's data—namely, *social disorganization*.

Nonetheless, it should be noted that the later work of Shaw and McKay did not stress social *disorganization*. Instead, they referred to concepts such as differential social organization (a term also used by Edwin Sutherland; see Chapter 6) and value differences to explain their position. The term social disorganization has persisted in the literature, however, and, for the sake of discussion, it will be the frame of reference for the rest of this section of the chapter.

According to Shaw and McKay the economic instability and social pathology which characterize delinquency rates lead to conflicting moral and value systems for young children. These conflicting standards are reflected in the influence that individuals and informal groups exert in the areas, in addition to, or opposed to, the traditional institutionalized social control forces emanating from churches, schools, and families. In delinquency areas, a young child is as likely to see economic success and personal reputation earned by criminal behavior as by school success and hard work in legal occupations (Shaw and McKay, 1969).

The extent to which children in a delinquency area may choose to identify with a conventional or criminal life-style depends on the particular strength of the legitimate social control forces in their lives, particularly those within their *family* settings. In addition, the choice of one life-style over another depends on the amount of support for a particular pattern of behavior the children receive from their associates and peers. Since, by definition, delinquency areas are characterized by a concentration of delinquents and criminals in a small geographical area, the chances would be slim of a child growing up in such a setting and not coming into contact with values and behavior that supported criminality.

The persistence of high delinquency rates in certain areas decade after decade prompted Shaw and McKay to suggest that a tradition of criminality eventually develops in these neighborhoods, which becomes transmitted from one generation to another. The medium of this transmission is largely the structure of juvenile and adult gangs in the areas. This conclusion was derived from in-depth case studies of juvenile delinquents (see also Shaw et al., 1938 and Shaw, 1966). In addition, Shaw and McKay noted that not only were most delinquent offenses committed in group settings but that, in most such settings, specific older and younger boys regularly appeared together in court records "backward in time in an unbroken continuity" (1969:175).

Evaluation

The empirical and theoretical work of Shaw and McKay has generated a substantial amount of literature in the field of delinquency (Wilks, 1967; Voss and Petersen, 1971; Finestone, 1976). Their work has also generated what some would regard as a successful delinquency intervention program, the Chicago Area

Projects, which have been operative for over 40 years (Kobrin, 1959; Finestone, 1976). The data and conceptualization surrounding the work of Shaw and McKay, however, have not been without critical comment. The adequacy of this approach to an understanding of juvenile delinquency can be evaluated according to three factors: (1) the influence of cultural factors in the effects of social disorganization on delinquency; (2) the presence of non-delinquency in "delinquency areas"; and (3) the question of whether socially disorganized areas produce delinquency traditions or attract delinquent individuals.

One of the strongest criticisms of social disorganization as an explanation of delinquency is that it tends to downplay the significance of ethnic and cultural factors. The replication of Shaw and McKay's work in different countries has generally supported their contention that delinquent rates are highest in areas marked by economic and population decline or instability (Morris, 1958; DeFleur, 1967). Such research, however, has not duplicated the American findings of decreasing rates from the center of the city outward. In Argentina, for example, the highest rates of delinquency have been found in interstitial and peripheral sections of the city, partly because the wealthy are often found near the center of the city, while the poorer sections of the city are found near its outskirts (DeFleur, 1967).

Besides differences in the physical location of delinquency, the influence of cultural factors can alter the basic effects area of residence may have on delinquent tendencies. In a strong critique of Shaw and McKay's work, Jonassen (1949) argues that Shaw and McKay's own data reveal marked ethnic differences in delinquency rates *within* areas. In addition, Shaw and McKay concede the importance of ethnic differences when they note the unusually low rates of delinquency among Oriental juveniles found in Hayner's studies of Pacific Northwest communities (Hayner, 1942; Shaw and McKay, 1969). The overall significance of ethnicity as a determining or mitigating factor in the explanation of delinquency, however, was not developed by Shaw and McKay.

The influence of race and ethnicity on rates of delinquency has been studied extensively and has indicated a variety of ways in which such cultural factors can influence delinquent behavior. The low rates of delinquency among Orientals have been noted by others (Smith, 1937; Chambliss, 1974) and have usually been interpreted as reflecting strong familial controls as well as a strong network of informal groups and organizations. Nonetheless, studies in the 1970s have indicated a large increase in the number of Oriental youth in American gangs (Miller, 1975).

The influence of cultural factors has also been examined relative to the delinquency producing effects of *cultural conflicts* (Sellin, 1938). Such conflicts are thought to have either direct effects, especially on second-generation juveniles, or assimilative effects, in which the extent of delinquency in a minority group becomes similar to that of a dominant group as cultural assimilation occurs (Smith, 1937; Young, 1967).

Cultural factors are also apparent in the type of delinquency in which members of various ethnic groups engage. This influence can derive both from the process of assimilation with other cultural groups (Sellin, 1938; Sutherland and Cressey, 1978) and from the distinctive experiences and value systems of particular racial and ethnic groups. In a study of the emergence of blacks and Hispanics in organized crime, for example, Ianni (1974) argues that the process of transmitting criminal values from adults to juveniles and from older to younger juveniles does not always occur in the streets of local neighborhoods but often through prison experiences. In fact, he argues that, while some similarities exist between Italian and black-Hispanic structures of organized crime, there are also numerous differences, some of which have a direct bearing on the type of criminal activity committed.

Thus, while it would be erroneous to attribute a deterministic influence to cultural factors, it would be equally erroneous to discount or ignore the effect of such variables on delinquency, as Shaw and McKay tended to do.

Another question about the conclusions of Shaw and McKay concerns the extent of nondelinquency in "delinquency areas."

Certainly, it is unrealistic to expect a theory to explain all cases of a phenomenon. Much of sociological theory and research is based on correlations and relationships, not total explanation and prediction. Inasmuch as Shaw and McKay's own data reveal that no more than 30 percent of the 10- to 16-year-old males appeared in juvenile court records, even in high delinquency rate areas, their contention that something about the culture of a geographical area contributes to its rate of delinquency is subject to challenge. Admittedly, the use of official court records lowers the percentage of recognized delinquency in a study, as compared to unofficial measures (Robison, 1936). The point remains, though, that the large percentage of "nondelinquents" in delinquent areas should be addressed if this theory is to be considered a major explanation of delinquency.

The development of a cultural tradition of delinquency transmitted through gangs was a primary effort of Shaw and McKay to explain *why* delinquency areas developed and continued. This explanation was largely based on case analyses, such as *The Jack-Roller* (Shaw, 1966). Although these analyses can be very useful in theory building, the method here often failed to define terms or to quantify concepts in replicable fashion. These types of shortcomings have prompted some, such as Kobrin (1971), to argue that the delinquency tradition argument is the weakest link in Shaw and McKay's theory.

Part of the reason for the unsystematic accounting of the development of delinquent traditions was Shaw and McKay's failure to develop more specifically some of the institutional and social psychological factors which they merely seemed to suggest in their work. Institutional factors, such as family, school, and religious disorganization, were often linked with delinquent traditions. By implication, the presence of greater controls through these institutions over juveniles residing in delinquency areas would lessen their chances of committing delinquency. Similarly, peer relationships and personalities, including self-concept, may also explain why many nondelinquents exist in delinquency areas. Later theoretical developments, such as Sutherland's theory

of differential association, Reckless' self-concept theory of delinquency, and a whole battery of theory and research on the effects
of institutional attachments and commitments (social control
through social bonds) on delinquency, have contributed considerably to our understanding and most certainly can be used to
distinguish those who have conflict with the law from those who
do not in delinquency areas. These theories are discussed in detail
in subsequent chapters.

The consideration of institutional and other specific variables,
however, might not always yield clear distinctions. An ecological
study of delinquency rates in Philadelphia, for example, compared officially defined delinquents with nondelinquents in a
"high delinquent area" of blacks according to the following
variables: presence of parents, presence of adult males in home,
sex of household head, sex of main decision maker, household
size, ordinal position, occupation and education of main wage
earner, home ownership, and room density (Rosen, 1978). The
basic conclusion of this study was that no variable distinguished
delinquents from nondelinquents in the area studied, prompting
the author to conclude that perhaps the "area" itself should be the
proper focus of attention. Nonetheless, this interpretation would
not resolve the question at hand, and presumably factors other
than those measured should be studied.

An issue closely related to the two already discussed is whether
the rates of delinquency for an area should be based on where the
delinquent act occurs or where the identified delinquent lives.
This would not be an issue if the two rates of delinquency were
the same, or if delinquents lived near the locus of their deviant
acts. The available evidence on this question is not clear. For
example, some argue that very often the area of a delinquent's
home is the same as the area where he commits offenses (Morris,
1958; Sutherland and Cressey, 1978; Fabrikant, 1979). These statements are qualified, however, to include mostly serious felonies
(such as murder, rape, and robbery), acts in large cities, or inadequate transportation facilities and opportunities. In addition, not
all research has found that delinquent acts are committed in
proximity to the residences of delinquents (Morris, 1958; DeFleur,

1967). In these cases, it is argued that delinquency areas are more likely to attract than produce delinquents.

In a similar sense, it could even be argued that areas tend to attract social misfits and the disadvantaged as a place to reside. As Sutherland and Cressey (1978) contend, however, the observation that delinquent areas remained such for nearly 30 years, despite numerous turnovers in dominant ethnic composition, provides strong support for the contention that they contain delinquent traditions. Moreover, the case study material mentioned earlier frequently reflects pride and determination in the people who live in these areas rather than fatalism and apathy. In fact, the whole premise of the Chicago Area Projects is based on the use of local lay leaders and other residents as the basic source of neighborhood reorganization.

While the separation of offense from residence is important for a fuller understanding of delinquency, the definition of delinquency based on residential location is better when the explanation is focused on the development *and* transmission of traditions within geographical areas. If one were solely interested in charting the distribution of delinquent offenses, then a definition of delinquency based on location of delinquent acts would be more appropriate. On this issue, then, it would seem that Shaw and McKay's methods and observations are justified.

In summary, the theory of social disorganization, as principally developed by Shaw and McKay, has merit in that it has pointed to social causes of delinquency that seem to be located in specific geographical areas. In this sense, the theory makes a contribution to an understanding of delinquency. On the other hand, the lack of specification of just why delinquent rates are concentrated in certain areas of a city reduces the merits of the theory. In effect, the theory would appear to be generally accurate, but incomplete. Social disorganization as an explanation of delinquency thus offers a good starting point, but leaves to other analyses—whether they are individualistic, cultural, institutional, or social psychological—the task of more clearly specifying differences between delinquents and nondelinquents, whether or not they live in delinquent areas.

ANOMIE AND DELINQUENCY: DISCONTINUITIES IN SOCIETY

Specific Assumptions

A sociological construct closely related to, but conceptually distinct from, social disorganization is *anomie*. Social disorganization often applies to localized institutional conditions, while anomie usually refers to larger, societal conditions. A major assumption of anomie as an explanation of delinquency and crime is that large numbers of people who find themselves at a disadvantage relative to legitimate economic activities are seen as being motivated to engage in illegitimate, delinquent activities. These individuals may be willing to work or otherwise be productive members of society but, because of the unavailability of employment or an opportunity to develop job skills, they turn to criminality, perhaps out of frustration with their situation or perhaps because of economic necessity.

Although anomie theory is oriented toward conditions in society generally, some researchers have attempted to combine the theory of anomie with the ecological method, that is, the study of neighborhood rates of delinquency. These studies are discussed in this section. With anomie theory, however, there is no basic assumption that delinquency becomes embodied in localized traditions, which reflect divergent economic classes and value systems. According to anomie theory, while such traditions may develop, they might more accurately be described as consequences of broader social conditions that affect a society's economy and the distribution of work and economic rewards within that society.

The relationship between anomie and delinquency may be presented as shown in Figure 6.

Societal (mostly economic) conditions that affect one's access to legitimate activities (anomie)   →   Pressures to engage in illegitimate (mostly economic) activity or delinquency

FIGURE 6

As Figure 6 shows, the relationship between anomie and delinquency is straightforward. On the surface, it makes no specifications concerning states of mind or intervening conditions. Many of those who have utilized this explanation of delinquency have attempted to "flesh it out," so to speak, but such modifications are not an actual component of anomie theory per se.

Key Concepts

Anomie   This construct refers to inconsistencies between societal conditions and individual opportunities for growth, fulfillment, and productivity within a society. The term *anomia* has been used to refer to those who experience personal frustration and alienation as a result of anomie within a society.

Opportunity Structure   This concept is defined as the availability of legitimate work and other activity to attain the goals that are inculcated into the people of a society.

Discussion

The introduction of the concept of anomie to sociology is generally attributed to the French sociologist Emile Durkheim. In a classic volume entitled *The Division of Labor in Society* (1933), Durkheim detailed a thesis which argued that societies normally develop or change from a relatively simple, uncomplicated state of existence to a complex state. The first condition Durkheim referred to as a state of *mechanical solidarity*, in which societies are held together, so to speak, by forces of similarities and likenesses. In this state of affairs, the biological endowments of people are roughly equal to the roles in life they are expected to perform (Durkheim, 1933).

As societies become larger and population more dense, and as economic and technological advances develop, the structure of social relationships changes to what Durkheim called *organic solidarity*. In this situation, society is held together through a system of functional interdependence. Roles and positions become divided and specialized, and people come to depend on one another for their survival.

Durkheim viewed this change as natural for a variety of reasons. For one thing, he equated the development of division of labor with the insatiable human desire to be happy. Thus, the more work is divided and specialized, the more people can produce and consume for their enjoyment. The natural development of division of labor, however, does not always occur smoothly. Under certain conditions, the division of labor develops "abnormally" and the society is said to be in a "pathological state."

Durkheim outlined three situations that could lead to an abnormal division of labor. The first comes from financial crises and failures, as well as industrial conflicts and disputes. The second comes from unnatural class and caste divisions, in which those in the lower classes rebel against the arbitrary boundaries placed on their aspirations and abilities. The third abnormal form of a division of labor occurs when duplication and lack of coordination within and among businesses result in a breakdown of social cohesion. In a sense, workers become alienated from their jobs.

In part, all three conditions of an abnormal division of labor have been associated with anomie by subsequent analysts (Taylor et al., 1973). Durkheim's own terminology, however, suggests that the term anomie is to be reserved for times of financial and industrial crises. In a lengthy discussion of the social causes of suicide, Durkheim specifically refers to *anomic* suicide as the result of a lack of societal regulation over people's desires and aspirations. Furthermore, this societal deregulation arises from economic crises, either depressions or rapid periods of prosperity (Durkheim, 1951).

While Durkheim failed explicitly to relate conditions of anomie to crime or deviance, with the exception of suicide, later writers did utilize the term to explain the presence of crime and deviance. The most significant of these contributions was provided by

Robert Merton, whose article on social structure and anomie, first published in 1938, has become a classic.

The basic argument of Merton's theory is that there often exists within a society a discrepancy, or disjunction, between its goals and its system of legitimate means for achieving those goals. In the United States, Merton reasons, the dominant goal is the achievement of economic success. At the same time, the system of legitimate opportunities for achieving success, such as the availability of educational and occupational pursuits, is not evenly distributed within the society (Merton, 1957). Although most people can obtain some type of job, the ability to secure a high-paying position, or one with advancement potential, is dependent on a variety of conditions that a large part of the population does not possess.

The goal of economic success is placed within the realm of culture, while the system of legitimate opportunities is classified as part of the society's social structure. Anomie is defined, according to this theory, as the disjunction between cultural goals and structured means for achieving these goals, as it affects a large number of people. For this reason, Merton's theory is also known as the means-end theory of deviance.

The reactions or adaptations to a state of anomie can vary within a society, according to Merton, and these reactions help describe the types of crime and deviance that exist in society. These responses are described in terms of accepting or rejecting cultural goals or structural means (see Figure 7).

In Figure 7, the first reaction is not considered deviant at all, but is termed *conformity*. This reaction is characterized by accepting, not necessarily achieving, both goals and means, and by attempting to abide by one's lot in life, so to speak. Merton argues that this reaction is the most common form of behavior in anomic, yet stable, societies. Thus, the theory would appear to be aimed at a minority of a population that is faced with a condition of anomie. In many ways, this is the same condition with which Shaw and McKay were faced in their explanation of delinquency as the result of social disorganization. It must be remembered, however, that the theories of both Merton and Shaw and McKay

FIGURE 7　A typology of modes of individual adaptation.

Modes of Adaptation	Cultural Goals	Institutionalized Means
I　Conformity	+	+
II　Innovation	+	−
III　Ritualism	−	+
IV　Retreatism	−	−
V　Rebellion	±	±

+ = acceptance; − = rejection; ± = rejection of prevailing values and substitution of new values.

(*Source*: Merton, 1957:140.)

were based on observations of *official* rates of criminality and deviance. While conformity may appear on the surface to be a dominant reaction among people in "crime-prone" situations, in actuality it may be a minority reaction. In any case, the point to be noted here is that conformity to rules and regulations, even when they appear to place one in disadvantageous and undesirable positions, is a form of behavior that many people adopt.

The other four reactions to anomie, as identified by Merton, are considered deviant, in one way or another. The first of these is called *innovation*, in which there is an acceptance of cultural goals but a rejection of legitimate means. The second is termed *ritualism*, in which the goals are sometimes rejected while the means are rigidly obeyed. Another reaction is *retreatism*, in which both the goals and the means are rejected. The final response is labeled *rebellion*, which involves not only a rejection of goals and means, but also a desire to substitute new goals and means in place of the established ones.

Of the four "deviant" responses to anomie just described, all but one point to some evident example of a criminal or delinquent act. The "innovator," for example, would be expected to engage in theft. Retreatism would involve illegal drug use. Rebellion would include property destruction and crimes of public disorder. The ritualist, however, displays no clear-cut example of criminal or delinquent behavior. It is plausible to connect ritualism with neuroticism and claim a deviant connection in that sense. Since Merton's purpose was to outline a general theory of deviance, the inclusion of ritualism as a basic "deviant" reaction would thus seem appropriate.

The concept of anomie has also been used in connection with ecological studies of delinquency. One such ecological investigation was Bernard Lander's (1954) analysis of juvenile court statistics among the census tracts of Baltimore. Some results were similar to the studies of Shaw and McKay. For example, he found large inverse correlations between the delinquency rates of a census tract and median education, median rental values, and the percentage of home ownership; positive correlations were found between delinquency and overcrowding and substandard housing in census tracts.

In other respects, however, Lander's study did not support Shaw and McKay's findings. Delinquency rates only generally conformed to concentric zone patterns, and they were not uniformly highest in or near industrial or commercial zones. In general, Lander's results questioned the validity of social disorganization and transitional zones as major explanations of the distribution of delinquency rates.

As an alternative explanation, Lander offered the concept of anomie, which he defined as community stability and the effective presence of agreement concerning proper conduct. Community, or neighborhood, stability is best exemplified by home ownership, a factor which had the highest overall correlation with delinquency. Thus, a stable, or less anomic, community would tend to have lower rates of delinquency *in spite* of socioeconomic characteristics potentially capable of producing delinquency, such as substandard housing, poverty, and overcrowding.

Evaluation

The Durkheim-Merton formulations of anomie have received a substantial amount of attention in the field of crime and deviance (Cole and Zuckerman, 1964). Much of this literature has indicated a general acceptance of anomie as an explanation of criminality. At the same time, several problems exist that limit the explanatory power of anomie theory.

One of the foremost concerns is how social conditions become translated into forces that can influence individual behavior. For Durkheim, the issue was not an idle one, but one which presented many problems to those who would wish to reduce suicide in their society. For the most part, Durkheim viewed the corporate entity, as opposed to other institutions such as government, education, the family, and religion, as the most practical source of efforts to control suicide (Durkheim, 1951). Whether such entities actually are society's best defense against suicide, the point to be stressed here is the recognition by Durkheim that individual adjustments to societal conditions should be considered as part of a full development of socially constructed theories of behavior.

While Durkheim argued that institutional collectivities are major connectors between social structure and individual behavior, Merton's views on the subject are more general. In the initial explication of his theory, Merton has conceded that little attention was paid to the individual interpretations of anomic conditions and the effect such interpretations might have on behavior (Merton, 1964). For him, however, the principal consideration of anomie theory is that it is based on conditions that characterize society, or the "social surround" (Merton, 1964).

Still, the question remains, what is the relationship between anomie and individual behavior? A tentative answer for Merton lies in the interaction patterns generated by individuals living in "collectivities" of varying degrees of anomie (Merton, 1964). Thus, the influence of societal conditions on individual behavior is evident in *interaction* patterns, however these may be specifically generated.[1]

In a lengthy analysis of reference groups, Merton discusses a concept that could influence patterns of interaction, although he does not pursue the connection with respect to his anomic theory of deviance. This concept is called *relative deprivation*, which refers to comparisons an individual makes of himself or his social situation relative to his associates, or others, who are in some respects similar to himself (Merton, 1957). This concept can be used to explain why some people in "anomic" situations do not resort to criminality to resolve their dilemma. They do not perceive the dilemma as others might or as a structural, "objective" assessment of the situation might suggest. According to the logic of relative deprivation, the poor, or those in the lower class, do not compare their condition with middle- and upper-class lifestyles, even when they are aware of such values and behaviors. Instead, the poor compare themselves with each other or those just above poverty. In other words, the poor, and other social classes as well, will compare themselves more to those with whom they interact and associate than to those whom they only know through mass media accounts. It may be argued, for example, that labor union workers compare their economic situation more with the members of other unions than with management. A young lower-class offender may not be comparing himself with a specific victim who is also poor and resides nearby, but he is evaluating himself in relation to the general conditions of his peers and associates, as opposed to those in the middle- or upper-middle class.

Actually, Durkheim's concern with institutional factors and Merton's use of relative deprivation could be combined to produce another anomic view of delinquency. If one does not focus on economic issues, it is possible to conceptualize anomie in terms of specific organizational goals and means. With respect to delinquency, therefore, the means-end theory may be more appropriately applied to school problems, peer relationships, and other youth-oriented concerns rather than to economic issues. An illustration of this point is provided by the following interview. Although the subject is a college senior, the topic of cheating on exams gives a good example of how anomie can create pressures that force people to break the rules.

Excerpt from an Interview with a 19-Year-Old,
Female, Fourth-Year Pre-Med Student (Class of 1975)*

Interviewer — James K. Skipper, Jr.

Interviewer: *How important do you consider grades in being admitted to graduate school?*

*Source: Previously unpublished data from a project on the "Academic and Personal Problems of Pre-Med Students," Medical College of Ohio at Toledo, 1975–76, James K. Skipper, Jr., Project Director.

Respondent: As a pre-med student I have to get grades—at least a 3.5. But so do all the other pre-med students here. We are all in competition with each other. What makes it hard is that we have to take a lot of classes together. Now you know the instructor is only going to give maybe 3 or 4 A's. But there may be 8 or 10 of us are trying to get those A's. We are all good students with little to choose between us. The pressure is tremendous and even greater for me because I am a woman. Most of the time just an extra couple of points on the exam is all that is separating the A's from the B's.

Interviewer: *Do you ever resort to cheating?*

Respondent: Why of course, any advantage you get, you take. If you don't when you get the chance, you know someone else will and you will be behind. It is not like regular cheating anyway. We are all good students. It is just a matter of getting that little edge for the grade: if you don't you may be just as good as the next guy, but he is going to get into medical school and you are not. That is just the way it is. It has nothing to do with ethics. It is just what you have to do to get admitted. You understand what I mean, don't you?

The ecological construct of anomie is in some respects so similar to the social disorganization perspective that a detailed evaluation of its logical properties would be redundant. There have been several replications of Lander's Baltimore study and they have essentially supported the ecological correlations reported earlier (Bordua, 1958–59; Chilton, 1964). These analyses, and other discussions of Lander's study (Gordon, 1967), however, question the legitimacy of using home ownership and percent nonwhite as indicators of anomie. In addition, statistical manipulations often produce diverse findings and can lead to the conclusion that socioeconomic variables, such as rental value and median education, are as strongly related to delinquency as Lander's anomie constructs.

Overall, it would appear that the ecological definition of anomie, and its relationship to delinquency, has run its course. This approach to delinquency seems to have no real "home," as it were, in theoretical classification schemes. Using anomie as an *ecological* concept is inconsistent with a social disorganization perspective. At the same time, to compare anomie with ecological characteristics is incongruous with the dominant usage of the term. Even Merton, for example, criticizes Lander's conceptualization on the ground that it represents, at best, only an indirect measure of social relationships, which represent only one component (actually, result) of anomie (Merton, 1957). The urgings of Chilton (1964) and Rosen and Turner (1967) for an end to ecological-anomic studies of delinquency appear to have been heeded. While the investigation of delinquency still sometimes utilizes ecological measurements, and is more often informed by anomie theory, the specific search for statistical indices of anomie in neighborhood or census tract settings has become virtually nonexistent.

SUMMARY

As social explanations of delinquency, social disorganization and anomie offer significant contrasts to individualistic explanations. In both instances, the logic of the theory appears to be fairly sound, if not complete. Furthermore, in the case of social disorganization, there has appeared a rather impressive collection of supporting evidence (the empirical assessment of the anomic theory of delinquency is discussed in Chapter 5).

A persistent problem of both explanations of delinquency, however, is the lack of explanation as to how social or societal conditions exert an influence over one's behavior. In this sense, both theories are incomplete. While they provide a solid base from which to launch other theoretical explanations of delinquency, they should not be interpreted as providing the ultimate sociological understanding of delinquency.

In particular, the theory of social disorganization has provided the basis for many significant contributions to delinquency theory and research in the latter half of the twentieth century. The value of social disorganization as an explanation of delinquency lies in its implication of institutional factors in the etiology of delinquency. Although these factors were largely invoked in an attempt to explain the ultimate acceptance of delinquent behavior in delinquency areas, subsequent research has pointed to institutional factors as significant influences on delinquency in their own right. In addition, the cultural transmission aspect of social disorganization utilizes interpersonal concepts in describing the process of learning and conveying criminal values. These concepts have also proved useful in explaining delinquency.

The theory of anomie, particularly Merton's means-end interpretation, is also not without promise as an explanation of delinquency. Anomie theory might best be applied to delinquency in the form of means and goals that are relevant to the status of youth, such as pressures and expectations associated with school, rather than solely in terms of economic issues. Nonetheless, a large part of the literature relating anomie to delinquency has focused on the distribution of economic opportunities in society, particularly among lower-class youth. The application of anomie theory, and other theories, to delinquency among lower-class youth is presented in the following chapter.

NOTE

1. Lemert (1964) argues that individual choices are also controlled by calculated risk assessments and awareness of the opportunity to commit illegal or deviant acts. In this analysis, cultural or societal conditions are relatively noninfluential in the explanation of individual behavior, especially in a complex, technologically advanced society, such as the United States.

REFERENCES

Bordua, David J., 1958–59, "Juvenile Delinquency and 'Anomie': An Attempt at Replication." Social Problems 6:230–238.

Burgess, Ernest W., 1942, "Introduction." Pp. ix–xiii in Clifford R. Shaw and Henry D. McKay, Juvenile Delinquency and Urban Areas. Chicago: University of Chicago Press.

———, 1967, "The Growth of the City: An Introduction to a Research Project." Pp. 47–62 in Robert E. Park, Ernest W. Burgess, and Roderick D. McKenzie (eds.), The City. Chicago: University of Chicago Press. First published in 1925.

Chambliss, William J., 1974, "Functional and Conflict Theories of Crime." MSS Modular Publications, Module 17:1–23.

Chilton, Roland J., 1964, "Continuity in Delinquency Area Research: A Comparison of Studies of Baltimore, Detroit, and Indianapolis." American Sociological Review 29:71–83.

Cole, Stephen and Harriet Zuckerman, 1964, "Inventory of Empirical and Theoretical Studies of Anomie." Pp. 243–283 in Marshall B. Clinard (ed.), Anomie and Deviant Behavior. New York: Free Press.

DeFleur, Lois B., 1967, "Ecological Variables in the Cross-Cultural Study of Delinquency." Social Forces 45:556–570.

Durkheim, Emile, 1933, The Division of Labor in Society, translated by George Simpson. London: The Free Press of Glencoe. First published in 1893.

———, 1951, Suicide, translated by John A. Spaulding and George Simpson. New York: Free Press. First published in 1897.

Fabrikant, Richard, 1979, "The Distribution of Criminal Offenses in an Urban Environment: A Spatial Analysis of Criminal Spillovers and of Juvenile Offenders." American Journal of Economics and Sociology 33:32–48.

Farris, R. E. L. and H. W. Dunham, 1939, Mental Disorders in Urban Areas. Chicago: University of Chicago Press.

Finestone, Harold, 1976, Victims of Change. Westport, Conn.: Greenwood Press.

Gordon, Robert A., 1967, "Issues in the Ecological Study of Delinquency." American Sociological Review 32:927–944.

Hayner, Norman S., 1942, "Five Cities of the Pacific Northwest." Pp. 353–387 in Clifford R. Shaw and Henry D. McKay, Juvenile Delinquency in Urban Areas. Chicago: University of Chicago Press.

Ianni, Francis A. J., 1974, Black Mafia. New York: Simon & Schuster.

Jonassen, Christen T., 1949, "A Re-Evaluation and Critique of the Logic and Some Methods of Shaw and McKay." American Sociological Review 14:608–617.

Kobrin, Solomon, 1959, "The Chicago Area Project—A Twenty-five Year Assessment." The Annals of the American Academy of Political and Social Science 322:20-29.

——, 1971, "The Formal Logical Properties of the Shaw-McKay Delinquency Theory." Pp. 101-131 in Harwin L. Voss and David M. Petersen (eds.), Ecology, Crime, and Delinquency. New York: Appleton-Century-Crofts.

Lander, Bernard, 1954, Towards an Understanding of Juvenile Delinquency. New York: Columbia University Press. Reprinted by AMS Press, 1970.

Lemert, Edwin M., 1964, "Social Structure, Social Control, and Deviation." Pp. 57-97 in Marshall B. Clinard (ed.), Anomie and Deviant Behavior, q.v.

Merton, Robert K., 1957, Social Theory and Social Structure, revised and enlarged edition. London: The Free Press of Glencoe.

——, 1964, "Anomie, Anomia, and Social Interaction: Contexts of Deviant Behavior." Pp. 213-242 in Marshall B. Clinard (ed.), q.v.

Miller, Walter B., 1975, Violence by Youth Gangs and Youth Groups as a Crime Problem in Major American Cities. Washington, D.C.: U.S. Government Printing Office.

Morris, Terence, 1958, The Criminal Area. London: Routledge and Kegan Paul.

Park, Robert E., 1936, "Human Ecology." American Journal of Sociology 42:1-15.

——, 1967, "The City: Suggestions for the Investigation of Human Behavior in the Urban Environment." Pp. 1-46 in Robert E. Park, Ernest W. Burgess, and Roderick D. McKenzie (eds.), The City, q.v.

Robison, Sophia M., 1936, Can Delinquency Be Measured? New York: Columbia University Press.

Rosen, Lawrence, 1978, The Delinquent and Non-Delinquent in a High Delinquent Area. San Francisco: R&E Research Associates.

Rosen, Lawrence and Stanley H. Turner, 1967, "An Evaluation of the Lander Approach to Ecology of Delinquency." Social Problems 15:189-200.

Sellin, Thorsten, 1938, Culture Conflict and Crime. New York: Social Science Research Council.

Shaw, Clifford R., 1966, The Jack-Roller. Chicago: University of Chicago Press. First published in 1930.

Shaw, Clifford R. and Henry D. McKay, 1942, Juvenile Delinquency and Urban Areas. Chicago: University of Chicago Press.

——, 1969, Juvenile Delinquency and Urban Areas, revised edition. Chicago: University of Chicago Press.

Shaw, Clifford R., Henry D. McKay, and James F. McDonald, 1938, Brothers in Crime. Chicago: University of Chicago Press.

Shaw, Clifford R., Frederick M. Zorbaugh, Henry D. McKay, and Leonard S. Cottrell, 1929, Delinquency Areas. Chicago: University of Chicago Press.

Smith, William Carlson, 1937, Americans in Process. Ann Arbor, Mich.: Edwards Brothers.

Sutherland, Edwin H. and Donald R. Cressey, 1978, Criminology, tenth edition. New York: Lippincott.

Taylor, Ian, Paul Walton, and Jock Young, 1973, The New Criminology. New York: Harper & Row.

Thomas, William I. and Florian Znaniecki, 1927, The Polish Peasant in Europe and America, Volume 2. New York: Knopf.

Voss, Harwin L. and David M. Petersen (eds.), 1971, "Introduction." Pp. 1–44 in Voss and Petersen (eds.), Ecology, Crime, and Delinquency, q.v.

Wilks, Judith A., 1967, "Ecological Correlates of Crime and Delinquency." Pp. 138–156 in The President's Commission on Law Enforcement and Administration of Justice, Task Force Report: Crime and Its Impact—An Assessment. Washington, D.C.: U.S. Government Printing Office.

Young, Pauline V., 1967, The Pilgrims of Russian-Town. New York: Russell and Russell. First published in 1932.

5

LOWER-CLASS-BASED THEORIES
OF DELINQUENCY

HISTORICAL OVERVIEW AND GENERIC ASSUMPTIONS

Beginning in the 1950s, several causal theories of juvenile delinquency were developed in an attempt to explain delinquent, and typically delinquent gang, behavior of lower-class males. Such explanations concentrated on the social nature of delinquency, much like the social disorganization and anomie theories offered 20 or 30 years earlier. Indeed, they may be viewed as modifications and extensions of sociological perspectives that developed in the 1920s. In this context, a "juvenile gang" is often described as a "delinquent subculture," or at least as being the gang part of such a subculture. For this reason, these are referred to as "subcultural theories" of delinquency. This terminology suggests one major assumption—namely, that most delinquent behavior occurs within a group or gang setting. Delinquents, it is said, typically act together, or when they act alone, their behavior is strongly influenced by groups, gangs, peers, and the general ambience of their lives and associations.

Another basic assumption of these theories is that delinquency is overwhelmingly a *lower-class, male* phenomenon. As Albert Cohen, the developer of one such theory, put it: "It is our conclusion, by no means novel or startling, that juvenile delinquency and the delinquent subculture in particular are overwhelmingly concentrated in the male, working-class sector of the juvenile population" (1955:371). Here, as elsewhere, Cohen uses the term "working class" more or less interchangeably with "lower class," although many sociologists make a rather strong distinction. Whatever the terminology, [all theories of lower-class juvenile misconduct are based on the assumption that delinquency, particularly gang delinquency, is concentrated in the lower class, as measured by a variety of economic and social factors.]

Of course, some investigators are skeptical of the validity of this assumption (Vaz, 1967). Surely, they argue, delinquency occurs among all social classes, and the official estimates of delinquency, which so regularly indict the lower classes, are more reflections of the biases of the police, courts, and others than the actual behavior of lower-class juveniles. Theorists who contend that the delinquency of lower-class youth is relatively high are not unmindful of such charges. Upon examination of the evidence, their conclusion remains, however, unchanged: serious and repetitive juvenile delinquency is predominantly a lower-class phenomenon.

Similar arguments and charges are sometimes raised with respect to the distribution of delinquency by gender, although the evidence here is not as much in doubt as with the question of social class. Much of the controversy regarding the increased involvement of females in crime and delinquency is built around the suspected influence of the changing sex roles of women on the opportunity and motivation for deviance (delinquency in this case) among the distaff side of the population (Adler, 1975; Simon, 1975; Steffensmeier and Steffensmeier, 1980). Data on the increase of female delinquency indicate that female rates of delinquency are still lower than male rates. Furthermore, the increase in female delinquency is primarily in property- and drug-related crimes. Females have not been involved in violent offenses to the same extent as males, and female delinquency has not been considered as threatening as male delinquency.

Certainly, there is enough delinquency among the lower-class male segment of the population, whether it has been officially recorded or not, to warrant concern and investigation. To the extent that delinquency occurs among lower-class youth, it may well be that experiences of the lower class, including values and life-styles, contribute significantly to this behavior.

A sound explanation of delinquency within a particular segment of the population, therefore, may be useful in the search for delinquency causation. Such an explanation would not only be useful in its own right, but it might also provide insightful clues for the explanation of delinquency among other groups of people.

There are three major concepts and ideas in the subcultural explanations of lower-class delinquency: the middle-class measuring rod theory of Cohen, the opportunity theory of Richard Cloward and Lloyd Ohlin (partly based on Merton's anomie theory of deviance), and the lower-class value system explanation of Walter Miller.

COHEN AND THE MIDDLE-CLASS MEASURING ROD

Specific Assumptions

The middle-class measuring rod theory has four basic assumptions: (1) that a relatively high number of lower-class youth (males in particular) do poorly in school; (2) that poor school performance is related to delinquency; (3) that poor school performance is mostly attributable to a conflict between the dominant middle-class values of the school system and the values of lower-class youth; and (4) that lower-class male delinquency is largely committed in a gang context, partly as a means of developing more positive self-concepts and nurturing antisocial values.

Key Concepts

Reaction Formation   This is a Freudian term that describes the process in which a person openly rejects that which he wants, or aspires to, but cannot obtain or achieve.

Middle-Class Measuring Rod   The evaluations of school performance or behavior according to norms and values thought to be associated with the middle-class, such as punctuality, neatness, cleanliness, nonviolent behavior, and so on, constitute a middle-class measuring rod.

Discussion

The gist of Cohen's (1955) argument is that social class membership is associated with social values and life-styles. With respect to child-rearing in the middle class, the working-class (and presumably lower-class) child is likely to be taught that behavior should be spontaneous and aggressive. Values are focused on the present with little emphasis placed on long-range planning. Socialization, or training, in the lower class is "easy going." The child learns to obey commands because of the immediate, practical value of obedience, not because of the intrinsic worth or "good" associated with conformity in and of itself, or because obedience will generate warm, affectionate reactions from a parent who is loving and on whom the child has become dependent.

By contrast, Cohen maintains that middle-class socialization or child-rearing stresses values and life-styles that are often quite opposite to those found within the lower class. Specifically, he suggests that middle-class values can be summed up in nine concepts: (1) drive and ambition, (2) individual responsibility, (3) achievement and success, whether at work, in the classroom, on the field, or in any other arena of competition, (4) the willingness to postpone immediate satisfaction of wants and desires for future profit or gain (the deferred gratification pattern), (5) rationality in the form of long-range planning and budgeting, (6) exercise of courtesy and self-control in association with others, particularly strangers, (7) control of violence and aggression, verbal or physical, in all social settings, (8) "wholesome" recreation, that is, constructive use of leisure time, such as in a hobby, and (9) respect for the property of others, perhaps the most basic value of all. Here, Cohen is suggesting that the middle-class members of society admire and try to promote more than simple, basic honesty. The value of property rights extends to the right of the owner of an article or thing to do as he or she wishes with it, with little interference from others.

While these two separate class-related value systems exist, middle-class values predominate within the school context. Consequently, the lower-class youth finds himself "measured" and evaluated by middle-class standards. This situation would present no problems to the lower-class young were it not for two conditions. First, middle-class values are the generally accepted ones in society, even among those of the lower class. Thus, standards of acceptance, achievement, and reward, as established by middle-class values and norms, are adopted and *aspired* to by members of the lower class. Second, personal failure alone, at the immediate level of the school setting, can lead to other problems, not excluding delinquency.

So strongly does the lower-class boy initially aspire to the middle-class standards of success that his repeated failures in the school system, both academically and otherwise, lead him to reject the school and the system of values it represents (a reaction formation). In this case, Cohen argues, the lower-class boy repudiates middle-class values and becomes malicious and hostile toward a now hated set of standards and all things which symbolize those standards. Cohen stresses three descriptive words to denote the extent to which the lower-class delinquent boy rejects middle-class status symbols: *malicious, negativistic,* and *nonutilitarian*. In other words, delinquent boys are "just plain mean." Middle-class standards are not only to be rejected, they are to be *flouted*. Thus, "good" children are to be terrorized, playgrounds and gyms are to be taken over for aimless use, golf courses are to be torn up, library books are to be stolen and destroyed, and so on. But perhaps the most graphic display of contempt and malice shown by lower-class gang boys toward the school system is defecating on a teacher's desk.

The final element of Cohen's theory is the introduction of a peer group or, more accurately, a gang context through which the rejected and resentful lower-class boy can nurture his growing feelings of hostility and bolster a damaged self-concept. At this point, Cohen is careful to specify that not all working- or lower-class boys caught in this predicament begin to associate with delinquent peers. Because of family, neighborhood, personality, and other conditions, some working-class males adopt a "college-boy" response, which is based on success at school and in the conventional, middle-class world altogether. Others, perhaps most, adopt a "corner-boy" response, which represents an acceptance of the lower-class male's situation and an attempt to make the best of a bad situation. The residue, a numerical minority, turn to delinquency.

The theoretical scenario of Cohen's explanation of delinquency is depicted graphically in Figure 8.

| Working-class socialization + Middle-class values of success | → | Lower-class failure in the school system (among many) | → | Loss of self-esteem and increased feelings of rejection | → |
| School dropout and association with delinquent peers (among some) | → | Increased hostility and resentment toward middle-class standards and symbols, thus reaction formation | → | Improved self-image in a gang context and through negative and malicious delinquent behavior | |

FIGURE 8

Evaluation

Recall that Cohen's theory is based on several assumptions. Evidence on the first assumption is fairly clear; lower-class youth generally *do* perform poorly in school relative to other students. From the early studies of sociologists at the University of Chicago, from which there came such works as *The Gang* by Frederick Thrasher (1927) and *Elmtown's Youth* by August Hollingshead

(1949), to more recent research of a wide methodological variety (Polk and Schafer, 1972; Harvey and Slatin, 1975; Liazos, 1978), there emerges the conclusion that lower-class youth (and often ethnic minority youth) perform poorly, academically and socially, in school. Indeed, much of this evidence suggests that lower-class juveniles are expected by teachers and school administrators to perform at academic levels below those of middle-class students, and the effect of such lower expectations on eventual performance cannot be ignored.

One example of the influence of school administration expectations on student performance is the tracking system, in which students are placed into a multi-year program of instruction which is typically divided into college-oriented and trade or technical training-oriented curricula. While a number of academic factors have been related to the assignment of juveniles to particular tracks, social factors have also been found to play a part in this selection, including social class (Schafer et al., 1972; Kelly, 1978).

The second basic point of Cohen's thesis, that school performance is related to delinquency, has also been supported by research. In fact, this has been one of the most consistently documented relationships in recent literature (Hirschi, 1969; Offord et al., 1978; Jensen and Rojek, 1980).[1]

An acceptance of Cohen's thesis leads to the conclusion that school failure leads to dropping out, which leads to delinquency. In one of the most careful analyses of this relationship, Delbert Elliott and Harwin Voss (1974) provide some very interesting information. They investigated the correlation between school dropout and delinquency by closely monitoring the annual school performance and delinquency records of 2000 students in California, from the ninth grade to one year after the expected date of graduation from high school (twelfth grade).

As with several other studies, these researchers found that those students who had dropped out of school during this monitored time had higher rates of delinquency than those who had graduated. The expected causal ordering of this relationship, however, was not supported. Instead, the study revealed that rates of delinquency (as measured by police contacts and self-reports) *peaked* in the time just *before* dropping out and *declined* in each subsequent check period. According to this study, then, dropping out may be a *delinquency-reducing solution* to school problems rather than the starting point for a delinquent career, as Cohen's theory suggests. This conclusion is further justified by the finding that delinquency rates of dropouts are lower for those who married and, to some extent at least, found employment. That is, dropouts who not only eliminate school problems by dropping out but who also bolster their efforts to assume adult status by marrying or gaining employment have the lowest rates of delinquency.

The causes of school problems which led to dropping out were analyzed according to a variety of possibilities, including self-esteem, academic abilities, feelings of isolation and alienation (at home, in the community, or at school), and peer associations. In general, Elliott and Voss conclude that academic achievement is strongly related to dropping out, as are isolation and alienation from the school. Social class is not examined relative to dropping out per se, but Elliott and Voss did find that social class is related to exposure to dropouts. Moreover, in another investigation of school dropout and delinquency, Elliott (1966) found that the relationship between dropping out and delinquency was stronger for lower-class boys than for middle-class youth, a finding which supports Cohen's thesis.

Nonetheless, the documentation of *class-related* school problems, the third assumption, is generally problematic. Several darts have been thrown at the ineffectiveness of public education to reach and develop the potential of *all* youth (Polk and Schafer, 1972; Liazos, 1978). Some of those criticisms, such as irrelevant instruction, improper motivation, and intolerance of nonconformity to rigid rules, would certainly suggest that *differential class values between pupils and school officials* might be a major influence on the higher failure rates of lower-class youth. But this class connection, which is clearly at the heart of Cohen's argument, has not been carefully researched or well documented.

The fourth major component of Cohen's theory, that delinquency is a gang phenomenon and that gang members derive psychological gratification from gang membership, has received mixed support from other studies. On the one hand, there is considerable research evidence that delinquency is *social* in nature, occurring in the presence of at least two adolescents. However, the extent to which delinquency, even lower-class male delinquency, is part of structured, antisocial gangs is debatable (Jensen and Rojek, 1980).

Aside from the question of how much of lower-class male delinquency is gang related, there is mixed opinion concerning the psychological states of gang members. Somewhat consistent with Cohen's thesis, Lewis Yablonsky (1970) contends that juvenile gangs, particularly lower-class violent gangs, are best described as "near groups" because their core members are psychopathic and unable to establish primary, stable relationships, even with each other, and hence do not have the close interweaving of members with one another that would characterize true groups. This view of gang personalities, however, is contrary to most other studies of gangs (Thrasher, 1927; Bordua, 1961; Short and Strodtbeck, 1965; Klein, 1971). Actually, very few delinquents, lower-class males or otherwise, are considered psychopathic or even seriously disturbed, as Yablonsky maintains. In addition, there is little evidence to support the contention that gang membership helps to bolster one's self-esteem (Jensen and Rojek, 1980). But whereas Cohen's thesis suggests inner conflict and psychological problems in the delinquent, it does not require that we find psychopathology to maintain its basic tenets. It does seem to require the search for an explanation related to neurosis to solve a class-based problem, and personality studies do not appear to validate that aspect of his theory.

On balance, the totality of Cohen's theory has not been empirically verified. There is little doubt that America is socially stratified and that class differences are observed with respect to school performance. However, that such differences are both the cause of school problems and, subsequently, of delinquency, particularly among lower-class males, has not been consistently substantiated. Nor has it been demonstrated that male youth who have failed in school seek peer associations through which aggressive and hostile acts of delinquency are committed against an overtly hated, but unconsciously admired, middle-class value system. It is also problematic to try to explain just how failure in school becomes interpreted in terms of a delinquent response, as opposed to what Cohen feels is a more common response among lower-class males, the adaptive, corner-boy response. As Hyman Rodman (1963), Elliot Liebow (1967), and others suggest, the disadvantaged often display an ability to incorporate a basic conformity to a dominant, middle-class value system with the exigencies of their everyday lives.

Cohen's thesis has merit, however, in that it has pointed to a critical source of adolescent problems and juvenile delinquency—lack of status and failure within the school system. And to the extent that he highlights the qualitative distinction between youthful and adult lawbreaking, both in motivation and pattern of conduct, Cohen made an important contribution to the understanding of delinquency. If this observation is accepted, then no theory of delinquency is adequate that does not account for Cohen's measuring rod.

CLOWARD AND OHLIN'S THEORY OF DIFFERENTIAL OPPORTUNITY STRUCTURE

Specific Assumptions

The differential opportunity theory has two basic assumptions: (1) that blocked economic aspirations cause poor self-concepts and general feelings of frustrations, and (2) that these frustrations lead to delinquency in specialized gang contexts, the nature of which varies according to the structure of criminal and conventional values in the juvenile's neighborhood.

Key Concepts

Differential Opportunity Structure   The uneven distribution of legal *and* illegal means of achieving economic success in a society, particularly as these opportunities or means are unequally divided by social class positions, represents a differential opportunity structure.

Criminal Gang   A juvenile gang primarily involved in theft activity is a criminal gang.

Conflict Gang   A conflict gang engages largely in violent behavior.

Retreatist Gang   A retreatist gang is primarily involved in drug-related behavior.

Discussion

In contrast to Cohen's explanation of lower-class delinquency, the explanation of Cloward and Ohlin (1960) suggests that lower-class male delinquents are goal-oriented beings, who are able rationally to assess their *economic* situation and to plan for their future accordingly.

This theory stems from a combination of two theoretical positions, which are discussed elsewhere in this book. One position is that of Robert K. Merton (1957), who argues that lower-class crime and delinquency result from a systematic exclusion of the lower class from competitive access to legitimate channels that lead to economic success in this society (see Chapter 4). The other position, brought forth by Edwin Sutherland (1939), maintains that criminal and delinquent behavior, like all other behavior, is learned, primarily in close, primary group relationships and associations (see Chapter 6). The specific content, degree, and duration of delinquent behavior depends on these associations.

Cloward and Ohlin combine the essential elements of Merton's theory of anomie and Sutherland's theory of differential association to propose that lower-class male gang delinquency is *generated* from blocked legitimate economic opportunities through America's conventional institutions, and that the specific *nature* of this delinquency is dependent on the *characteristics of the neighborhoods* in which the delinquent adolescents live (and to a slighter extent, on other significant associations, particularly with peers, that the adolescents make). These characteristics affect the opportunities for committing *illegal* acts. A major contribution of this theory is the contention that the opportunity to commit illegal acts is distributed unevenly throughout society, just as are opportunities to engage in conformist behavior.

Essentially, Cloward and Ohlin argue that lower-class gang delinquency occurs in three dimensions: *criminal, conflict,* and *drug-oriented* or *retreatist.* They also contend that the *predominance* of one or the other delinquent behavior patterns is largely dependent on the *integration of conventional and organized illegitimate values and behavior systems and the integration of offenders of different ages in a neighborhood.* Previous studies of gangs and general delinquent behavior in lower-class neighborhoods have emphasized the close connection that often exists between gang behavior and conventional, legitimate business and governmental concerns (Kobrin, 1951; Whyte, 1955). Furthermore, years earlier Thrasher, Shaw, and others of the influential school of sociology located at the University of Chicago had consistently documented associations between delinquent gangs of different age levels and between older gangs and adult offenders (Thrasher, 1927; Shaw, 1930; 1931; Shaw and McKay, 1942). Cloward and Ohlin took this work a step further by systematically connecting neighborhood integration patterns with specific types of gang behaviors and by tying all of this in with Merton's theory of means-end societal discrepancies as the generating force of delinquent gangs.

According to the theory, a *criminal* pattern of gang behavior emerges when there is the presence of organized, adult criminal activity in a lower-class neighborhood. In this situation, adult criminals become the success role models of the juvenile gangs. These adult role models serve as the tutors for the juveniles and as the developers of criminal skills within that group. The relationship between the adult criminals and conventional adults in these neighborhoods is described as "stable." A pattern of accommodation and mutual interdependence emerges between these two adult groups, which filters down to the juvenile gangs that flourish in the area. This accommodation is exemplified by the "fence," who makes a little extra income by disposing of stolen goods through a conventional business. Of course, local political and criminal justice officials are also accommodative of the criminal behavior in their neighborhoods, often offering protection and other preferred treatment to the criminals in exchange for personal gain and community stability. The integration and accommodation between criminal and conventional forces in a neighborhood combine to produce an emphasis on neighborhood stability and order. Thus, gang behavior will become theft oriented, not violence oriented. Behavior is supposed to be businesslike and disciplined, not irrational or tempestuous. As Cloward and Ohlin put it, "there is no place in organized crime for the impulsive, unpredictable individual" (1960:167). And while gang behavior is not organized crime in the sense in which that term is widely used, to connote powerful families in virtual control of large-scale criminal activity, Cloward and Ohlin find that the organization and discipline necessary in fruitful gang conduct preclude the impulsive and irrational people.

In some lower-class neighborhoods a stable, organized pattern of adult criminality fails to develop, although the discrepancy between societal success goals and accessibility to legitimate means of achieving success still exists for the local residents. Furthermore, in these areas living conditions in general are unstable and transient. Adult role models for juveniles, either criminal or conventional role models, do not develop. The result is the emergence of what Cloward and Ohlin call a *conflict* form of gang behavior. In this type of gang, violence becomes predominant. The violent behavior in these gangs, however, is *not* characterized as stemming primarily from psychopathic personalities or from reaction formation, although the youths in these gangs are described as "acutely frustrated." The major reason for the emergence of conflict gangs in these lower-class neighborhoods is the absence of a stable system of social control, which can be exerted either by criminal adult or conventional adult models. Adolescents use violence as a means of obtaining some kind of status and success because nonviolent, theft-oriented avenues of success are not available to them.

To illustrate their point, Cloward and Ohlin assert that violence within gangs declines when a detached street worker is assigned to work with them. This reduction in violence might reflect not only the abilities of the street worker, but also recognition by the gang members that the street worker represents the end of rejection and the beginning of access to legitimate success opportunities in their lives.

In some neighborhoods, *whether or not they are characterized by stable adult success opportunities (criminal or conventional)*, gangs develop that are dominated by drug use. These are the *retreatist* gangs, according to Cloward and Ohlin. Their members are described as "double failures" because they cannot succeed either in the conventional or the criminal world. The authors caution that not all double failures become members of retreatist gangs. Some scale down their aspirations and become "corner boys," as Cohen has suggested. The extent to which adolescents adopt a corner-boy or a retreatist response varies not only according to the personality of the youth, but particularly according to his associations and circumstances.

An indication that retreatism is largely a response to one's associations and circumstances is provided in the assertion of Cloward and Ohlin that retreatist gangs often emerge *after* involvement with criminal or conflict gangs. In fact, they suggest that inappropriate behavior by some in the gang, abusive drug behavior or otherwise, can lead to a rejection by the gang members and the subsequent development of a retreatist life-style. It is also for this reason that Cloward and Ohlin hedge on the description of these doubly rejected youths as members of a retreatist gang or subculture. Although most gangs use drugs, it is doubtful whether there are many drug-oriented gangs, as such. It would be more accurate, therefore, to use the word "response" or "adaptation" when referring to retreatism through drug use.

In summary, the basic components of Cloward and Ohlin's theory of lower-class gang delinquency may be diagrammed as shown in Figure 9.

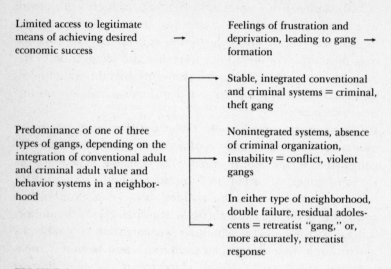

FIGURE 9

Evaluation

The assumption that blocked economic aspirations affect attitudes and cause frustration has been tested in a variety of ways and has basically been found lacking. Interviews with lower-class youth, delinquent youth, or gang members simply fail to support the basic assumption that lower-class youth hinge their feelings and behavior on the door of perceived economic opportunity in their lives. One reason for this conclusion is the interaction among aspirations, *expectations*, and behavior. In a comparative study of high school seniors from working- and middle-class neighborhoods in Atlanta, for example, Wan Sang Han (1969) found that working-class and middle-class students aspired to essentially the same goals several years after graduation. When asked what they *expected* to have after graduation, however, there were marked differences among the students. Working-class seniors expected to have less than they desired. Middle-class students, on the other hand, still continued to expect what they desired 10 years upon graduation, almost as if they considered these goals a right or a natural phase of life.

An attempt to assess the interrelationship among a juvenile's aspirations and expectations and subsequent delinquency was reported in the previously discussed study by Elliott and Voss (1974). These researchers assessed the actual and anticipated amount of success or failure among their sample with respect to educational and occupational status. Simply put, the results of this test failed to demonstrate a relationship between failure and self-reported delinquency in support of the thesis of Cloward and Ohlin. If anything, what little relationship did emerge tended to support an opposite conceptualization—that lowered perceptions of occupational success *follow* delinquency rather than precede delinquency. A similar conclusion was reached by another investigation of self-reported delinquency, with the qualification that delinquency was more strongly related to perceived lower educational opportunities than to occupational aspirations (Quicker, 1974).

Elliott and Voss did find that educational and occupational perceptions of success were lower for lower-class youth than for middle-class adolescents. The relationships were not very strong, however, and should not be used in support of class-linked theories of delinquency.

A study of gang delinquency in Chicago provides conflicting evidence concerning the relationship between delinquency and perceived opportunities for success (Short, 1964). On the one hand, the analysis revealed that lower-class gang boys, both white and black, had higher rates of official delinquency and higher average discrepancies between occupational aspirations and expectations than nongang boys, although the discrepancies were small. When the boys' aspiration levels were compared with their fathers' occupational levels, however, it was found that white gang members had the smallest discrepancy of all groups studied, including black gang juveniles, lower- and middle-class black youth, and lower- and middle-class white boys. With respect to perceived educational opportunities, the highest rates of delinquency were recorded for those juveniles who perceived educational opportunities as closed to them, in agreement with the theory. However, among those who perceived educational opportunities as closed, those who had the lowest aspirations also had the highest rates of delinquency, contrary to the thesis.

Other studies, either of delinquency in general (Hirschi, 1969) or of gang delinquency (Short et al., 1965), provide further evidence refuting Cloward and Ohlin's argument. In these studies, the most delinquent juveniles are those with both low aspirations and expectations rather than those with high aspirations and low expectations, as the thesis would predict.

Perhaps the difficulty in this area lies with the imprecision of paper and pencil measures of values. It may well be that lower-class and middle-class adolescents, as well as adults, *do* have different goal perceptions and that the perception of blocked opportunities may lead to feelings of hostility and frustration. On the other hand, the perceptions and values of those in the lower class, including lower-class delinquents, are adapted from basic support of middle-class or conventional standards. Those in the lower class must come to grips with the reality of the situation and "stretch" or alter their values to accommodate their present behavior (Rodman, 1963). Excellent literary and ethnographic descriptions of this process are found in Joyce Carol Oates' *Them* (1969) and Elliot Liebow's *Tally's Corner* (1967). Paper and pencil tests, it may be argued, simply cannot measure or describe the complexities of these relationships.

The second assumption of Cloward and Ohlin's argument, that lower-class gangs become specialized according to the type of neighborhood in which they exist, has received more support in the literature than the first assumption.

Irving Spergel (1964) examined the nature of juvenile gangs in three predominantly lower-class neighborhoods and concluded that gang specialization did appear. The specific content of these gangs, however, did not duplicate Cloward and Ohlin's criminal, conflict, and drug typology. For example, Spergel could not detect a specific drug subculture, or juvenile gang, in any of the three neighborhoods, although drug use was practiced in a limited way in each area.[2] In addition, Spergel's analysis differentiated the criminal subculture of Cloward and Ohlin into a *racket* subculture and a general *theft* subculture.

Spergel's study also demonstrated a connection between gang delinquency and neighborhood integration, both conventional-criminal integration and age-level integration. The racket (career theft, organized crime) subculture was found in a neighborhood having residential stability and organized crime. In this neighborhood, Spergel noted a connection between both conventional and criminal adult activities and between the criminal activities and the dominant forms of conduct in the juvenile gangs, such as loan sharking, policy or numbers games, off-track betting, drug selling, and prostitution. The gang members from "Racketville" exhibited a stronger criminal orientation (although no more delinquent behavior) than the gang members in the other two neighborhoods. A dominant role model for the delinquents in Racketville was the adult racketeer, and the major means of getting ahead for them were "connections," as opposed to luck, ability, or education.

A fighting or conflict subculture was found in an area with high rates of public assistance, psychiatric treatment, infant mortality, congestion, physical deterioration, and low income. The delinquents in these neighborhoods also had the least amount of stability of all three areas. Consistent with Cloward and Ohlin's predictions, the integration of "Slumtown" was very low. Petty criminals occupied the streets. Respected adults in the area, conventional or criminal, were hard to locate. Deference to older delinquents by younger ones was also not in evidence.

The third neighborhood studied by Spergel, "Haulburg," was lower-class by some economic criteria, but in many ways more middle-class than the other two areas, standing midway between Racketville and Slumtown in terms of neighborhood integration and adult criminal organization. Gang behavior in Haulburg was composed of some violence but more theft, such as car theft, apartment burglary, and store holdups. This type of gang was not predicted by Cloward and Ohlin, but the relationship between this gang's behavior and its neighborhood characteristics does not contradict the thesis.

A study by James Short and Fred Strodtbeck in Chicago also generally supports the idea of gang specialization, although the specific nature of the specialization is, again, not in perfect agreement with Cloward and Ohlin (Short and Strodtbeck, 1965). In this study no criminal subculture, as such, was discovered. Instead, several cliques within conflict gangs would break off and engage in "semi-professional theft," such as burglary, auto stripping, and shoplifting. To some extent, Short and Strodtbeck feel that there may be a "parent delinquent subculture" which characterizes all gangs in general and from which more specialized gang activity may develop.

On many other accounts, however, this research lends little support to Cloward and Ohlin's thesis. There was no evidence that these gang boys were driven by frustrations derived from perceived blocked economic aspirations.

Because dominant themes among these gangs were fighting and sexual activity, Short and Strodtbeck point out that a major concern among lower-class gang members is the development and maintenance of a "rep" for both physical and sexual prowess. This concern is highlighted by the general description of adolescent gang behavior as "risk-taking," with little long-term profit making involved.

More recent research using mathematical models has also shown that delinquent behavior is specialized (Wolfgang et al., 1972; Bursik, 1980; Rojek and Erickson, 1982). This research does not focus on lower-class gang behavior, however, nor does it specify any connection between delinquency specialization and neighborhood integration patterns.

Overall, it would seem that Cloward and Ohlin's theory has not stood up to the test, a view fortified by an effort in New York City to utilize it as the basis for a massive program, known as Mobilization for Youth, which did not seem to have a significant effect on reducing serious delinquency (Empey, 1982). The paper and pencil tests of the aspiration-expectation component of the thesis are not adequate to measure complex psychological processes. It is most difficult to capture all the nuances in human behavior and its motivation by asking people to respond yes, no, or maybe to short questions or statements. Gang members may indeed share the feelings and attitudes predicted by the theory; it is difficult to know for sure when using attitude scales.

There is support, however, for the contention that lower-class gang behavior is specialized and that the specialization is somewhat connected with neighborhood characteristics. In fact, connection between gang delinquency and neighborhood organization is the strongest feature of Cloward and Ohlin's theory. In other words, the theory offers a reasonably good explanation of the *content* of gang delinquency, with the possible exception of drug use in gangs; it falls short in providing an adequate explanation of *why* the delinquency originally develops.

MILLER'S THEORY OF LOWER-CLASS CULTURE AND DELINQUENCY

Specific Assumptions

The lower-class culture explanation of delinquency rests on two very basic assumptions: (1) that clear-cut lower-class focal concerns or values exist, independent of other values, and (2) that female-dominated households constitute an integral feature of lower-class life-styles and, as such, represent a primary reason for the emergence of street-corner male adolescent groups in lower-class neighborhoods.

Key Concepts

Focal Concerns   Predominant values and norms that guide the day-to-day behavior of people are referred to as focal concerns; in this context, such concerns are thought to be characteristic of various social classes, with attention devoted to the lower class.

One-Sex Peer Unit   This is a social unit that serves as an alternative source of companionship and male role model development outside the home.

Discussion

Both Cohen, on the one hand, and Cloward and Ohlin, on the other, have brought forward what have been termed "strain" theories. For different reasons, both propose that a basic cause of lower-class gang delinquency is a structurally imposed barrier or obstacle to success in the society. That such a structural strain is not a requisite for an explanation of lower-class gang delinquency is the contention of Walter Miller.

In 1958, Miller summarized the tenets of what was to become a highly politicized explanation of lower-class gang delinquency. Essentially, his thesis was that lower-class gangs are male-oriented and street-oriented groups, and that these characteristics do not develop by chance. The characteristics of lower-class gangs, including their behavior, reflect the characteristics *not* of the gangs' neighborhoods but, instead, of a generic lower-class cultural system.

According to Miller, the key components of the lower-class culture are best described as "focal concerns," of which there are six: (1) trouble, (2) toughness, (3) smartness, (4) excitement, (5) fate, and (6) autonomy.

Trouble involves run-ins with authority, police, bureaucratic personnel, or others. It also includes, for men, problems associated with fighting or sexual activity accompanied by drinking and, for women, complications associated with sexual activity.

Toughness is characterized as a concern for physical prowess and strength, so-called masculine traits (as exhibited by bravery and sexual skills, often symbolized through tattooing and shown by lack of emotion).

Smartness represents an ability to outwit someone through mental gymnastics. It involves being able to "play the game," to hustle the John, so to speak, particularly in the setting of the street.

Excitement represents a heightened interest in the "thrill"— particularly experienced through alcohol, sex, gambling, "making the rounds," and "going out on the town." It is considered a periodic adventure, often followed by, or preceded by, a period of inaction, referred to as "hanging out."

Fate includes the feeling that one's future is out of his hands, beyond his control, not necessarily because of religious powers, but more because of the strong forces of destiny or magic.

The last focal concern, autonomy, contains paradoxical elements. On the surface, Miller argues that autonomy represents a strong desire on the part of lower-class people to be independent of external controls (the "boss" or a spouse, for example). Underneath all this manifested independence, however, is a consistent pattern of seeking out nurturing situations, such as a steady job or a comforting wife, or perhaps a period of confinement, particularly after a round of trouble or excitement.

The focal concerns of a lower-class culture relate to delinquency in two ways. First, the values of lower-class life often result in the absence of the father, or any other significant male role model, in the home. Thus, many adolescent boys leave the home in search of male identities in street gangs, called by Miller "one-sex peer units" (1958:14). Second, within the gang, needs and behaviors develop that are *consistent with* the focal concerns of the lower class. According to Miller, lower-class gang members are not psychologically disturbed. Instead, gang members typically represent the most "able" male youngsters in a neighborhood, both in terms of physical abilities and "personal competence."

The motivation for delinquency, in this theoretical context, is the need among most adolescents, but heightened for lower-class males because of female-oriented households, to "belong" and to be positively recognized—that is, to have "status" among their peers. Fulfillment of these needs is sought in street-corner gang membership. Because the behavior in these gangs is guided by lower-class focal concerns, it will "automatically" go against certain laws, such as laws regulating aggressive behavior. Rather than being nonconformist and "driven," gang members are behaving in stable, conforming, and "normal" fashion, according to the norms and values of their "most significant cultural milieu" (Miller, 1958:18).

Diagrammatically, Miller's thesis can be presented as shown in Figure 10.

Lower-class focal concerns
+
Female-dominated households
→
Desire of lower-class male adolescents to seek male identity and status in "one-sex peer unit" street-corner gangs
→

Behavior in accordance with lower-class focal concerns
→
Behavior that is often delinquent and criminal

FIGURE 10

Evaluation

With respect to the first assumption of the theory, the reader might be of the opinion that the focal concerns described above are, to some extent, as much a part of the middle class as the lower class. This situation indicates a blending of class-related cultural values and life-styles. The blending can occur as a result of the incorporation of middle-class values among the lower class, or vice versa. Indeed, the incorporation of lower-class values by middle-class adolescents has been used by Miller to explain middle-class delinquency (see Chapter 11).

There are many social commentators who basically agree with the notion that there is a lower-class culture, a set of life-styles and values unique to the lower class. A popularized version of this concept is the "culture of poverty," most often associated with Oscar Lewis' ethnographic studies of poverty in Latin American cultures (Lewis, 1961; 1966). Later, Edward Banfield (1968) took up this theme in describing the ills of the modern urban center. In this treatise, Banfield suggests that poverty represents a cycle in which lackadaisical attitudes and present-time orientations produce low educational aspirations and achievements, which result in low occupational attainment, which is equated with low social class attainment and, often, with poverty.

In addition, Marvin Wolfgang and Franco Ferracuti (1967) contend that violence, manifested criminally in such acts as homicide and assault, is part of a subculture of values and norms that legitimate the use of violence in various social situations. Moreover, this theory explicitly locates the subculture of violence among young males in the lower social classes of Western societies as well as in the populations of many developing nations. While there has been inconsistent support for this theory, the fact remains that it represents another attempt to locate specific values and behavioral norms in the lower social classes of developed countries.

Whether the life-style of the poor represents a cultural set of values consciously passed along from one generation to the next, or whether this life-style is a rational, logical adaptation to a continous set of problems and obstacles to achievement, is subject to debate (Liebow, 1967). In either case, research evidence accumulated since the end of World War II has supplied *some* support for a basic tenet of Miller's thesis—that a definite set of values and life-styles exists among the poor of Western societies.

The rich, detailed ethnographic accounts of the lower class do not, of course, duplicate the specific focal concerns outlined in Miller's thesis. More importantly, these accounts rarely discuss crime and delinquency as separate aspects of lower-class behavior, sometimes barely at all. Poverty engenders a variety of problems, it would seem, while crime and delinquency, in this view, are manifestations of the larger problem of poverty.

It is with regard to the second assumption of Miller's thesis that any direct attention has been applied. This assumption, again, is that a common facet of lower-class culture and life-styles is the matriarchal home, and the presence of female-oriented households contributes directly to lower-class male delinquency. Attempts to test this proposition, however, have largely focused on the issue of race rather than social class. This attention to the relationship between family structure and delinquency, *by race*, is largely attributable to a controversial report issued by Daniel Patrick Moynihan in 1965. In essence, Moynihan argued that the contemporary urban black population was becoming divided into two definite sections, a stable middle class and a deteriorating lower class. This deteriorating lower-class segment of blacks was directly related to the presence of *female-dominated households*, which, in turn, was traceable in American history to the breakup of the black family structure during the period of slavery (Moynihan, 1965). The presence of female-dominated households leads Moynihan to conclude that the lower-class black family is inordinately involved in a "tangle of pathology" (1965:29), which includes, among a host of social problems, a high rate of delinquency. A major attack on Moynihan was not a repudiation of his factual information as much as a shifting of responsibility for the plight of blacks from the contemporary white-dominated society to an unalterable historical legacy.

Now, instead of describing the roots of *lower-class* male delinquency, a central component of Miller's thesis had been transformed into a *racial* issue, at the apex of racial problems in America, no less.[3] Besides this transformation, Moynihan failed to make any reference to Miller's thesis in his report, a point which further allowed the ensuing controversy to take on racial tones rather than class issues.

The issue of family structure and delinquency has a lengthy research tradition of its own.[4] For the moment, it is sufficient to discuss attempts to test the assumption that female-dominated households lead to, or correlate with, delinquency among blacks, or within the lower class. Actually, the presence of female-dominated households within the lower class or among blacks is less than half, on an absolute scale (Rosen, 1969), although it is higher than among whites. The gap, moreover, may be closing, not only with more white mothers as heads of families, but middle-class white mothers, at that. On the surface, therefore, there would appear to be little support for the contention that female-dominated households lead to higher rates of delinquency among lower-class or black adolescents.

It has been pointed out, however, that the *relative* proportion of female-dominated homes among blacks or the lower class is much greater than among middle-class whites (Moynihan, 1965; Rosen, 1969), and thus the relatively higher rates of delinquency among these groups may be related to matriarchal homes. When this assumption has been tested, it has received contradictory support. Some research has noted no evidence that young males from lower-class or nonwhite homes are delinquent because of female dominance in the households, whether delinquency is measured in official terms or through self-reports (Rosen, 1969; Berger and Simon, 1974). Other studies indicate that lower-class juvenile males have stronger images of masculinity and are more aggressive than middle-class youth (Fannin and Clinard, 1967), and that incarcerated delinquents from female-based homes are more concerned with masculine images and are more hostile than delinquents from other home situations (Silverman and Dinitz, 1974).

On the whole, Miller's thesis remains speculative and interesting, often substantiated more by common sense and haphazard observations than by systematic research. Although there is some evidence that a lower-class culture of poverty does exist, it is difficult to determine how influential this set of values and norms may be on behavior, including delinquent behavior, when counterposed with middle-class norms and values. Furthermore, there is *not* a preponderance of female-dominated households in the lower class, and there is little evidence that such households are directly related to delinquency in any case.

SUMMARY

It would be easy to criticize all of the theoretical positions on lower-class delinquency on the grounds that *none* of them provides an adequate explanation of delinquency among all adolescents, particularly middle-class juveniles. This type of criticism, however, is irrelevant in that the theories were not intended to explain middle-class delinquency. A theory should be evaluated in terms of what it purports to explain, not in terms of anything else.

Considering only the basic assumptions and explanatory goals of the subcultural theories of lower-class delinquency, several difficulties emerge in attempts to establish the veracity of their propositions. In addition to the previously discussed shortcomings of each theory, any attempt to explain a complex behavioral phenomenon on a grand and largely static condition is unlikely to be persuasively supported by research evidence. Why, for example, do most delinquent youth, in gangs or otherwise, "reform," so to speak, and abstain from criminality when reaching young adulthood, as the theorists themselves suggest is the case? Surely one would not argue that *social class* conditions change so dramatically for these youth in a span of four or five years. The paradox here is that the larger, social-class conditions remain relatively stable while the behavior these conditions are proposed to influence changes.

Of the three theories discussed in this chapter, the one that is best able to handle this paradox is Cohen's middle-class measuring rod theory. In this case, delinquent youth would be expected to move away from delinquency when pressures to achieve through the school system were lessened, such as upon reaching adulthood. In fact, research has shown that delinquency is immediately reduced when the youth are removed from the stress-producing conditions of school. The value of Cohen's thesis, however, resides in its connection with an institutional factor, the school setting, as a basic element in the causation of delinquency.

The utility of Cohen's theory underscores another significant shortcoming of subcultural theories of delinquency. That is, whatever the content of class values may be, their *interpretation* is almost always derived from interpersonal and institutional experiences. It is one thing to suggest that social class values and norms exist; it is quite another matter to maintain that such values serve as the prime motivators of thought and behavior, separately from other social or personal conditions. Such powers of persuasion would be difficult enough to establish in a culture literally dominated by social class distinctions. Frankly, to attribute to social class factors an overriding influence on behavior in any complex, modern Western society is unrealistic.

All of these comments should not be construed as suggesting that social class values do not exist, or that such values may not be mutually incompatible. Of course, there are different values in different social classes. The accommodations people make relative to class values, or conflicts among values, however, reduce the explanatory power of social class-generated theories of behavior.

The strength of these theories lies in their *sensitizing* qualities. That is, each suggests that a broad-based societal condition is responsible for a significant proportion of delinquent behavior. To rest an explanation of delinquency *solely* on such factors is inadequate. To ignore societal conditions in the explanation of delinquency, however, would be myopic and, most probably, unproductive. In other words, attention to institutional conditions, such as school problems or family relationships, in the explanation of delinquency may be generated from an analysis of the structure of social class values. Indeed, the desire to focus attention on social class values and life-styles is quite strong among sociologists. The use of social class as a basis for explaining delinquency is addressed again in Chapter 9, when the radical approach to youthful misconduct is examined, although the issues raised from Marxist and other radical perspectives are not the same as those discussed here.

NOTES

1. The subject of school-related factors and delinquency is also discussed in Chapter 7, which looks at control theories. The relationship between poor school performance and delinquency is mentioned at this point only to document the validity of this aspect of Cohen's thesis.
2. The inability to find an exclusive drug or "retreatist" subculture is not too surprising to some (Lindesmith and Gagnon, 1964). Drug use and addiction have long preceded the blocked economic opportunity conditions spelled out in Cloward and Ohlin's thesis. In addition, relatively high rates of addiction have been found among upper-

middle-class occupational groups, such as physicians, whose legitimate opportunities for economic success would be much greater than for lower-class juveniles (Lindesmith and Gagnon, 1964). Furthermore, the effects of drugs, including addictive drugs, vary according to the social situations in which drug use occurs and can range over a variety of reactive moods. Thus, to conceptualize drug use as a retreatist reaction to failure is inaccurate.

3. Another example of transforming the problem of delinquency into a racial issue is the previously discussed analysis of IQ, race, and delinquency presented by Gordon (1976); see also Sagarin (1980).

4. Parsons (1954), for example, presents an interesting theoretical connection among family structure, sex roles, and aggression. Parson's discussion, however, covers Western society in general and is not confined to criminal behavior among lower-class males. His ideas are examined more fully in Chapter 11, which looks at middle-class delinquency. In addition, the connection between family factors and delinquency is also analyzed in Chapter 7, which has as its topic control theories.

REFERENCES

Adler, Freda, 1975, Sisters in Crime. New York: McGraw-Hill.

Banfield, Edward C., 1968, The Unheavenly City. Boston: Little, Brown.

Berger, Alan S. and William Simon, 1974, "Black Families and the Moynihan Report: A Research Evaluation." Social Problems 22: 145–161.

Bordua, David J., 1961, "Delinquent Subcultures: Sociological Interpretations of Gang Delinquency." Annals of the American Academy of Political and Social Science 33:119–136.

Bursik, Robert J., Jr., 1980, "The Dynamics of Specialization in Juvenile Offenses." Social Forces 58:851–864.

Cloward, Richard A. and Lloyd E. Ohlin, 1960, Delinquency and Opportunity. New York: Free Press.

Cohen, Albert K., 1955, Delinquent Boys. New York: Free Press.

Elliott, Delbert S., 1966, "Delinquency, School Attendance, and Dropout." Social Problems 13:307–314.

Elliott, Delbert S. and Harwin L. Voss, 1974, Delinquency and Dropout. Lexington, Mass.: D. C. Heath.

Empey, Lamar T., 1982, American Delinquency, second edition. Homewood, Ill.: Dorsey.

Fannin, Leon F. and Marshall H. Clinard, 1967, "Differences in the Conception of Self as a Male among Lower and Middle Class Delinquents." Pp. 101–112 in Edmund W. Vaz (ed.), Middle-Class Juvenile Delinquency. New York: Harper & Row.

Gordon, Robert A., 1976, "Prevalence: The Rare Datum in Delinquency Measurement and Its Implications for the Theory of Delinquency." Pp. 201–284 in Malcolm W. Klein (ed.), The Juvenile Justice System. Beverly Hills, Calif.: SAGE.

Han, Wan Sang, 1969, "Two Conflicting Themes: Common Values Versus Class Differential Values." American Sociological Review 34:679–690.

Harvey, Dale G. and Gerald T. Slatin, 1975, "The Relationship Between Child's SES and Teacher Evaluations." Social Forces 54:140–159.

Hirschi, Travis, 1969, Causes of Delinquency. Berkeley: University of California Press.

Hollingshead, August E., 1949, Elmtown's Youth. New York: Wiley.

Jensen, Gary F. and Dean G. Rojek, 1980, Delinquency. Lexington, Mass.: D. C. Heath.

Kelly, Delos H., 1978, "Status Origins, Track Position and Delinquency." Pp. 446–452 in Leonard D. Savitz and Norman Johnston (eds.), Crime in Society. New York: Wiley.

Klein, Malcolm W., 1971, Street Gangs and Street Workers. Englewood Cliffs, N.J.: Prentice-Hall.

Kobrin, Solomon, 1951, "The Conflict of Values in Delinquency Areas." American Sociological Review 16:653–661.

Lewis, Oscar, 1961, The Children of Sanchez. New York: Random House.
——, 1966, La Vida. New York: Random House.

Liazos, Alexander, 1978, "School, Alienation, and Delinquency." Crime and Delinquency 24:355–370.

Liebow, Elliot, 1967, Tally's Corner. Boston: Little, Brown.

Lindesmith, Alfred R. and John Gagnon, 1964, "Anomie and Drug Addiction." Pp. 158–188 in Marshall B. Clinard (ed.), Anomie and Deviant Behavior. New York: Free Press.

Merton, Robert K., 1957, Social Theory and Social Structure, revised and enlarged edition. New York: Free Press.

Miller, Walter B., 1958, "Lower-Class Culture as a Generating Milieu of Gang Delinquency." Journal of Social Issues 14:5–19.

Moynihan, Daniel Patrick, 1965, The Negro Family. Washington, D.C.: U.S. Department of Labor.

Oates, Joyce Carol, 1969, Them. New York: Vanguard.

Offord, D. R., Mary F. Poushinsky, and Kathryn Sullivan, 1978, "School Performance, I.Q., and Delinquency." British Journal of Criminology 18:110–127.

Parsons, Talcott, 1954, "Certain Primary Sources and Patterns of Aggression in the Social Structure of the Western World." Pp. 298–322 in Talcott Parsons (ed.), Essays in Sociological Theory, revised edition. New York: Free Press. First published in 1947.

Polk, Kenneth and Walter B. Schafer (eds.), 1972, School and Delinquency. Englewood Cliffs, N.J.: Prentice-Hall.

Quicker, John C., 1974, "The Effect of Goal Discrepancy on Delinquency." Social Problems 22:76–86.

Rodman, Hyman, 1963, "The Lower Class Value Stretch." Social Forces 42:205–215.

Rojek, Dean G. and Maynard L. Erickson, 1982, "Delinquent Careers: A Test of the Escalation Model." Criminology 20:5–28.

Rosen, Lawrence, 1969, "Matriarchy and Lower-Class Negro Male Delinquency." Social Problems 17:175–189.

Sagarin, Edward, 1980, "Taboo Subjects and Taboo Viewpoints in Criminology." Pp. 7–21 in Edward Sagarin (ed.), Taboos in Criminology. Beverly Hills, Calif.: SAGE.

Schafer, Walter, Carol Olexa, and Kenneth Polk, 1972, "Programmed for Social Class: Tracking in High School." Pp. 33–54 in Kenneth Polk and Walter E. Schafer (eds.), q.v.

Shaw, Clifford R., 1930, The Jack-Roller. Chicago: University of Chicago Press.

———, 1931, The Natural History of a Delinquent Career. Chicago: University of Chicago Press.

Shaw, Clifford R. and Henry D. McKay, 1942, Juvenile Delinquency and Urban Areas. Chicago: University of Chicago Press.

Short, James F., Jr., 1964, "Gang Delinquency and Anomie." Pp. 98–127 in Marshall B. Clinard (ed.), q.v.

Short, James F., Jr., Ramon Rivera, and Ray A. Tennyson, 1965, "Perceived Opportunities, Gang Membership, and Delinquency." American Sociological Review 30:56–67.

Short, James F., Jr. and Fred L. Strodtbeck, 1965, Group Process and Gang Delinquency. Chicago: University of Chicago Press.

Silverman, Ira and Simon Dinitz, 1974, "Compulsive Masculinity and Delinquency: An Empirical Investigation." Criminology 11:498–515.

Simon, Rita, 1975, Women and Crime. Lexington, Mass.: Lexington Books.

Spergel, Irving, 1964, Racketville, Slumtown, and Haulburg. Chicago: University of Chicago Press.

Steffensmeier, Darrell J. and Renee Hoffman Steffensmeier, 1980, "Trends in Female Delinquency: An Examination of Arrest, Juvenile Court, Self-Report, and Field Data." Criminology 18:62–85.

Sutherland, Edwin H., 1939, Principles of Criminology, third edition. Philadelphia: Lippincott.

Thrasher, Frederick M., 1927, The Gang. Chicago: University of Chicago Press.

Vaz, Edmund W. (ed.), 1967, Middle-Class Juvenile Delinquency. New York: Harper & Row.

Whyte, William F., 1955, Street Corner Society. Chicago: University of Chicago Press.

Wolfgang, Marvin E. and Franco Ferracuti, 1967, The Subculture of Violence. London: Tavistock.

Wolfgang, Marvin E., Robert Figlio, and Thorsten Sellin, 1972, Delinquency in a Birth Cohort. Chicago: University of Chicago Press.

Yablonsky, Lewis, 1970, The Violent Gang, revised edition. Baltimore: Penguin.

6

INTERPERSONAL AND SITUATIONAL EXPLANATIONS

HISTORICAL OVERVIEW

Interpersonal and situational theories of delinquency are historically placed in time between the development of individualistic theories and the more recent labeling and radical perspectives. The interpersonal theory of Edwin Sutherland, *differential association*, was developed during the 1920s, from Sutherland's earlier education at the University of Chicago and from his continued contact with those associated with ecological studies of criminality in Chicago, such as Henry McKay (Schuessler, 1973; Sutherland, 1973).

In Chapter 4, which examined social disorganization and anomie, it was stressed that community- and social-based explanations of delinquency were unable to explain the behavior of individuals. In other words, these relatively macro-level explanations did not provide a theoretical mechanism for the translation of environmental factors into individual motivations.

Sutherland was well aware of the deficiencies of the ecological studies of crime in Chicago. He was also well informed of the ethnographic studies of Shaw and McKay, which represented an effort to supply some of the missing links in a total explanation of delinquency. Sutherland's theory of differential association, therefore, was an attempt to "bridge the gap," so to speak, between the atomistic, individualized explanations of the turn of this century and the emerging environmental theories of delinquency of the 1920s and 1930s.

In a similar vein, the situational explanation of delinquency, most often associated with David Matza's use of the term *drift* (Matza, 1964), represents an effort to focus on the connection between internally based and societally based theories of delinquency. A major difference between Matza's situational explanation and other explanations of delinquency developed in the twentieth century, including Sutherland's, is the importance of human will and choice in behavior. According to Matza, all explanations of delinquency are too deterministic. While it is true that some external, or perhaps uncontrollable, factors influence human behavior, it is also true that people have the capacity to modify these influences and to choose what will affect their decisions and behavior. Since human behavior is extremely complex, the specific determination of any particular delinquent act must be based on the influences that are in effect in a particular situation.

Matza's explanation of delinquency was proposed during the mid-1960s, at a time when sociologists were becoming more and more dissatisfied with sociological and psychological causal explanations. The theory itself stands as a transitional statement between the earlier, deterministic depictions of delinquency and later perspectives on delinquency, which have tended to focus more on factors that influence the description of behavior as delinquent rather than on the causes of the behavior in the first place.

GENERIC ASSUMPTIONS

A major assumption of interpersonal and situational theories of delinquency is the belief that human behavior, including delinquent behavior, is flexible and not fixed. Behavioral inclinations change according to circumstances or situations. A second assumption of these theories is that neither the delinquent nor the society in which he lives is deviant or "bad." Delinquency arises from the same general social conditions as does nondelinquent behavior, and the same person may be committing both kinds of acts at different times. A third assumption of these theories is that most delinquent behavior is committed in a group or gang context. While the particular situation in which delinquent behavior appears may fluctuate, the general setting will most typically include group norms and behavioral patterns.

Figure 11 depicts the causal flow of delinquency according to these assumptions.

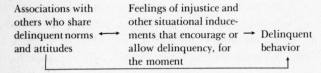

FIGURE 11

Two points should be stressed relative to Figure 11. First, both peer associations and situational factors may independently lead to delinquent acts, even though they are thought to be related to each other. Second, the proper terminology to use in connection with these theories is delinquent *behavior*, because such activity is presumed to be situational, not indicative of long-term behavioral patterns or personal character (Sagarin, 1975); that is, the behavior is delinquent, but the individual ought not to be characterized *as a delinquent*, in the sense of a continuing identity.

DIFFERENTIAL ASSOCIATION

Specific Assumptions

The best known interpersonal theory of delinquency (and adult crime as well) is the theory of differential association, developed by Edwin H. Sutherland. Unlike the developers of many other theories of delinquency, Sutherland outlined the major components of his theory in the form of propositional statements. These propositions also represent the basic assumptions of the theory, and they are discussed in detail here. Some of the major overriding assumptions of the theory, however, include the following: (1) all behavior is learned (that is, not genetically programmed) and, hence, delinquent acts are learned behavior; (2) the learning of delinquent behavior primarily occurs in small, informal group settings; and (3) the learning of delinquent behavior develops from collective experiences as well as from specific situational, current events.

Key Concepts

Differential Association   According to the concept of differential association, a youth commits an act of delinquency in response to an *excess* of attitudes favoring law or norm violation, *at that time*, and that principally he has attained this excess in association with others. Since this idea also appears in the list of propositions which collectively define the theory, it will be elaborated on later.

Differential Social Organization   This concept represents an alternative to social disorganization. Rather than arguing that certain environmental settings are disorganized, Sutherland reasoned that such areas are organized differently from other areas. In other words, there is some organization in any social setting, whether or not that setting is conducive to criminality. This concept reflects the societal dimension of the theory of differential association. At the individual level, young people commit delinquent acts in accordance with delinquent associations. At the community or societal level, norms, values, and behavior patterns are differentially organized to make it more or less likely that a juvenile will come into contact with, and be influenced by, delinquent values.

Discussion

Sutherland formally proposed the theory of differential association in 1939, in a new edition of his already successful textbook, *Principles of Criminology*. This first enunciation of the theory contained seven propositions. In subsequent editions of that book, as well as in other publications, the theory was revised to include nine propositions. These nine statements represent the theory as it is currently conceptualized (Sutherland and Cressey, 1978:80–83; italics specify words from the original).

Proposition 1. *Criminal behavior is learned*, not inherited. Put in another way, people do not commit crime because of in-born predispositions. Instead, they utilize previously acquired experiences in the commission of crime and delinquency.

Proposition 2. *Criminal behavior is learned in interaction with other persons in a process of communication.* This communication can either be verbal (or direct) or symbolic.

Proposition 3. *The principal part of the learning of criminal behavior occurs within intimate personal groups.* This statement allows for the influence of impersonal, mass media influences on behavior, but it clearly stresses the overwhelming importance of personal relationships on norms and action.

Proposition 4. *When criminal behavior is learned, the learning includes (a) techniques of committing the crime, which are sometimes very complicated, sometimes very simple*, and *(b) the specific direction of motives, drives, rationalizations, and attitudes.* Thus, the learning of criminal behavior involves not only how the behavior is to be committed, but also why it is to be done.

Proposition 5. *The specific direction of motives and drives is learned from definitions of the legal codes as favorable or unfavorable.* "Definitions," in this statement, refer to attitudes toward the law. This statement also recognizes that definitions or attitudes are not consistently or entirely favorable or unfavorable, but are most often, at least in American society, mixed and conflicting for an individual.

Proposition 6. *A person becomes delinquent because of an excess of definitions favorable to violation of law over definitions unfavorable to violation of law.* This statement represents the main point of the theory. It stresses the transient nature of delinquency and it casts the delinquent in a situational mold. This statement further illustrates a point made in connection with Proposition 5—that exposure to delinquent norms and behavior is likely to be inconsistent and mixed with simultaneous exposure to nondelinquent norms and behavior.

Proposition 7. *Differential associations may vary in frequency, duration, priority, and intensity.* These terms exhibit an effort to qualify the effect of definitions concerning the law on behavior. Frequency and duration have the same meanings they do in common usage. Priority indicates that associations (whether delinquent or nondelinquent) formed in early childhood may take precedence in influence over later associations. Intensity refers to the prestige of an association or, actually, to the power of influence one person or group may have over another.

Proposition 8. *The process of learning criminal behavior by association with criminal and anticriminal patterns involves all of the mechanisms that are involved in any other learning.* Learning among humans, in other words, is complex and includes much more than mere imitation or copying. At the same time, delinquent and criminal acts are learned in the same manner as all other human acts. The behavior may be different, but the learning process through which the behavior develops is the same.

Proposition 9. *While criminal behavior is an expression of general needs and values, it is not explained by those general needs and values, since noncriminal behavior is an expression of the same needs and values.* Theft and honest labor both have the same goal—making money to obtain some measure of happiness and satisfaction in life. Thus, the goals of delinquents and nondelinquents are often the same; the means, however, are different. Of course, this view of criminality is not unique to Sutherland but has been offered by other sociologists, most notably by Robert Merton in the means-end theory of deviance discussed in Chapter 4. Sutherland offers this proposition, however, in an effort to persuade criminologists not to separate delinquent and nondelinquent acts on the basis of different drives and goals. If we all behave according to the same general goals, then other factors must be identified to explain delinquent and nondelinquent choices for reaching the same goal.

Some criminologists have suggested modifications of the concept of differential association for the purpose of greater precision or in order to expand the scope of the theory. Melvin DeFleur and Richard Quinney (1966), for example, reformulated the nine propositions. Using the logic and symbols of set theory, DeFleur and Quinney argue that the theory of differential association could be formally tightened if it were based on the concepts of symbolic interaction and attitude formation. Their basic statement of crime causation, based on the principle of differential association, is that criminal behavior stems from the learning of "criminal motivations, attitudes and techniques" through the processes of symbolic interaction in close-knit, informal primary groups (DeFleur and Quinney, 1966:14).

Daniel Glaser (1956) offers the concept of "differential identification" as a more inclusive conceptualization of differential association. The theory of diffrential identification is stated as follows: *"a person pursues criminal behavior to the extent that he identifies himself with real or imaginary persons from whose perspective his criminal behavior seems acceptable"* (Glaser, 1956:440; italics in the original). The concept of differential identification stresses the importance of group memberships and social roles in shaping one's behavioral choices. In addition, the concept allows for the influence of *reference groups*—groups to which a youth looks for general evaluation and approval, whether or not he is in direct contact with the group (see also Haskell, 1960).

However, the largest number of suggested reformulations of differential association has been based on the principles of behavioral conditioning or "learning theory." In heeding the earlier advice of C. R. Jeffery (1965) to couch the concepts and principles of differential association in terms of operant behavior theory, Robert Burgess and Ronald Akers (1966) proposed a step-by-step *restatement* of differential association according to such ideas as reinforcement and punishment. The use of these concepts does not offer a new theory, but they were substituted in an effort to place the key elements of the theory into testable constructs. Thus, instead of saying that criminal behavior is learned mostly in primary groups, Burgess and Akers contend that criminal behavior is primarily learned "in those groups which comprise the individual's major source of reinforcements" (1966:146). This theme has also been applied by Reed Adams (1973) in a call for the use of learning principles in general criminological research.

While all of these suggested revisions have added some insight into Sutherland's formulations of differential association, they have not significantly altered the basic principles of the theory. The identification of reference group and nonsocial influences on attitudes and behavior is quite important, but not entirely unrecognized by Sutherland. Essentially, the reformulations of differential association according to the concepts of set theory or learning theory have formally stated what was already implicit, if not explicit, in Sutherland.

In addition, not all are in agreement that the formalistic features of learning theory offer the most insightful interpretation of human learning (Halbasch, 1979). The argument here is that Sutherland's theory of differential association allowed for the influence of human emotion and interpersonal feedback in the explanation of behavior, whereas behaviorist concepts imply an animalistic, noninterpretive response to stimuli, characteristics which do not apply to humans. For these reasons, the following evaluation of differential association is based on the theory as proposed by Sutherland.

Evaluation

The theory of differential association has not been totally accepted by criminologists. Some of the sharpest attacks have focused on the contention that criminal behavior is learned. It is argued by some that this view is either too simplistic, in consideration of the complexity of crime patterns and motivations, or that the gist of the statement adds nothing new to an understanding of criminality, and that it downplays the influence of individualistic factors. According to these criticisms, the theory may serve as a better explanation of why juveniles do *not* commit acts of delinquency than of why they do commit offenses (Glueck, 1962; Radzinowicz, 1966).

Sutherland and his collaborator, Donald R. Cressey, have catalogued challenges to differential association on at least a dozen points of wording, logic, and scope (Sutherland and Cressey, 1978). According to Sutherland and Cressey, some of these criticisms arise from errors of interpretation. For example, a common misinterpretation of the theory is that it deals only with actual contacts or associations with criminal or delinquent behavior. Were this the case, the theory would not be able to account for the conforming behavior of most police officers and court personnel, as well as the differential involvement in delinquency of children from the same family. Differential association, however, refers to association with attitudes and values (definitions) that are connected with patterns of behavior, through secondary as well as primary contacts, and criminality results from an excess of procriminal definitions over neutral or anticriminal definitions.

Another erroneous criticism, according to Sutherland and Cressey, is the failure of differential association to account for why people have the associations they have. Two rebuttals are offered for this charge. One, the concept of differential social organization, defined earlier, does somewhat account for variations in associations. Unfortunately, the significance of this concept has been lost in comparison to the attention given to differential association. Consequently, research concerning differential association has virtually ignored this principle. Second, the individualized aspect of the theory is self-contained and does not have to account for why or how associations develop. Technically, this assertion is correct. It would seem, however, that if a theory as broad in scope as differential association is to be accepted, it needs to stress why associations arise as well as what the consequences of the associations might be.

Another argument is that differential association does not account for the influence of personality variables in the development of definitions relative to law violation. This criticism is a rather strict one inasmuch as the theory does allow for individual interpretations and applications of definitions of legal codes. At one time, Sutherland felt it necessary to incorporate personality traits into his theory, but later reflections caused him to question the wisdom of such modifications (Sutherland, 1973). Part of the difficulty with incorporating personality variables into the theory lies in determining which traits to include and under what conditions to include them—that is, how they are to be measured. To move beyond such particular traits and to charge that the theory generally ignores individual interpretations is, again, erroneous. The question then becomes not whether individual responses to situational conditions affect behavior, but what kinds of responses affect behavior and in what ways.

Other complaints against the theory concern the measurement of key concepts. For example, if, as the theory suggests, certain characteristics of associations are to have more influence on behavior than other characteristics, such as intensity and priority, how are such qualities to be measured and compared? Similarly, how is an *excess* of definitions to be objectively measured *and applied* to a particular act (Sutherland and Cressey, 1978)?

Of all the criticisms levied at the theory of differential association, the problem of measurement is the most serious. Several investigators have commented on the difficulty of measuring a person's definitions of the law, their sources, and their qualifications (Cressey, 1952; Short, 1960; Stanfield, 1966). A major problem of measurement with this theory is its historical and situational focus. Since most criminal offenders are discovered after the fact, so to speak, reconstruction of thoughts and moods at the time the act was committed is exceedingly difficult to develop. When one adds to this difficulty the problem of reconstructing prior events and influences on one's attitudes and behavior, the task becomes almost impossible.

Despite these methodological difficulties and shortcomings, there have been empirical attempts to test the validity of the theory, with juveniles as well as adults. One empirical assessment of differential association relative to delinquency is the well-documented fact that most delinquency is committed in a group context (Jensen and Rojek, 1980; Weis, 1980). The overall significance of this finding for the theory of differential association, however, is questionable. For one thing, the relationship does not speak to the issue of shared attitudes and values, nor to the matter of excess of definitions favorable to law violation, either within the group or individually. In addition, the group nature of delinquency does not specify temporal conditions of causality—that is, whether the associations occurred before or after delinquency was first or most often committed.

Specifically, with reference to delinquency, those issues concerning the relationship between peer group associations and delinquency have been empirically studied. These investigations have *generally supported* the basic propositions of the theory (Short, 1957; 1960; Reiss and Rhodes, 1964; Voss, 1964; Jensen, 1972; Hepburn, 1977). For the most part, however, the research has indicated that differential association is only one of two or three causal explanations that is supported. In a study of nearly 1600 white male junior and senior high school students in California, for example, Gary Jensen (1972) found support for the *independent* effects of differential association variables and family supervision variables on self-reported delinquency. That is, each set of factors had a separate, unique influence on delinquent behavior. Differential association variables were measured according to number of close delinquent friends, perceptions of "trouble" in the neighborhood, official delinquency rates of the schools attended, and measures of the acceptance of attitudes or definitions favorable to the violation of laws.

In summation, the theory of differential association appears to offer a reasonable explanation of individual delinquency within environmental contexts, although the numerous critical comments concerning its scope and logic cannot be ignored. Empirically, the theory is difficult to test, yet several attempts to assess its validity have generally been supportive. That differential association is not the only valid explanation of delinquency is indicated by the importance of other variables simultaneously compared with differential association variables. In addition, some have challenged the often-noted group nature of delinquency by asserting that delinquency is *inversely* related (delinquents have low group involvement) to peer group associations (Hirschi, 1969), or that attachment to peers is *unrelated* to delinquency (Jensen and Rojek, 1980).

DRIFT AND DELINQUENCY

Specific Assumptions

Matza's concept of drift shares many of the assumptions found in the theory of differential association. A central difference between the two theories, however, is that the notion of drift assumes delinquency to be based largely on the exercise of a juvenile's choices, depending on the situation or circumstances at a particular moment. The importance of individual judgment on behavior in this explanation differs from virtually all other theories of delinquency, which stress the influence of deterministic forces, individualistic or environmental, on the behavior of juveniles.

Another assumption of drift theory, which tends to separate it from differential association, is that delinquents are angered over a sense of injustice they feel from discriminatory law enforcement practices and community reactions to their misbehaviors. In other words, delinquents are somewhat psychologically alienated from society.

Key Concepts

Drift The concept of drift asserts that delinquent behavior and law-abiding behavior are both characteristics of delinquents. Thus, juveniles drift in and out of delinquency, depending on the situation and their mood or feelings. They do not have a commitment to delinquency, even when deeply immersed in the behavior.

Neutralization   A central factor in the decision to commit a delinquent act is the juvenile's ability to neutralize, or explain away, the moral reprehension felt to be associated with the act. There are several types of neutralizations. Their existence may be encouraged by feelings of injustice, but the factor of neutralization is a key link between emotional states and delinquent behavior.

Discussion

According to Matza, delinquency is best viewed as occasional and associated with particular situations and circumstances. In other words, juveniles do not commit acts of delinquency because a group set of norms dictates that they do, but because the nature of a particular time, place, and setting encourages the commission of delinquent acts at that time. Group membership may promote a delinquent response in certain situations, but it does not mandate such behavior.

Because of their status in Western societies, juveniles are lodged in a transitional state between total dependence on adults and freedom of thought and action. Opposition to adult rules is likely to develop among juveniles and will sometimes be expressed in the form of delinquency. The emergence of delinquent subcultures, however, with totally oppositional values to that of conventional, adult values is not likely to happen. Delinquent (oppositional) subcultures do not emerge because adolescents are too closely supervised by, or otherwise connected with, adults for that to happen.

This view of delinquency is also characterized as drift, in which delinquency is seen as the result of vacillation within a juvenile between the conforming expectations of adults and the peer-dominated, situational demands and opportunities that encourage delinquency. In this view, delinquency is committed not because a juvenile is driven by wicked internal or external forces, but because it seems more profitable and correct to do at the moment.

Juveniles are able to drift into and out of delinquency through a number of rationalizations or neutralizations (Sykes and Matza, 1957; Matza, 1964). These rationalizations and neutralizations, respectively, provide excuses for having committed delinquency and justifications for committing delinquency before the fact. Gresham Sykes and Matza (1957) concentrate on the justifications for delinquency and propose five types of "techniques of neutralization": (1) *denial of responsibility*, in which the juvenile fails to accept personal blame for his actions, attributing them instead to forces beyond his control, such as having bad parents or living in poverty; (2) *denial of injury*, in which the juvenile does not deny the act but maintains that no one was really physically hurt or economically harmed; (3) *denial of a victim*, in which the harm of injury caused by the act is felt to be deserved because the "victim" deserved it, such as stealing from a "crooked" store owner; (4) *condemnation of condemners*, which involves a view of disapproving others as hypocrites and hidden deviants, a view which sometimes becomes cynical of authority figures, such as the police and school officials; (5) *appeal to higher loyalties*, which argues that the immediate demands of the group take precedence over familial, community, or societal values and rules, and that these group demands sometimes call for the commission of delinquent acts.

While Sykes and Matza did not dwell on the factors that contribute to the techniques of neutralization, subsequent comments have tended to focus on the existence of a "subterranean" adult value system which tacitly encourages the pursuit of thrills and irresponsibility among juveniles (Matza and Sykes, 1961). This underground system of values, as it were, also contributes to adolescent justifications for delinquency by allowing one to charge that "Everyone is doing it, so why can't I?"

The later work of Matza (1964) implicates the lack of family supervision in the development of neutralization techniques, but more emphatically suggests the role of peer-dominated social settings and the operations of the juvenile justice system in the emergence of such justifications.

Peer-group situations are characterized by the concept of "situation of company," in which the delinquent is depicted as constantly exposed to tests or "soundings" designed to challenge his masculinity and group loyalty. Ironically, however, Matza contends that each member of the group personally adopts conventional adult values but that public expressions to the contrary lead to group shared misunderstandings of just what others in the group actually feel.

To summarize, Matza's theory of drift suggests that most delinquents are not alienated from adult, conventional values but, instead, that they are susceptible to both the conforming influences of adults and the delinquent influences of peer pressure. Opportunities for delinquency emerge out of situational contexts. These opportunities can assume more importance for a juvenile when he has established a set of justifications, or moral neutralizations, which temporarily sanction delinquent behavior. The neutralization of conventional values, in turn, is facilitated by several factors, including perceived discriminatory enforcement of the law and perceived implicit adult acceptance of many "delinquent" acts, which represent what conventional adults often do or encourage rather than what they publicly proclaim to be their values and attitudes.

Evaluation

The theory of drift assumes that juveniles live in a state of flux and uncertainty, and this notion is convincing (Goodman, 1962). Furthermore, some research has documented the general acceptance of middle-class, conventional values among juvenile gang members and their leaders (Short and Strodtbeck, 1965; Krisberg, 1974). In addition, Cohen's (1955) argument that a common trait in juvenile gangs is short-run hedonism is consistent with Matza's conceptualization of drift (although on other particulars Cohen and Matza are at odds). Even though these characteristics apply to gang delinquency, it is possible that they apply to other examples of delinquency as well.

An implicit assumption of Matza's drift theory is that delinquency will decline as adolescents approach adulthood. This is a very involved issue and it is definitely influenced by the effects of official intervention and treatment efforts on the part of society in an effort to "reform" delinquents. Certainly gang members tend to disassociate from the gang as adulthood approaches, and delinquency, gang or otherwise, does decline with advanced age status, through marriage, employment, or perhaps general maturation (McCord et al., 1959; Briar and Piliavin, 1965). Edwin Schur (1973) advocates an approach of "radical nonintervention" toward delinquents, an approach which is in part based on Matza's theory, including the implicit notion of natural reformation.

Those who have attempted to study specifically the concepts of drift and neutralization, however, have not supported Matza's assertions. In an investigation of rural and urban youth and institutionalized delinquents, Michael Hindelang (1974) failed to find any support for Matza's contention that delinquents are basically disapproving of delinquency but go along with it because they think their friends would approve. Those who admitted involvement in delinquency were more likely to approve personally of such behavior than those not involved in delinquency, and this finding remained constant for a variety of offense behaviors, for males and females, rural and urban youngsters, and institutionalized youth as well as juveniles in public schools (see also Hindelang, 1970). Richard Ball (1983) found that neutralization was less related to "basic norm violation" among young adolescents than was their self-concept.

Peggy Giordano (1976) surveyed the attitudes of public school students and juveniles who had been processed through various stages of the juvenile justice system (police contact, court contact, institutionalization, and so on). She found no significant attitudinal differences between the students and the official delinquents. These delinquents did not perceive their handling as unfair or unjust. If anything, they developed more positive feelings toward the juvenile justice system as they experienced more contact with it. Such results question the foundation on which Matza's theory of drift and neutralization is based.

A difficulty with Matza's theory lies in its focus on psychological motivations and intentions regarding behavior, both before *and* after the act. In this respect, Matza's theory of drift shares the same difficulty with Sutherland's theory of differential association—namely, the assessment of one's *prior* state of mind from a vantage point far removed from the commission of an act.

Matza's conceptualization of the delinquent adolescent portrays a rather free-floating individual who is being buffeted about by diverse influences. While this view may be somewhat appealing, it seems to allow for too much individual freedom of choice without suggesting a rationale for explaining the choices which are made. Some have suggested that drift theory is actually a type of social control theory of delinquency (see Chapter 7), in which the delinquent is seen as relatively uncommitted or unattached to conventional social institutions and peer groups (Briar and Piliavin, 1965; Schur, 1973). In fact, this type of theoretical framework does seem to be beneficial to a better understanding of delinquency if the two perspectives are merged. For example, drift theory proposes that juveniles may be delinquent at any given time. It does not provide a systematic account, however, of why delinquency is defined as acceptable by a group or an individual. Social control theory argues that delinquency occurs after disaffiliations develop between juveniles and representatives of social institutions, such as parents and school authorities. Youngsters who are thus unattached are more likely to be attracted to delinquency than others. Those who "drift" into delinquency are those who are relatively more disenchanted with traditional institutions in society.

SUMMARY

Differential association and drift as explanations of delinquency differ from previously discussed explanations in that they are essentially *social psychological*. That is, the primary cause of delinquency lies *with* the individual, but not within him. While these theories maintain that individuals commit delinquent acts, they also acknowledge the importance of social factors in the decision to commit delinquency. Furthermore, the influential individuals or groups typically are significant others (meaningful people in one's life, such as peer group members and authority figures).

In Sutherland's theory of differential association, the influence of significant others on a juvenile is in the direct encouragement of delinquency. For Matza and his theory of drift, the influence of significant others can be either an actual encouragement of delinquency or an indirect contribution to delinquency through the development of resentment of authority figures.

Both theories attempt to provide a link between the broad, ill-defined effects of social class and social structure and the atomistic, overly deterministic conceptualizations of biological and psychological theories of delinquency, such as psychoanalytic interpretations. In this respect, they make a contribution to the explanation of delinquency.

A difficulty with both theories, however, lies with the measurement and testing of basic concepts and propositions. Of the two theories, differential association is presented in a more rigorous fashion, and it has been researched more thoroughly than has Matza's drift theory. Nonetheless, it seems as if both explanations are trying to explain too much by attempting to account for the vagaries of human behavior from an open and situational point of view.

Both differential association and drift appear to be well grounded in their attempts to understand the more proximate causes of delinquency. It would appear, however, that both theories would be enhanced by being attached to a more measurable and fixed social entity, as opposed to broadly conceived societal factors. This type of foundation may perhaps best be supplied by control theories, particularly *social* control theories, of delinquency. These explanations are considered in the next chapter.

REFERENCES

Adams, Reed, 1973, "Differential Association and Learning Principles Revisited." Social Problems 20:458–470.

Ball, Richard A., 1983, "Development of Basic Norm Violation: Neutralization and Self-Concept Within a Male Cohort." Criminology 21:75–94.

Briar, Scott and Irving Piliavin, 1965, "Delinquency, Situational Inducements, and Commitment to Conformity." Social Problems 13:35–45.

Burgess, Robert L. and Ronald L. Akers, 1966, "A Differential Association-Reinforcement Theory of Criminal Behavior." Social Problems 14:128–147.

Cohen, Albert, 1955, Delinquent Boys. Glencoe, Ill.: Free Press.

Cressey, Donald R., 1952, "Application and Verification of the Differential Association Theory." Journal of Criminal Law, Criminology and Police Science 43:43–52.

DeFleur, Melvin and Richard Quinney, 1966, "A Reformulation of Sutherland's Differential Association Theory and a Strategy for Empirical Verification." Journal of Research in Crime and Delinquency 2:1–22.

Giordano, Peggy C., 1976, "The Sense of Injustice? An Analysis of Juveniles' Reactions to the Justice System." Criminology 14:93–112.

Glaser, Daniel, 1956, "Criminality Theories and Behavioral Images." American Journal of Sociology 61:433–444.

Glueck, Sheldon, 1962, "Theory and Fact in Criminology: A Criticism of Differential Association." Pp. 91–95 in Marvin E. Wolfgang, Leonard Savitz, and Norman Johnston (eds.), The Sociology of Crime and Delinquency. New York: Wiley.

Goodman, Paul, 1962, Growing Up Absurd. New York: Random House (Vintage).

Halbasch, Keith, 1979, "Differential Reinforcement Theory Examined." Criminology 17:217–229.

Haskell, Martin R., 1960, "Toward a Reference Group Theory of Juvenile Delinquency." Social Problems 8:220–230.

Hepburn, John R., 1977, "Testing Alternative Models of Delinquency Causation." Journal of Criminal Law and Criminology 67:450–460.

Hindelang, Michael J., 1970, "The Commitment of Delinquents to Their Misdeeds: Do Delinquents Drift?" Social Problems 17:502–509.

——, 1974, "Moral Evaluations of Illegal Behaviors." Social Problems 21:370–385.

Hirschi, Travis, 1969, Causes of Delinquency. Berkeley: University of California Press.

Jeffery, C. R., 1965, "Criminal Behavior and Learning Theory." Journal of Criminal Law, Criminology and Police Science 56:294–300.

Jensen, Gary F., 1972, "Parents, Peers, and Delinquent Action: A Test of the Differential Association Perspective." American Journal of Sociology 78:562–575.

Jensen, Gary F. and Dean G. Rojek, 1980, Delinquency. Lexington, Mass.: D. C. Heath.

Krisberg, Barry, 1974, "Gang Youth and Hustling: The Psychology of Survival." Issues in Criminology 9:115-129.

Matza, David, 1964, Delinquency and Drift. New York: Wiley.

Matza, David and Gresham M. Sykes, 1961, "Juvenile Delinquency and Subterranean Values." American Sociological Review 26:712-719.

McCord, William, Joan McCord, and Irving K. Zola, 1959, Origins of Crime. New York: Columbia University Press.

Radzinowicz, Leon, 1966, Ideology and Crime. New York: Columbia University Press.

Reiss, Albert J., Jr. and A. Lewis Rhodes, 1964, "An Empirical Test of Differential Association Theory." Journal of Research in Crime and Delinquency 1:5-18.

Sagarin, Edward, 1975, Deviants and Deviance. New York: Praeger.

Schuessler, Karl, 1973, "Introduction." Pp. ix-xxxvi in Karl Schuessler (ed.), Edwin H. Sutherland on Analyzing Crime. Chicago: University of Chicago Press.

Schur, Edwin M., 1973, Radical Non-Intervention. Englewood Cliffs, N.J.: Prentice-Hall (Spectrum).

Short, James F., Jr., 1957, "Differential Association and Delinquency." Social Problems 4:233-239.

———, 1960, "Differential Association as a Hypothesis: Problems of Empirical Testing." Social Problems 8:14-25.

Short, James F., Jr. and Fred L. Strodtbeck, 1965, Group Process and Gang Delinquency. Chicago: University of Chicago Press.

Stanfield, Robert E., 1966, "The Interaction of Family Variables and Gang Variables in the Aetiology of Delinquency." Social Problems 13:411-417.

Sutherland, Edwin H., 1939, Principles of Criminology, third edition. New York: Lippincott.

———, 1973, "Development of the Theory." Pp. 13-29 in Karl Schuessler (ed.), Edwin H. Sutherland on Analyzing Crime. Chicago: University of Chicago Press.

Sutherland, Edwin H. and Donald R. Cressey, 1978, Criminology, tenth edition. New York: Lippincott.

Sykes, Gresham M. and David Matza, 1957, "Techniques of Neutralization: A Theory of Delinquency." The American Journal of Sociology 22:664-670.

Voss, Harwin L., 1964, "Differential Association and Reported Delinquent Behavior: A Replication." Social Problems 12:78-85.

Weis, Joseph G., 1980, Jurisdiction and the Elusive Status Offender. Washington, D.C.: U.S. Government Printing Office.

7

CONTROL THEORIES

HISTORICAL OVERVIEW

Control theories of delinquency cover a wide range of topics. Lamar Empey (1982) characterizes nineteenth-century and early-twentiety-century individualistic theories of delinquency as "control" theories, especially psychoanalytic explanations. Travis Hirschi (1969) traces the ideas of control theory as far back as Durkheim in the nineteenth century. The core ideas of control theories, therefore, have a rather long history. Most often, however, control theories of delinquency are equated with self-concept research and social control mechanisms, such as family and school experiences. In this context, control theories may be historically placed in the 1950s and early 1960s, with the development of Walter Reckless' self-concept or containment explanation of delinquency. In the late 1960s Travis Hirschi extended Reckless' ideas to broader social contexts, thus leading to the social or psychosocial perspective, which became synonymous with control theory (see also Toby, 1957).

The idea that juveniles commit delinquency because some controlling force is absent or defective has been generally supported for some time. The *focus* of attention on social or social psychological control factors, however, is relatively new. Although family factors were prominent in late-nineteenth and early-twentieth-century explanations of delinquency (Sanders, 1970; Krisberg and Austin, 1978), they were either not carefully researched or were of secondary importance to the psychoanalytic interpretation of delinquency as an *individual* problem.

Among sociological perspectives, interest in family factors gave way to broader social and economic conditions in the 1940s and 1950s and all but disappeared from the literature (Wilkinson, 1974). Current interest in family variables, as well as other institutional factors, such as religious and school influences, is often couched in terms of the control perspective.

For the most part, therefore, control theories of delinquency represent a relatively modern development. This statement is most particularly appropriate for social control factors, the subject of considerable research and discussion since the early 1970s.

GENERIC ASSUMPTIONS

Control theories all assume one basic point. Human beings, young or old, must be held in check, or somehow controlled, if criminal or delinquent tendencies are to be repressed.

A related assumption of control theories is that delinquency is to be expected, considering all of the pressures and inducements toward delinquency to which most juveniles are exposed. To control theories, the explanation of delinquency is based not on the question of "*Why* did he do it?" but, instead, "Why did he *not* do it?" In other words, control theories assume that the tendency to commit delinquent acts is well-nigh universal. Since delinquent behavior is to be expected, the crucial explanation of it is to be found in searching for *missing* factors in delinquents that separate them from nondelinquents.

The first two assumptions logically point to a third generic assumption; namely, delinquency is the result of a *deficiency* in something, the *absence* of a working control mechanism. Delinquents are seen neither as driven nor as perfectly "normal." They are simply seen as youth who are relatively uncontrolled or unattached, psychologically or socially.

The specific type of control factor or system deemed absent or faulty among delinquents is what distinguishes various types of control theories. In the main, there are two general types of control systems, personal and social. Personal control systems involve individualistic factors, especially psychological ones. They are best exemplified by psychoanalytic concepts and the notion of self-concept or esteem. Social control variables involve attachments to basic social institutions, such as families, schools, and religious practices. Attachments are often measured in a variety of ways but typically are conceptualized as emotional (such as the amount of affection between parent and child) and behavioral (such as grades in school).

A fourth assumption of control theories is that there is general societal consensus concerning conventional beliefs and norms, especially as these are associated with various institutions in society.

The assumptions of control theories lead to the diagrammatic explanation of delinquency shown in Figure 12.

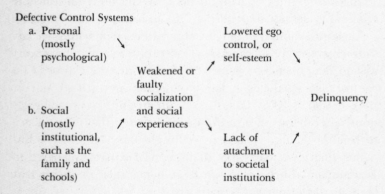

Defective Control Systems

FIGURE 12

From Figure 12, one could state that the weakened personal or social control factors contribute to delinquency through socialization (basically childhood) experiences and current social situations. The defective control systems affect the learning of social norms and the implementation of norms in terms of appropriate behavior. It is also possible, of course, that weakened personal and social controls may be interconnected. Lowered self-concepts and antisocial attitudes may stem from negative family and school experiences, and vice versa. This possibility, however, is not a necessary component of control theory.

PERSONAL CONTROLS

Psychoanalysis Revisited

Psychoanalysis can readily be viewed as a control perspective. The emphasis on early childhood socialization experiences, especially within the family, and the focus on the superego, holding sway over instinctive id impulses, are consistent with the control conceptualization of delinquency.

Psychoanalysis, however, offers problems to some who would categorize it as a control theory. To some extent, this concern is a reflection of the individualistic nature of the psychoanalytic approach. Nonetheless, the assumptions of psychoanalytic theory fall within the general assumptions of control theories.

Containment Theory

Other than psychoanalysis, the "containment" perspective, developed by Walter Reckless, has probably attracted the greatest attention as a personal control theory of delinquency. Properly classified as a social-psychological explanation of delinquency, similar to Sutherland's differential association, containment is linked to the idea of self-concept.[1] Unlike differential association, however, containment theory stresses the importance of the personalized feelings of youth rather than their associations.

Specific Assumptions

Containment theory is based on the assumption that delinquency is a result of poor self-concepts. This view is in contrast with that of the labeling perspective, which argues that negative self-concepts are the result of having been labeled delinquent.

Besides the view that negative self-images contribute to delinquency, containment theory is based on the assumption that a boy's positive view of himself provides an insulation against the pressures and the pulls toward delinquency, regardless of social class or other environmental conditions.

Third, containment theory is based on a multifaceted image of behavior. That is, people are conceptualized as being composed of several layers of drives, pressures, pulls, and insulators or buffers. All of these forces affect the individual simultaneously, and they come both from within and outside of the person. The most important of these forces, however, is the internal insulator, the self-concept.

Key Concepts

Containment   The principal concept of this explanation is that drives and pulls (forces in general) toward delinquency must somehow be contained—that is, checked or controlled—if delinquency is to be averted.

Self-concept   This concept usually refers to an image, whether of one's place in society or of one's value to others or to society in general. The most typical way of measuring self-concept is through the use of attitude and personality scales, including subjective and limited-response scale items.

Discussion

Although Reckless began to investigate the relationship between self-concept and delinquency in the mid-1950s (Reckless et al.,

1956), the theory of containment was not published in systematic form until the early 1960s. According to Reckless, containment theory is essentially a theory of the *middle range*. By this, Reckless means that it is designed to explain those forms of delinquent and criminal behavior that fall outside the highly personalized acts resulting from organic and personality disorders, such as brain damage, on the one hand, and organized criminality, such as organized crime and delinquent gangs, on the other hand. According to Reckless, these behaviors constitute from one-fourth to one-third of the acts of crime and delinquency. The rest, the bulk of criminal and delinquent activity, he terms the "middle range of norm violation," the range to which containment theory applies (Reckless, 1961).

During the 1960s, the theory became couched in terms of pressures, pulls, pushes, and containments or buffers, all focused on the individual. Reckless identified four types of pressures and containments: (1) outer, or social, pressures and pulls; (2) external containments; (3) inner containments; and (4) inner pushes, that is, organic or psychological forces (Reckless, 1967). These four factors are conceptualized by Reckless as circles, or layers, emanating from the self. Thus, the self serves as a container of internal pushes, while prosocial contacts serve as buffers against external pressures and containers against external pulls.

External pressures include "diverse living conditions" such as poverty, unemployment, minority group status, and discrimination. Outer pulls consist of bad companions, deviant prestige figures, juvenile gangs (subcultures), and mass media inducements. Internal pushes include a veritable host of faults and problems, such as tensions and frustrations, aggressiveness, need for immediate gratification, rebelliousness, feelings of inadequacy, compulsions, phobias, brain damage, and psychoses.

With all of these pushes and pulls operating on juveniles, it is a wonder that they do not all become delinquent and remain that way. Society, however, offers various external or outer constraints on lawbreaking behavior. The most important of these outer containments, according to Reckless, are "nuclear groups," such as the family and community, whose influences people experience in varying degrees. Two other aspects of external containment are the structure of roles and expectations in society and the sense of acceptance and belonging relative to a group or society.

The inner restraint on delinquent behavior is associated with the self-concept. The theory maintains that a low or negative self-concept contributes to delinquency. Reckless also mentions three other types of inner containment: goal orientation, frustration tolerance, and norm commitment and retention. Orientation to long-range, socially approved goals, high frustration tolerance, and high levels of norm commitment and tolerance are all thought to inhibit delinquency.

Of the two general types of containment, inner and outer, Reckless clearly feels that inner containment is more important for the control of delinquency, at least in industrialized societies. In less developed societies, external pressures toward crime and deviance are not very great. In addition, Reckless reasons that "undisturbed and developing" countries are tightly structured, particularly by religious restraints, and the individualized component of the self is rarely developed.

In summary, containment theory proposes that delinquency can be produced by a variety of forces and factors, both internal and external. That such behavior does *not* occur is attributable to insulations or buffers, both social and personal. Of these two types of containments, the most important in inhibiting delinquency is inner containment, especially self-concept.

Evaluation

Reckless felt that containment theory offered a better explanation of delinquency than other theories for the following reasons: (1) it can be applied to particular individuals; (2) the various external and internal constraints can be observed and measured, both qualitatively and quantitatively; (3) the theory explains both delinquency and conformity; (4) it likewise explains a wide variety of criminal or delinquent activity; and (5) it is a possible basis for the treatment and prevention of delinquency (Reckless, 1967).

The connection between negative self-concepts and delinquency has been fairly uniformly established through empirical research. Reckless and his associates, for example, have presented evidence from studies of juveniles in Columbus, Ohio, which demonstrates that predicted delinquents ("bad" boys) have lower self-concepts than predicted nondelinquents ("good" boys), as measured by official records (Reckless et al., 1956; Reckless et al., 1957). Furthermore, "good" boys not only remain freer of official contacts with police and courts than do bad boys, but they consistently evidence more positive levels of self-concept, from the age of 12–13 well into adolescence (Scarpitti et al., 1960; Dinitz et al., 1962).

The data reported by Reckless and his students were characterized by the following conditions: (1) the "good" and "bad" boys were initially selected by teachers' predictions, and (2) the measures of the boys' self-concepts were cross-validated by their teachers and mothers. Although these conditions can be defended, taken together they call into question the validity of self-concept or containment as an explanation of delinquency. Some have argued, for example, that cross-validation of personally expressed self-concept with teachers' and mothers' judgments confuses the issue between what a person actually thinks of himself and what he thinks others think or expect of him (Schwartz and Tangri, 1965; Orcutt, 1970).

Michael Schwartz and Sandra Tangri (1965) examined the issue of self-concept by utilizing a semantic differential test, whereby juveniles were asked to rate themselves on a "good-bad" continuum along several dimensions. These perceptions were then correlated with judgments of how respondents felt mothers, friends, and teachers thought of them. The research was conducted on 101 school-nominated "good" and "bad" sixth-grade boys in an all-black school in a high delinquency area of Detroit. The results lent some support to containment theory in that those designated as "good" boys had higher personal self-concepts than those felt to be "bad" boys. Comparisons of self-concept with perceptions of opinions of others, however, indicated that self-image was correlated with different significant others (meaningful people in one's life) and these significant others tended to vary between "good" and "bad" boys. The self-concepts of "good" boys, for instance, were influenced by perceived teachers' images, while "bad" boys' self-images were strongly associated with perceived mothers' judgments (see also Schwartz and Stryker, 1970).

The issue of self-concept is clearly a complex one, and its measurement and application to delinquency, while important, are still incomplete for a thorough examination of containment theory.

Besides the issue of self-concept, some have questioned the validity of identifications of delinquency by teachers and principals (Orcutt, 1970). A critical question is the accuracy of the predictions. The original reports of the Columbus students indicated substantial agreement between group predictions and subsequent official contact with the police or the courts (Scarpitti et al., 1960; Dinitz et al., 1962). Additional investigations, however, question the accuracy of such predictions. In a longitudinal study of delinquency prevention, for example, Reckless and Simon Dinitz (1972) found that of more than 1000 predicted delinquents (bad boys) over 40 percent had had no police contact within four years. If nominations or predictions of future delinquency are to be used as a primary measure of delinquency, there must be consistent and substantial agreement between the prediction and the subsequent behavior for the procedure to be acceptable.

In addition to conceptual and methodological concerns involving attempts to test containment theory, some investigators have raised the issue of relative importance. It is generally conceded in these studies that self-concept measures can distinguish between delinquents and nondelinquents, but that other factors may be more important in the explanation of delinquency. These findings have tended to occur, furthermore, when self-report measures of delinquency have been employed. Several studies (for example, Voss, 1969; Jensen, 1973; and Rankin, 1977) present data that suggest that inner containment may be less powerful as an explanation of delinquency than other factors, such as peer group associations (differential association), family relationships, and social class. At the same time, these investigations suggest that self-concept measures be combined with other variables to improve the explanation of delinquency.

In summary, it cannot be denied that self-concept has an effect on behavior, delinquent or nondelinquent, deviant or nondeviant (Wells, 1978). Changes in self-concept can lead to changes in behavior.[2] While various conceptual and methodological problems have characterized containment theory and attempts to test it, the theory has generally been supported with empirical investigation. Self-concept, or containment, however, appears to be less important as an explanation of delinquency than other factors, particularly when unofficial measures of delinquency are used. One such influence, peer group associations, has already been discussed. Another set of conditions, social control or bond variables, is considered next.

SOCIAL CONTROLS—THE SOCIAL BOND

Specific Assumptions

The difference between personal and social control theories of delinquency lies in the assumption of social control theory that social bonds and attachments are a stronger protection against delinquency than are personality characteristics.

Key Concept

Social Bond   Essentially, this concept refers to the connection between the individual and the society, usually through social institutions. Travis Hirschi (1969) conceptualizes the social bond as consisting of four parts: attachment, commitment, involvement, and belief.

Discussion

According to Hirschi, the four elements of the social bond collectively explain the social control theory of delinquency. *Attachment* refers to the psychological and emotional connection one feels toward other persons or groups and the extent to which one cares about their opinions and feelings. According to Hirschi, attachment is the social counterpart to the psychoanalytic concept of superego or conscience.

Commitment is the result of a cost-benefit approach to delinquency. It refers to the investments accumulated in terms of conformity to conventional rules (such as time, money, effort, and status) versus the estimated costs, or losses, of investments associated with nonconformity. Commitment, therefore, is viewed as a rational aspect of the social bond, the social counterpart to the psychoanalytic concept of the ego.

Involvement refers to participation in conventional and legitimate activity. In a school, for example, it would include extracurricular activities such as school plays, clubs, organizations, and athletic events.

Belief involves the acceptance of a conventional value system. In the logic of control theory, it is argued that a weakening of conventional beliefs, for whatever the reason, increases the chances of delinquency.

Although Hirschi recognizes several possibilities of the interconnectedness of these four elements of the social bond, he suggests that they generally vary together. It is possible, for example, for attachment and commitment to vary inversely. In other words, attachment to parents and peers may prevent a juvenile from developing commitments to school and legitimate occupational pursuits, particularly if he is from a lower- or working-class environment. Hirschi contends, however, that attachment and commitment are *positively* associated, regardless of social class position. Moreover, he maintains that commitment, involvement, attachment, and belief are also positively associated with one another. No component is theoretically more important than another, although research may suggest the ascendancy of one over another under specified conditions.

Evaluation

The evaluation of social control theory will be conducted according to the relationship between delinquency and three institutional settings: religion, the family, and the school. The focus will be on the extent to which bonds (in a general sense) to these institutions are associated with delinquency.

Religion and Delinquency   For some time, criminologists have been interested in the connection between religious participation and beliefs and criminality. Since the 1930s, research has been conducted on the relationship between religious variables and delinquency. Earlier studies, which focused on officially defined delinquents, tended to yield conflicting results. Some studies found delinquents to be *more* involved with religion than non-delinquents; others found delinquents to be *less* active in religious behavior than nondelinquents; and still another group of results found no relationship between religious variables and delinquency (Jensen and Rojek, 1980).

Despite the inconsistencies of systematic research on the subject, popular opinion has held that there exists an inverse relationship between religion and delinquency; that is, delinquents are less religiously active than nondelinquents.

The view that delinquency and "religiosity" are inversely related did have some support in the literature. One of these studies was the previously discussed comparative analysis of 500 delinquents and 500 nondelinquents (Glueck and Glueck, 1950). The Gluecks noted that less than 40 percent of the delinquents attended church regularly, as compared with over 67 percent of nondelinquents. At the same time, neither delinquents or nondelinquents were markedly negligent of their "church duties," that is, not attending church at all. The Gluecks, though, paid scant attention to the relationship between church attendance and delinquency, presumably because their findings did not clash with general expectations.

A few years after the Glueck study, F. Ivan Nye reported an intensive investigation of the relationship between family factors and self-reported delinquency (1958). Part of that investigation included the relationship between other variables and delinquency, including church attendance. Basically, Nye found that nondelinquents, and their parents, attended church significantly more often than delinquents. Similar to the Gluecks, however, Nye found that the biggest separation between delinquents and nondelinquents occurred at the regular attendance point. The differences between delinquents and nondelinquents, while apparent, were not as large among those who never or only occasionally attended church as among those who attended church regularly. The socialization value of church attendance was questioned in the Nye study because he could find no association between delinquency and length of church attendance.

The Nye study also found religion to be connected with delinquency through family relationships. Nondelinquents, for example, tended to discuss religious issues with their parents. The importance of these relationships lies more in their description of the connection between family factors and delinquency rather than of the connection between religion and delinquency.

The investigation of religious factors and delinquency lay virtually dormant until the late 1960s when a study called "Hellfire and Delinquency" was published (Hirschi and Stark, 1969). Using both a self-report delinquency scale with over 4000 junior and senior high school students in California, as well as police records, Travis Hirschi and Rodney Stark measured the association between delinquency and church attendance, acceptance of moral values, respect for law and the police, and belief in the existence of a supernatural power and sanctions in life after death. Their results were as follows: (1) there was little or no association between church attendance and either an acceptance of moral values or respect for law and the police; (2) there was a strong, positive association between church attendance and belief in supernatural sanctions; (3) there were strong inverse associations between both self-report and official delinquency and acceptance of moral values and respect for law and the police; (4) there was no association between either measure of delinquency and belief in supernatural sanctions; and (5) there was no relationship between either type of delinquency and church attendance. These results led Hirschi and Stark to conclude that religion and church attendance had no effect on delinquency, particularly in the face of worldly influences.

The report by Hirschi and Stark left several issues unresolved. For example, is religion unrelated to delinquency in all locations, for all faiths and denominations, and for all types of delinquency? These and other issues were addressed by a plethora of investigations in the 1970s, many of which were attempted replications or extensions of the Hirschi and Stark research. For the most part, these studies tended to reveal some association between religion and delinquency, but the association depended on various situations.

In one extension of Hirschi and Stark's research Steven Burkett and Mervin White (1974) investigated the relationship between self-reported delinquency and religion among a sample of 750 high school students in the Pacific Northwest. Although the same measures of religion were used as in the Hirschi and Stark study, the measure of delinquency was extended to include alcohol (beer) and marijuana offenses (no official records of delinquency were used). In virtually all particulars, the results of the study were consistent with those of Hirschi and Stark. When the offenses of alcohol and marijuana use were considered, however, Burkett and White found strong inverse relationships with church attendance, moral values, and respect for "wordly authority"—that is, those who exhibited such behavior and attitudes were relatively less involved with drug use.

Burkett and White concluded from their study that religious participation does seem to deter some delinquency, especially those acts for which there is not consistent condemnation in the secular society. Interestingly, they further concluded that rather than religion being one of the *least* effective institutions for controlling delinquency, it may be one of the *most* effective, since its influence tends to be greater for those offenses for which secular controls have weakened.

In a partial replication of the Hirschi and Stark study, Paul Higgins and Gary Albrecht (1977) examined the relationship between church attendance and self-reported delinquency among 1400 high school students in Atlanta. They concluded that, contrary to Hirschi and Stark, delinquency was inversely related to church attendance. This relationship, furthermore, was influenced by the variable of respect for the juvenile court system (except for nonwhite females). That is, the greater the church attendance, the more respect for the juvenile court, and the less delinquency. Higgins and Albrecht speculated that their findings might have reflected the inclusion of more serious offenses than Hirschi and Stark had investigated, but discounted this explanation in favor of a geographical one. In other words, they ultimately concluded that religion has more of an influence on behavior in areas where religion occupies a more central place in the lives of people, such as in the South.

Other research has indicated some relationship between religion and delinquency, usually drug use and status offenses (Jensen and Rojek, 1980). Some would contend, then, that the conclusion of Hirschi and Stark was based on incomplete evidence. There *does* seem to be some connection between religious factors and delinquency, particularly drug and status offenses, and particularly in the South.

The relationship between delinquency and particular religious faiths, however, is still an issue. Many of the earlier investigations either did not specify a particular faith or considered only Christian faiths as a single category. Some studies have found delinquency rates to be lower among Jews (where there is widespread secularism and relatively lesser orthodoxy) than among Catholics or Protestants (Jensen and Rojek, 1980). On the other hand, Hirschi and Stark, as well as Burkett and White, reported no differences in delinquency rates by denomination, although no data were presented in support of these conclusions. Another analysis indicated that church attendance and delinquency were more inversely related among "fundamentalistic" or "highly ascetic" faiths, such as the Church of Christ or Church of God, than among other religions (Jensen and Erickson, 1979). It would appear more accurate to argue at this point that the religious convictions of members are more central to an explanation of their behavior than the fact that they belong to or attend one denomination or another.

In summation, it may be unrealistic to expect the influence of religion on juvenile delinquency to be greater than that of competing secular forces. At the same time, it would be equally unrealistic to suppose that religion has no effect on juvenile behavior. Most of the recent research discussed above indicates that there *is* an association between the two variables, especially in areas where religion is still generally influential and with delinquent offenses for which secular sanctions have become ambivalent.

Family Factors   Perhaps one of the most persistent explanations of delinquent behavior is the breakdown of the family. From the concerns of those in the Child-Saving Movement of the nineteenth century (Platt, 1977) to the present, the family has been regarded as a major variable in the presence or absence of delinquency. This interest in the family as a factor in delinquency is shared by students of sociology and psychology. Many of the individualistic theories of delinquency, such as psychoanalytic explanations, for example, incorporate aberrations in family interaction as these occur early in life. Shaw and McKay's social disorganization theory of delinquency also viewed the breakdown of family controls as an important contribution to the development of social disorganization in a neighborhood.

The centrality of family relationships in the explanation of delinquency, however, has not always been accepted, particularly among sociologists. Karen Wilkinson (1974) argues that interest in the "broken home" and delinquency among sociologists can be divided into three periods: (1) a period of keen interest and research activity (1900–1932); (2) a period of rejection of the relationship between the broken home and delinquency (1933–1950); and (3) a period of renewed interest in the connection between the broken home and delinquency (1951–1970s).

Partly, this fluctuation reflects various interpretations of empirical analyses of the relationship. Wilkinson argues, however, that the emphasis, or deemphasis, on family conditions is also related to other matters, such as ideological biases of researchers, political views about the state of the family and the effects of divorce, and disputes between such fields as psychology and sociology over the importance of family intactness versus social class or other sociological concepts in the explanation of delinquency.

The interest in family factors and delinquency has typically involved both the structure of the family and the nature of relationships occurring within the family. The structure of the family includes the broken home—that is, a home where one (or both) natural parent is permanently absent because of events such as death, desertion, or divorce—but, as a force influencing the behavior of youths, this may be changing. The quality of family relationships involves such factors as parental conflicts, parent-child relationships, and discipline and supervision patterns. Both of these factors—the structure of the family and the nature of family relationships—are now discussed in connection with delinquency.

Broken Homes   The relationship between delinquency and a home broken by divorce, desertion, or death has been extensively investigated. For the most part, these studies have found that delinquents come from broken homes significantly more often than nondelinquents. Martin Haskell and Lewis Yablonsky (1982), for example, report the findings of eight studies from 1929–1971 that investigated the relationship between broken homes and delinquency. The range of delinquents from broken homes was 23.6 percent to 61.5 percent, while the range for nondelinquents was from 12.9 to 36.1 percent.

Similarly, Lawrence Rosen and Kathleen Neilson (1978) reported small but statistically significant *associations* between broken homes and male delinquency for 15 studies conducted between 1932 and 1975.

One of the clearest differences between delinquents and nondelinquents concerning broken homes is provided by Sheldon and Eleanor Glueck's comparison of 500 delinquents and 500 nondelinquents (1950) previously discussed. Over 60 percent of the delinquents came from broken homes, as compared with slightly more than one-third of the nondelinquents.

From a review of several studies of broken homes and delinquency and an analysis of over 44,000 official delinquents in

Philadelphia, Thomas Monahan (1957) concluded that the broken home is definitely related to delinquency.

Although the evidence seems clear that the broken home is associated with delinquency, several doubts exist concerning the importance of this relationship. First, virtually all of the studies supporting a relationship between broken homes and delinquency have used official police, court, or institutional records as the measure of delinquency. The reported relationships may thus reflect the decisions of juvenile justice officials to report and process juveniles from broken homes more often than juveniles from intact homes. That this bias might exist is supported by the observation that there is only a small relationship between the broken home and *self-reported* delinquency (Nye, 1958; Hirschi, 1969).

Second, not all of the studies that have examined the relationship between official measures of delinquency and the broken home have concluded that a significant association exists. In the period between 1933 to 1950, rejection of this relationship, for example, was partially based on Shaw and McKay's (1932) analysis of official delinquency and broken homes. Essentially, they found the relationship to be insignificant, particularly when controlling for such variables as age and ethnicity.

Third, the relationship between broken homes and delinquency has almost always been investigated from the point of view of delinquents rather than broken homes. As a causal variable, however, the broken home should also be analyzed relative to the proportion of juveniles from broken homes who are delinquent. Rosen and Neilson (1978) have attempted just such an analysis. They found that the overall probability of finding a *delinquent* (officially identified) from a broken home was less than the probability of finding a broken home among delinquents. The *relative* probabilities, however, were the same. That is, delinquents were about three times as likely to be found among broken homes as among intact homes, and broken homes were about three times more likely to be found among delinquents as among non-delinquents. Thus, they found evidence that both refuted and supported a causal connection between broken homes and delinquency. Overall, however, the investigators found a weak association between the two.

Family Relationships While some doubt exists concerning the connection between broken homes and delinquency, there is considerable evidence that points to a correlation between family relationships and delinquency. Family relationships, in this context, are usually measured in terms of interaction, affection, supervision, and discipline between and among parents and children.

Many investigators who have found a correlation between official delinquency and broken homes have also concluded that an association exists between delinquency and a variety of family relationships. The Gluecks, for example, concluded that future delinquency in a young boy (preschool age) could be predicted from knowledge of five family factors, not including the broken home: (1) discipline by father (overstrict, erratic, or lax discipline was positively associated with delinquency); (2) supervision by mother (classified as "suitable," "fair," or "unsuitable" with unsuitable supervision connected with delinquency); (3) affection of father for son (hostile or indifferent attitudes were positively related to delinquency); (4) affection of mother for son; and (5) cohesiveness of family (inversely related to delinquency; Glueck and Glueck, 1950:260–261).[3]

The importance of family relationships, such as supervision and affection patterns, does not necessarily preclude a contribution of the broken home to delinquency. However, the importance of the broken home may be in its effect on family relationships, which, in turn, have a more forceful impact on delinquency. It is the nature of what goes on in the family, therefore, that influences delinquency more than whether or not one parent is absent from the home.

As indicated earlier, the relative influence of family relationships over the broken home is illustrated in studies utilizing self-report measures of delinquency. Nye (1958), for example, closely examined numerous family factors, including the broken home, and self-reported delinquency among 780 high school students in several medium-sized Washington (state) communities. In all, he tested over 70 associations separately for mother-daughter, mother-son, father-daughter, and father-son relationships. Nearly 95 percent of the associations were consistent with the assumptions of control theory, and about 50 percent of these associations were statistically significant. These parent-child relationships covered such topics as the acceptance or rejection of parents by children, and vice versa, methods of parental discipline and punishment, family recreational patterns, and so on. In general, those adolescents whose parents treated them firmly but with love and respect tended to be considerably less delinquent than those juveniles whose parents continually nagged or scolded them or treated them as pawns by making expressions of love or acceptance contingent on good behavior.

Interestingly, Nye found little relationship between the physically, or legally, broken home and delinquency. He did, however, find a significant inverse association between delinquency and happiness and marital adjustment, regardless of whether the home was physically broken.

Hirschi's (1969) analysis of self-report delinquency among 4077 junior and senior high school students in California also failed to demonstrate an association between broken homes and delinquency. Hirschi did find, however, associations between delinquency and several measures of family relationships, such as affectional identification with parents, intimacy of communication with father, and identification with father. In general, Hirschi found that delinquency was inversely related to the bonds of attachment within the juvenile's family. This relationship was supported, moreover, regardless of race or social class. Furthermore, Hirschi's data led to the conclusion that ties to the family were inversely related to delinquency, even when parents were "unconventional" (on welfare or unemployed) and regardless of the existence of delinquent friends. Attachments to parents and delinquent companions, however, were independently related to delinquency, which supports both social control theory and differential association.

Hirschi's findings were generally replicated by Michael

Hindelang (1973) in a study of self-report delinquency among 900 adolescents in a rural area of upstate New York. Specifically, attachment to parents was inversely related to delinquency (the broken home was not investigated in this study).

In addition, Haskell and Yablonsky (1982) devote considerable attention to the empirically supported connection between "family dynamics" and delinquency and conclude that internal patterns of interaction within the family are more important in the explanation of delinquency than are structural features of the family, such as broken homes.

Overall, it would appear that the association between delinquency and broken homes is as much a reflection of the attitudes and decisions of juvenile justice personnel as it is a reflection of the delinquency-producing tendencies of broken homes. The nature of parent-child interactions and the general atmosphere within the home, however, have been consistently related to delinquency. Accordingly, it would be a mistake to accept the conclusions of many sociologists during the middle of this century —namely, that family-connected variables have no place in the explanation of delinquency. Clearly, family relationships are important and it is logical to locate the etiological significance of these factors within the framework of social control theory.

School Experiences and Delinquency   Achievement, participation, and overall involvement in school-related activities have been connected with delinquency for a long time. The negative association between grades in school (achievement) and delinquency was discussed in Chapter 5, in connection with Albert Cohen's middle-class measuring rod theory of delinquency. The influences of intelligence and learning disabilities have also been discussed in earlier chapters. It would appear that little more could be added to establish the significance of school situations in the explanation of juvenile delinquency. Because school activities constitute such a large focal point for adolescent behavior (Jensen and Rojek, 1980), and because attachment and commitment to school represent another major component of the social control theory of delinquency, it is appropriate to reconsider such issues at this point. The purpose of the following discussion is to comment on the *comparative* influence of these conditions, since the primary influence has already been established.

One of the clearest comparative assessments of the influence of school factors on delinquency is provided by Hirschi (1969). In particular, Hirschi compared "attachment to parents (father)" with "attachment to school" and found that those who were unattached to their parents were also disaffiliated with school (including their teachers). He also found that possessing favorable attitudes toward school, including favorable attitudes toward teachers, was associated with lower rates of delinquency, regardless of the strength of attachments to the father (Hirschi, 1969:131–132). In other words, while attachment to parents is definitely related to delinquency, its effects tend to be overshadowed by affiliations with school.

In a study of 482 official delinquents and 185 nondelinquents in Utah and Los Angeles, Lamar T. Empey and Steven G. Lubeck (1971) found that both family variables (broken homes, parental harmony, relations with parents) and school factors (particularly grades in school) were highly associated with delinquency in both settings. When the two sets of conditions were simultaneously compared, however, the data clearly indicated that school (as measured by dropouts) had a stronger direct effect on delinquency than family (as measured by boy-parent harmony) in Los Angeles. In Utah, the direct effect of dropout was somewhat stronger than the effect of harmony with parents, but the differences were not as pronounced as in Los Angeles.

It would thus appear that school experiences are not only directly associated with delinquency, but that they are also relatively more associated with delinquency than other institutional variables, namely family relationships.

Other Considerations   The foregoing discussions lead to the general conclusion that religious, family, and school variables are associated with both official and self-report measures of delinquency. In this sense, therefore, social control theory is supported by the data.

In addition to institutional influences on delinquency, social control theory also argues that delinquency is related to delinquent attitudes and beliefs. This position has received considerable support in the formulations and testing of differential association and neutralization theory, as discussed in Chapter 6. In addition, empirical assessments of social control theory per se have clearly supported the hypothesized relationship between delinquent attitudes and delinquent behavior (Hirschi, 1969; Hindelang, 1973).

Attempts to assess the causal priority of lack of attachment to conventional beliefs or ties in the community have established the existence of these disaffections and disaffiliations prior to delinquent behavior, or in spite of associations with delinquent peers (Hirschi, 1969; Empey and Lubeck, 1971; Jensen, 1972; Linden and Hackler, 1973; Hepburn, 1977; Phillips and Kelly, 1979).

Moreover, recent attempts to compare various elements of social control theory with structural theories of delinquency (such as anomic and lower-class culture theories) have indicated that social control variables are at least as powerful as structural variables in the explanation of delinquency, and often more so (Cernkovich, 1978; Eve, 1978; Kornhauser, 1978; Knox, 1981).

In numerous ways, therefore, the assumptions of social control theory have received considerable support in the literature. By no means have all of the issues and associated questions relative to social control theory been resolved. First, not all investigations of delinquency have supported the tenets of social control, especially with respect to the topic of conformity (Rankin, 1977).

Second, the strength of institutional attachments of conformity (or the lack of such attachments in relation to delinquency) must be considered in terms of cultural and historical values and conditions. A study of official delinquency and family factors in Israel, for example, found the two to be unrelated (Rahav, 1976). In addition, an analysis of self-reported delinquency indicated that youth in rural areas were less delinquent than youth in urban locations. Moreover, delinquents in general exhibited stronger social bonds than did nondelinquents. However, rural youths were no more committed to the legitimacy of authority and institutions in society than were urban juveniles. Commitment, or social bonds, therefore, did not explain the differences in delinquency rates between rural and urban youngsters (Lyerly and Skipper, 1981).

Third, the importance of other factors in the explanation of delinquency is indicated by the amount of delinquent behavior explained by social control variables (when this assessment has been possible to ascertain). Lamar Empey maintains that no more than 25 percent of the differences in delinquency rates can be explained by social control (bond) factors (1978). While this figure is a little low, few estimates exceed 50 percent, a figure which is impressive relative to other explanations of delinquency but far from allowing one to conclude that social control factors *determine* delinquency.

Fourth, the specific qualities of religious participation, family interactions, and school activities that foster delinquency are far from having been consistently identified. Certain situations are now strongly suggestive of delinquency, such as lax, inconsistent, or physically abusive parental discipline techniques. The thrust of the research thus far, however, has been on the general influence on delinquency of ties and affections with social institutions rather than on specific types of attachments, commitments, or activities that might more or less contribute to delinquency.

The overall assessment of the social control theory of delinquency is that it has generally been supported by research. The idea that a social bond to conventional activities and values inhibits delinquency is persuasive in its empirical support and is one of the most promising explanations of delinquency yet developed.

SUMMARY

Control theories of delinquency, including those of Reckless, Hirschi, and others, have more empirical support than other explanations of youthful antisocial activity. They consist of concepts that are measurable and that are based on logical properties which have informed popular and scientific opinions regarding delinquency for decades. While many questions relative to these theories remain unsolved, the research conducted thus far suggests that control theories are supported and worthy of continued investigation. This conclusion is particularly valid for the proposition that attachments and commitments to conventional institutions in society (the social bond) are associated with low rates of delinquency.

Of course, control theories cannot explain all acts of delinquency, nor can they predict what specific types of delinquency will develop. In addition, even though it has been established that positive self-concepts and attachments to conventional beliefs and institutions in society "protect," or "insulate," one from delinquent involvement, a key question still remains: "How are self-concepts and attachments produced and changed?" Containment and social control theories must yield to other explanations for an answer to this question, and it has been shown that numerous theories have approached this issue from many different viewpoints. In essence, control theories assume an intermediate, intervening position between delinquency and a variety of preconditions. Regardless of specific contributing factors, therefore, it would appear appropriate and potentially more fruitful to focus attention on the immediate precursors to delinquency—namely, self-concepts and social bonds.

NOTES

1. Others have viewed Reckless' theory as an example of a *social* control theory of delinquency (Gibbons, 1981). Using the conceptualizations developed in the current text, however, containment theory is more appropriately classified as an example of personal control theories.
2. On this point, it should be noted that Reckless and Dinitz (1972) conducted an extensive and scientifically sound delinquency prevention program, based on self-concept improvement. While no significant differences appeared between experimental and control subjects, containment theory per se was not rejected because the treatment program also produced no significant changes in self-concept.

3. Another investigation of official delinquency also found support for an association between "intrafamily problems," including broken homes, and delinquency, particularly in an urban area (Los Angeles) as compared to the state of Utah (Empey and Lubeck, 1971). Multivariate analysis, furthermore, indicated that family relationships, especially as measured by "boy-parent harmony," were more predictive of delinquency than was parental separation.

REFERENCES

Burkett, Steven R. and Mervin White, 1974, "Hellfire and Delinquency: Another Look." Journal for the Scientific Study of Religion 13:455–462.

Cernkovich, Steven A., 1978, "Evaluating Two Models of Delinquency Causation: Structural Theory and Control Theory." Criminology 16:335–352.

Cohen, Albert K., 1966, Deviance and Control. Englewood Cliffs, N.J.: Prentice-Hall.

Dinitz, Simon, Frank R. Scarpitti, and Walter C. Reckless, 1962, "Delinquency Vulnerability: A Cross Group and Longitudinal Analysis." American Sociological Review 27:515–517.

Empey, Lamar T., 1978, American Delinquency. Homewood, Ill.: Dorsey,
———, 1982, American Delinquency, revised edition. Homewood, Ill.: Dorsey.

Empey, Lamar T. and Steven G. Lubeck, 1971, Explaining Delinquency. Lexington, Mass.: D. C. Heath.

Eve, Raymond, A., 1978, "A Study of the Efficacy and Interactions of Several Theories for Explaining Rebelliousness Among High School Students." Journal of Criminal Law and Criminology 69:115–125.

Gibbons, Don C., 1981, Delinquent Behavior, third edition. Englewood Cliffs, N.J.: Prentice-Hall.

Glueck, Sheldon and Eleanor Glueck, 1950, Unraveling Juvenile Delinquency. Cambridge, Mass.: Harvard University Press.

Haskell, Martin R. and Lewis Yablonsky, 1982, Juvenile Delinquency, third edition. Boston: Houghton Mifflin.

Hepburn, John R., 1977, "Testing Alternative Models of Delinquency Causation." Journal of Criminal Law and Criminology 67:450–460.

Higgins, Paul C. and Gary L. Albrecht, 1977, "Hellfire and Delinquency Revisited." Social Forces 55:952–958.

Hindelang, Michael J., 1973, "Causes of Delinquency: A Partial Replication and Extension." Social Problems 20:471–487.

Hirschi, Travis, 1969, Causes of Delinquency. Berkeley, Calif.: University of California Press.

Hirschi, Travis and Richard Stark, 1969, "Hellfire and Delinquency." Social Problems 17:202–213.

Jensen, Gary F., 1972, "Parents, Peers, and Delinquent Action: A Test of the Differential Association Perspective." American Journal of Sociology 78:562–575.

———, 1973, "Inner Containment and Delinquency." Journal of Criminal Law and Criminology 64:464–470.

Jensen, Gary F. and Maynard L. Erickson, 1979, "The Religious Factor and Delinquency: Another Look at the Hellfire Hypothesis." Pp. 157–177 in Robert Wuthnow (ed.), The Religious Dimension. New York: Academic Press.

Jensen, Gary F. and Dean G. Rojek, 1980, Delinquency. Lexington, Mass.: D. C. Heath.

Knox, George W., 1981, "Social Disorganization Models of Deviance," Pp. 78–92 in Gary F. Jensen (ed.), Sociology of Delinquency. Beverly Hills, Calif.: SAGE.

Kornhauser, Ruth Rosner, 1978, Social Sources of Delinquency. Chicago: University of Chicago Press.

Krisberg, Barry and James Austin (eds.), 1978, The Children of Ishmael. Palo Alto, Calif.: Mayfield.

Linden, Eric and James C. Hackler, 1973, "Affective Ties and Delinquency." Pacific Sociological Review 16:27–46.

Lyerly, Robert Richard and James K. Skipper, Jr., 1981, "Differential Rates of Rural-Urban Delinquency: A Social Control Approach." Criminology 19:385–399.

Monahan, Thomas P., 1957, "Family Status and the Delinquent Child: A Reappraisal and Some New Findings." Social Forces 32:250–258.

Nye, F. Ivan, 1958, Family Relationships and Delinquent Behavior. New York: Wiley.

Orcutt, James D., 1970, "Self-Concept and Insulation against Delinquency: Some Critical Notes." Sociological Quarterly 2:381–390.

Phillips, John C., and Delos H. Kelly, 1979, "School Failure and Delinquency: Which Causes Which?" Criminology 17:194–207.

Platt, Anthony, 1977, The Child Savers, second edition. Chicago: University of Chicago Press.

Rahav, Giora, 1976, "Family Relations and Delinquency in Israel." Criminology 14:259–270.

Rankin, Joseph H., 1977, "Investigating the Interrelations among Social Control Variables and Conformity." Journal of Criminal Law and Criminology 67:470–480.

Reckless, Walter C., 1961, "A New Theory of Delinquency and Crime." Federal Probation 25:42–46.

————, 1967, The Crime Problem, fourth edition. New York: Appleton-Century-Croft.

Reckless, Walter C., Simon Dinitz, and Ellen Murray, 1956, "Self Concept as an Insulator Against Delinquency." American Sociological Review 21:744–746.

Reckless, Water C., Simon Dinitz, and Barbara Kay, 1957, "The Self Component in Potential Delinquency and Potential Nondelinquency." American Sociological Review 22:566–570.

Reckless, Walter C. and Simon Dinitz, 1972, The Prevention of Juvenile Delinquency. Columbus: Ohio State University Press.

Rosen, Lawrence and Kathleen Neilson, 1978, "The Broken Home and Delinquency." Pp. 406–415 in Leonard D. Savitz and Norman Johnston (eds.), Crime in Society. New York: Wiley.

Sanders, Wiley B. (ed.), 1970, Juvenile Offenders for a Thousand Years. Chapel Hill: University of North Carolina Press.

Scarpitti, Frank R., Ellen Murray, Simon Dinitz, and Walter C. Reckless, 1960, "The 'Good' Boy in a High Delinquency Area: Four Years Later." American Sociological Review 25:555–558.

Schwartz, Michael and Sandra S. Tangri, 1965, "A Note on Self-Concept as an Insulator Against Delinquency." American Sociological Review 30:922–926.

Schwartz, Michael and Sheldon Stryker, 1970, Deviance, Selves and Others. Washington, D.C.: American Sociological Association.

Shaw, Clifford R. and Henry D. McKay, 1932, "Are Broken Homes a Causative Factor in Juvenile Delinquency?" Social Forces 10:514–524.

Toby, Jackson, 1957, "Social Disorganization and Stake in Conformity: Complementary Factors in the Predatory Behavior of Hoodlums." Journal of Criminal Law, Criminology and Police Science 48:12–17.

Voss, Harwin L., 1969, "Differential Association and Containment Theory: A Theoretical Convergence." Social Forces 47:381–391.

Wells, L. Edward, 1978, "Theories of Deviance and the Self-Concept." Social Psychology 41:189–204.

Wilkinson, Karen, 1974, "The Broken Home and Juvenile Delinquency: Scientific Explanation or Ideology?" Social Problems 21:726–739.

8

LABELING THEORY

HISTORICAL OVERVIEW

The view that formal and informal societal reactions to delinquency can influence the subsequent attitudes and behavior of delinquents was recognized early in this century. Frederick Thrasher's work on juvenile gangs in Chicago (1936) was one of the first instances in which the consequences of official labels of delinquency were recognized as potentially negative. A few years later, Frank Tannenbaum (1938) introduced the term "dramatization of evil," in which he argued that officially labeling someone as a delinquent can result in the person *becoming* the very thing he is described as *being*. A few years after Tannenbaum's book was published, Edwin Lemert (1951) developed the concepts of *primary* and *secondary* deviance (to be defined below), which became the central elements of the first systematic development of what has come to be known as labeling theory.[1]

Interest in this theory was dormant during the 1950s, since numerous structural theories were introduced to explain delinquency, particularly lower-class gang delinquency (see Chapter 5). Increasing dissatisfaction with these, and other, theories and the growing awareness of middle-class delinquency, much of which was not officially recorded, prompted many criminologists to return to the earlier views of Thrasher, Tannenbaum, and Lemert. This renewed interest was particularly spawned by Howard Becker's analysis of deviance in the early 1960s (later revised in 1973). Essentially, Becker proposed that deviance was "created" by rule enforcers, who often acted with bias against the poor and powerless members of society. This idea, coupled with the earlier notion of changing self-images, during the 1960s and early 1970s became a central focus of much research and commentary that focused on the subjects of crime, delinquency, and deviant acts.

GENERIC ASSUMPTIONS

One of the basic assumptions of labeling theory is that initial acts of delinquency are caused by a wide variety of factors. These factors, however, are relatively unimportant in the scheme of things, which leads to a second assumption. That is, the primary factor in the repetition of delinquency is the fact of having been formally labeled as a delinquent. This assertion is accompanied by another idea, which may be presented as a third assumption. Repeated acts of delinquency are influenced by formal labels because such labels eventually alter a person's self-image to the point where the person begins to identify himself as a delinquent and act accordingly. Contrary to Reckless' containment theory, therefore, the view of the labeling perspective is that a negative self-image *follows* the act of delinquency rather than precedes delinquency. A fourth assumption of the labeling approach is that the official application of the label of delinquent is dependent on a host of criteria in addition to, or other than, the behavior itself, such as the offender's age, sex, race, and social class, as well as the organizational norms of official agencies and departments. These assumptions are diagrammed in Figure 13.

Of course, one does not have to be officially labeled criminal or delinquent in order to label himself as such. Moreover, an official label that calls one delinquent can be applied *irrespective* of any

Varied causes and influences	→	Deviant (delinquent) behavior	→	Problematic imposition of the official label of "delinquent"	→
Development of delinquent self-image	→	Delinqency, often in accordance with an identity of oneself as a delinquent, and sometimes in new and more serious forms			

FIGURE 13

nonconformist act. For the most part, however, the advocates of the labeling approach to delinquency have maintained that usually some type of nonconformity precedes an official label and that most self-labeling occurs after official labeling.

KEY CONCEPTS

The focus of this chapter is on the *effects* of labeling on delinquent self-images and behavior rather than on the antecedents of the labeling per se. Two concepts that are important in this regard are *primary* and *secondary* deviance, as introduced by Lemert (1951).

Primary Deviance This term refers to original acts of nonconformity that may be caused by any of a number of factors. Primary deviance is generally considered to be undetected, or not recognized, as deviant by others. Primary deviants have not adjusted their behavior to accommodate societal reactions to their deviance.

Secondary Deviance On the other hand, this term refers to deviance that is committed *as the result* of the problems of self-identity and social interaction, which are generated by the identification of the actor as a deviant. It is a new and often more serious form of deviance that is committed, in addition to the original causes of the primary deviance. Thus, secondary deviance is nonconformity created by the "pains of labeling."

DISCUSSION

Lemert's (1951) discussion of the labeling, or "societal reaction," theory was applied to deviant behavior in general. Lemert conceived of such behavior, which he termed "sociopathic," as meaningful only in the sense that it elicited an "effective" form of social disapproval. Deviation is neither *inherently* good or bad; such descriptions emanate only from the societal response to the behavior.

Lemert conceptualized the reaction process from two angles: the members of society and the deviant. The members of society are considered important in this process from the standpoint that it is they, particularly agents of social control, who are responsible for the labeling in the first place.

The second component of the labeling process, the deviant, is considered important because of the consequences the label of deviant produces for the labelee. It is with this aspect of the labeling process that Lemert introduced the concepts of primary and secondary deviation, and on which he concentrated his discussion.

The term "process" becomes meaningful in Lemert's discussion with the view that secondary deviation is reached through a series of steps, beginning with primary deviation, progressing through a series of penalties, to further deviance, then increased penalties, and eventually an acceptance by the actor of a deviant status.

The process of moving from primary to secondary deviance is conceived of as very complex. Numerous issues have been raised concerning the steps involved, and these issues have influenced considerable discussion regarding the logical adequacy of labeling theory (see, for example, Sagarin, 1975; Montanino, 1977; and Gove, 1980a).

One of the most central issues in the process of becoming a secondary deviant is the connection between behavior and the societal reaction to it. While labeling theorists may not be overly concerned with the basic causes of delinquency, those who advocate this theory must be able to distinguish between behavior, which is caused by some "primary" (pre-label) factor, and that which is committed largely in reponse to a label or an identification of one as a delinquent.

Howard Becker (1973) has attempted to deal with this question by conceptualizing three situations of deviant (or delinquent) behavior: the pure deviant, the falsely accused deviant, and the secret deviant. The pure deviant is a norm violator and is recognized as such by others. Falsely accused deviants are those whose acts are actually conforming, but who are incorrectly thought by others to be deviant (the victims of the "bum rap," so to speak). In the secret deviant situation, one violates a rule or a law but is not noticed or perceived by others as having committed an act of deviance.

It might appear that the term "secret deviance" is a contradiction within the assumptions of labeling theory (Gibbs, 1966). If an act is not to be considered deviant unless it is so recognized and labeled by others, as Becker maintains, then how is secret deviance possible? Becker addresses this question by suggesting that we call nonconformist behavior that is not reacted to by members of society "rule-breaking" behavior. Deviant behavior, however, is that which is so recognized in society, and secret deviance is behavior that would very likely be labeled as deviant if it were observed.

The use of a new term to answer a strong question does not always resolve the problem. If a considerable amount of undetected delinquency occurs, for example, it could suggest that delinquency is as much in response to primary factors as to the effects of labeling, if not more so. In fact, research does suggest that a great deal of "hidden" delinquency exists (see Chapter 11 on middle-class delinquency). It is still possible, of course, to argue that repeated delinquency occurs primarily because of the problems generated by official detection and labeling. But the existence of a significant amount of hidden delinquency, or "rule-breaking" behavior, questions the extent to which delinquency can be attributed to the effects of labeling (Hirschi, 1980).

Another issue with labeling theory is the matter of how the label is handled by the labelee. Does one resist the negative effects of labeling or become positively influenced by the label? Some people are able to deny the "deviant" implications that the judgments of others may denote. In addition, it is possible, some may say even likely, that being labeled a delinquent would lead to reformed behavior—the juvenile would decide to "mend his ways" to avoid further problems and adjustments occasioned by a label (Thorsell and Klemke, 1972; Becker, 1973). The list of possibilities is lengthy and demonstrates again the complexities of the theory.

The consideration of the labelee's reactions to his identification as a deviant leads many to associate labeling theory with an interactionist perspective (Becker, 1973; Lemert, 1974; Sagarin, 1975); that is, labeling theory attempts to account for the mutual effects of the actor and his audience. Thus, the theory is concerned not only with what the actor and reactor do, but with how each one's actions affect the behavior of the other.

In addition to conceptualizing deviant behavior in terms of personal interaction, some commentators on labeling theory have noted the importance of groups and associations in the actor's acceptance of societal reactions to his behavior. Becker, for example, argues that a "final step in the career of a deviant" is the identification with an "organized deviant group" (pp. 37–39). Others (Sagarin, 1969; Trice and Roman, 1970) have also acknowledged the influence that social groups with a deviant label may have on one's accepting a personal label of deviance. These authors have suggested that group support of a labeled deviant may either nudge him further into an identity as a deviant or serve as a catalyst for a transformation from an unacceptable role, in society's eyes, to a more positive social status. An example of the latter situation would be an alcohol abuser who joins Alcoholics Anonymous and pronounces himself an alcoholic in order to handle the problem (Trice and Roman, 1970).

EVALUATION

Despite numerous debates and discussion, several have argued that there are essentially two basic issues with which labeling theory is concerned: (1) the development and enforcement of rules and laws, and (2) the effects of labeling one a delinquent in terms of one's subsequent self-concept and behavior (Schur, 1971; Gove, 1980b; Kitsuse, 1980). The first issue concerns the various influences that shape society's laws and the manner in which they are enforced. With respect to the study of delinquency, these questions have typically been addressed to the demographic characteristics of the juvenile (for example, age, sex, race, or social class), the organizational climate of social control agencies (such as police departments and juvenile courts), and the interaction between juveniles and agents of social control (police, judges, probation officers, and so on). Some contend that this issue has become a dominant area of concern in criminology, but that it has become associated with conflict theory, particularly neo-Marxist, or radical theory (Hirschi, 1980). Because the question of discrimination against minorities is so important, its evaluation is placed in the following chapter, which addresses the radical theory of criminality.

The second basic issue of labeling theory, the consequences of labeling on one's self-concept and behavior, has received considerable attention in the literature and is definitely accessible to evaluation. It is recognized that concentrating on self-concepts and attitudes and visible behavior does not do full justice to the complexities of labeling theory and to the process of moving from primary to secondary deviance or of becoming enmeshed in a life of criminality, a "career" deviant (Becker, 1973). A systematic assessment of these factors, however, will provide some information concerning the validity of labeling theory.

Labeling and Self-Concept

The relationship between a formal delinquency label and consequent identity problems has been analyzed through both qualitative and quantitative research problems. Qualitatively, the connection between labeling a juvenile a delinquent and the development of a delinquent identity, or antiauthority attitudes, has been established by examinations of the court processing of juveniles (Emerson, 1969; Cicourel, 1976) as well as observations of juvenile gangs (Werthman, 1970). Thrasher and Tannenbaum also qualitatively assessed the connection between self-concept and formally being labeled, or "tagged," as a delinquent. In addition, Matza's view that delinquents develop a cynical and disrespectful attitude toward the police and juvenile courts was based essentially on qualitative assessments of juvenile reactions (see Chapter 6).

A quasi-experimental participant observation study of delinquency in a small town reported a connection between official (and unofficial) labeling and delinquent self-images. William Chambliss (1973) conducted a longitudinal study of two juvenile gangs—eight children of respectable, upper-middle-class families who formed a gang called the "Saints" and six youths from lower-class families who belonged to a gang called the "Roughnecks."

Although none of the Saints had ever been arrested, their observed involvement in delinquency was as thorough (although not for violent offenses) as the Roughnecks, who had been arrested repeatedly. Furthermore, the overall reputation of the Saints, in the community and among school officials, was generally good. The acknowledged transgressions of the Saints were often passed off as "pranks" and mischievousness to be expected of boys. The Roughnecks, on the other hand, were viewed by the police, school officials, and other members of the community as headed for "trouble," a "bad bunch of boys " (Chambliss, 1973:27–28).

More to the point of this discussion, Chambliss' observations indicated that the juveniles generally adopted, or lived up to, their reputations in the community. The Saints never saw themselves as delinquents. Instead, they saw themselves as merely out to have a good time, to raise a little hell, as it were, all of which never really hurt anyone. The Roughnecks, however, made their delinquency quite visible to the public and openly flouted their hostility toward the respectable members of the community. According to Chambliss, members of the Roughnecks not only viewed themselves as delinquents, but they also sought out as friends and associates other juveniles with similar self-concepts.

It would appear from qualitative analyses that official labels do produce, or at least contribute to, a delinquent self-image. More empirical or quantitative measures of self-concept, however, have provided only mixed support for the contention that a formal delinquency label produces a delinquent identity.

Jack Foster and his colleagues (1972), for example, interviewed 196 male youths who had either been arrested or referred to juvenile court. The juveniles were interviewed in their homes within 20 days after their arrest or court appearance. Basically, the boys reported no changes in personal relationships or parental attitudes toward them as a result of their involvement with the law. In addition, over 90 percent of the boys felt no difficulties would develop with respect to finishing school as a result of their official records of delinquency. About 40 percent of the boys felt that their chances of getting a suitable job might have been hurt by their legal involvements, but this feeling seemed more pronounced among those boys who had been sent to court. Overall, the investigators concluded that the labeled youths either did not feel any great liabilities as a result of their labels or were able to minimize, in their own minds, the possible effects of such labels because of their age, generally good behavior, and the current practice of keeping juvenile records confidential in the United States.

While the Foster study did not specifically address the issue of self-concept, the results clearly lent no support to the contention that associations and identities are affected by a formal label of delinquency (see also Giordano, 1976). Other research has, however, concluded that a formal delinquency label has no direct effect on self-concept. Leonard Gibbs (1974) compared the delinquent images and levels of self-esteem of a sample of 21 juveniles who had been arrested and subsequently referred to juvenile court for auto theft with a sample of 56 officially nondelinquent high school students. He found that the official delinquents looked on themselves as more delinquent after an arrest than after a court appearance. At both stages of processing, however, the official delinquents viewed themselves as more delinquent than the nondelinquents. With respect to self-esteem, Gibbs reported that the levels were higher after court processing, but not after arrest.

Altogether, in five of eight comparisons the results ran counter to the assumptions of the labeling perspective.

In another comparative study, John Hepburn (1977) analyzed the self-concepts and attitudes of 105 nondelinquent males versus 96 officially delinquent (arrested) males. Hepburn found that the delinquents, compared to the nondelinquents, had greater definitions of themselves as delinquents and greater commitment to future delinquency and to delinquent others, but lower self-concepts and less respect for the police. However, when the effects of several variables were considered simultaneously, such as socioeconomic status and self-reported delinquency, it was found that an arrest record had no direct effect on self-concept or delinquent identification. Hepburn concluded that whatever association may exist between a formal label of delinquency and a negative or low self-concept is spurious, in that self-image is best explained by the overall situation of a juvenile's life, including his self-reported delinquency.

In spite of the somewhat negative impression one may have after a review of this literature, in terms of the validity of the labeling perspective, there have been some conclusions in support of labeling, particularly with respect to certain categories of juveniles (Jensen, 1972; Ageton and Elliott, 1974). Using the same data base as in Travis Hirschi's study, Gary Jensen (1972) found that among adolescent males official delinquency (as measured by police records) was much more strongly related to having a delinquent self-concept among whites than among blacks. Furthermore, the lack of a relationship among blacks between an official label and a delinquent self-concept persisted among all social class levels. Among blacks, Jensen concludes, an official label of delinquency might not carry much significance for a delinquent identity either because such labels are fairly common or because the label is applied by "outsiders" (see also Gould, 1969).

On the assumption that a delinquent identity does not always mean a low self-esteem, Jensen also compared self-esteem with official delinquency, by race. This analysis showed no relationship at all, for either blacks or whites. However, the relationship did vary by social class among blacks. It was positive (the greater the official delinquency, the higher the self-esteem) among lower-class blacks but negative among middle- and upper-middle-class blacks. In this instance, Jensen argues, a delinquency label carries no negative value for lower-class blacks but is a stereotype that middle-class blacks wish to avoid or renounce.

Suzanne Ageton and Delbert Elliott (1974) extended Jensen's analysis by examining the relationship between official delinquency (police contact) and delinquent orientation over a six-year time period (the same data base used in the Elliott and Voss study discussed earlier). The authors concluded that a greater change toward a delinquency orientation, subsequent to police contact, occurred among males, both lower- and upper-class youths (which negated the effect of social class generally), and whites. Furthermore, Ageton and Elliott concluded that the *most* significant factor in the development of a delinquent orientation was police contact, as opposed to sex, class, and race. Even this conclusion must be tempered by the finding that the relationship between police contact and delinquent orientation, although statistically significant, was rather low.

In an effort to clarify the seeming contradictions of three earlier studies, Jensen (1980) reaffirmed his conclusion, and that of Ageton and Elliott, that official labels have more impact on the self-images and attitudes of those less heavily involved in delinquency. It may be that juveniles who have had previous contact with juvenile justice officials have come to terms with whatever effect such contact has upon their self-images. Future arrests or court appearances are thus unlikely to have a significant impact on a juvenile's self-concept, especially in comparison with youth who are arrested or sent to court for the first time.

Studies of those released from juvenile reformatories also report inconsistent findings relative to the effects of incarceration on self-concepts and attitudes. There is some evidence that suggests that a *treatment*-oriented institution is related to the development of *positive* self-images, while *custody*-oriented facilities tend to foster *negative* self-images and cynical attitudes toward staff members and authority figures in general (Street et al., 1966). Other studies, however, have not consistently documented any pronounced attitudinal or identity changes among youth as a result of confinement in juvenile detention centers or reformatories (Eynon and Simpson, 1965; O'Connor, 1970; Gibbons, 1981).

In summary, it is true that labeled delinquents do have negative or delinquent self-concepts (see Chapter 6) and that qualitative analyses suggest that such self-images are the product of official labeling. Quantitative analyses, however, have failed to confirm consistently the existence of measurable changes in identity or attitude as a result of official labeling, at any stage of processing. These studies do suggest, though, that the effects of official labeling that do exist are strongest among those least involved in delinquent activity (see also Lipsitt, 1968; Snyder, 1971; Mahoney, 1974; Jensen and Rojek, 1980).

The studies thus far reported have not lent themselves to a careful comparison of the effects of official labeling on juveniles because they have been unable to take a cohort of youths and follow them up for a considerable period of time, including those years *before* they were labeled. To varying degrees, research has approximated this ideal design. Nonetheless, most studies have allowed for a "labeling effect" to appear more often than would a thorough longitudinal design. Given these circumstances, a truly inconsistent set of findings casts considerable doubt on the significance of formal labels on the identities and attitudes of juveniles.

Labeling and Delinquent Behavior

In Chapter 6, it was noted that a common finding in the literature on juvenile delinquency is the tendency for miscreant juveniles to become more conformist with age, to "mature out" of delinquency. This pattern is reinforced by the fact that the "peak" age of arrest, among *all* those arrested, is about 16, with rates of arrest declining in older age categories. High arrest rates for adolescents are particularly notable for property offenses and for offenses that are exclusively committed by juveniles, such as running away (Jensen and Rojek, 1980; Siegel and Senna, 1981; Empey, 1982).

Studies of juvenile arrests and referrals to juvenile court also indicate that the peak age of delinquency is around 16 (Wolfgang et al., 1972; Smith et al., 1980). Marvin Wolfgang and co-workers (1972), for example, studied the arrest records of over 10,000 males born in 1945 who lived in Philadelphia between their tenth and eighteenth birthdays (the "cohort" study). They noted that nearly all arrest rates, for both whites and nonwhites, peaked at age 16 for both serious and nonserious offenses.

On the surface, it would appear that being arrested or sent to court would have only limited behavioral effects on delinquency, inasmuch as most official delinquents mature out of their law-breaking activities around the age of 16. The effects of an official label might be greatest, however, if applied early in a child's life. This view is consistent with the previous observation that official labeling is greater among less delinquent youth. It is also in agreement with the often-noted tendency for the rate of official delinquency to be inversely related to the age of the first official record of delinquency (Wolfgang et al., 1972).

Of course, it is possible to argue, in support of labeling theory, that a small proportion of juveniles continue to violate the law in response to the problems of having a record of delinquency. Wolfgang's cohort study provides some support for this contention. Whereas half of the boys with an arrest record had been arrested only once, and many two or three times, a small group of "chronic offenders," defined as youths who had five arrests or more, was identified. While these boys represented only 18 percent of all those arrested, they accounted for over half of all the arrests (Wolfgang et al., 1972). Attempts to connect the chronic offenders specifically with official labeling, however, proved inconclusive.

Additional research on the topic has yielded conflicting results. Some have found that juveniles who have been sent to court have lower rates of subsequent delinquency than those handled less formally (McEachern, 1968). Others have found that juveniles referred to court have higher subsequent rates of delinquency than others (Meade, 1974). Studies of those released from juvenile institutions indicate that about half (particularly males) violate parole or are referred to court within 12 to 15 months (Gibbons, 1981; Ohlin et al., n.d.). The rates for females, however, tend to be lower. These findings suggest that the behavioral effects of institutionalization are not pronounced, in any direction, at least for males.

Part of the reason for these inconsistent results is the fact that delinquency is indeed related to a host of factors other than official labels. In addition, as long as delinquent behavior is measured in terms of official records, the results are likely to be influenced by a self-fulfilling prophecy—in which the label generates a suspicion of future misdeeds, which leads to a higher probability of official processing, which affirms the original label, and so on.

One way to offset the influences of the self-fulfilling prophecy is to examine the association between labeling and self-report delinquency. Such studies have often noted a small but direct relationship between official records of delinquency and the frequency or seriousness of self-reported delinquency (Williams and Gold, 1972; Elliott and Ageton, 1980; Hindelang et al., 1981). To some extent, therefore, those who are caught and labeled as delinquent are indeed already delinquent, by their own admission. The label may thus be as much a reaction to delinquent behavior as it is a cause of delinquency. The difficulty with accepting such assessments is, again, the fact that they are not based on longitudinal investigations that measure behavior *before* a label has been applied. Moreover, specific attempts to compare the subsequent self-reported delinquency of those who have been labeled delinquent versus those who have not been so labeled have yielded inconclusive results (Jensen and Rojek, 1980).

The conclusion with respect to the behavioral effects of labeling is essentially the same as with the attitudinal effects of labeling. That is, what results may develop are more likely to occur among originally less delinquent youth and are more likely if the label is applied earlier in life. Otherwise, a strong connection between officially labeling a juvenile a delinquent and subsequent delinquent behavior is unsubstantiated.

It is possible that the effects of labeling one a delinquent would not be noticeable over the short term, but would be more pronounced with repeated contacts with juvenile justice authorities over time (Klein, 1974; Thornton et al., 1982). In fact, this situation appears to be the contention of some of the earlier developers of labeling theory, such as Lemert and Becker. As indicated earlier, research that compares behavioral and attitudinal differences among juveniles who have reached various stages of juvenile justice processing would cast doubt on such a conclusion. Again, however, the issue would be better addressed with longitudinal research or by studying groups of youngsters over an extended period of time.

SUMMARY

The significance of labeling juveniles as delinquent appears to be questionable, as far as subsequent identities and behavior are concerned. The rapid rise in the popularity of labeling theory during the 1960s perhaps reflects more the dissatisfaction among social scientists and criminologists with extant explanations of deviance and criminality than with the validity of the labeling perspective's assumptions. In this period, assumptions were accepted without careful empirical examination. Subsequent analyses, however, have cast doubt on the validity of many of those assumptions.

In retrospect, the view that a label creates behavior appears oversimplified. While it is true that many of the assumptions of the more popular theories of delinquency are not empirically supported, the alternate view proposed by labeling theorists is also not supported.

The assumptions of the labeling perspective, however, are not totally indefensible. Several studies, both qualitative and quantitative, suggest the existence of an effect of official labels on delinquent identities and behavior. In addition, research indicates a relatively strong effect of official labels among those less committed to antisocial behavior at the time the label was applied, and this would be truer of juveniles than of adult criminals. Furthermore, all of these conditions have been assessed relative to *official* labels. Had unofficial labels been examined, it is possible that the changes would have been more pronounced (see also Mahoney, 1974). To this extent, the arguments of labeling theorists have provided an important view in the understanding of criminality. The somewhat negative overall assessment of this theory, however, stems primarily from the inconsistent results that have been derived from research so designed as to reveal even weak labeling effects. Although such effects obviously occur, they are neither as inevitable nor as dramatic as the assumptions of the theory would predict.

NOTE

1. To some, the views of this approach are not accepted as a "theory" but, instead, as a perspective or an orientation. Using the definition of theory given in Chapter 1, however, the assumptions of "labeling" are within the realm of a theory and thus to call this approach a theory is appropriate for the purposes of this book.

REFERENCES

Ageton, Suzanne, and Delbert Elliott, 1974, "The Effects of Legal Processing on Self-Concept." Social Problems 22:87-100.

Becker, Howard S., 1973, Outsiders. New York: Free Press. First published in 1963.

Chambliss, William, 1973, "The Saints and the Roughnecks." Society 11:24-31.

Cicourel, Aaron, 1976, The Social Organization of Juvenile Justice, second edition. New York: Wiley.

Elliott, Delbert S. and Suzanne S. Ageton, 1980, "Reconciling Race and Class Differences in Self-Reported and Official Estimates of Delinquency." American Sociological Review 45:95-110.

Emerson, Robert M., 1969, Judging Delinquents. Chicago: Aldine.

Empey, Lamar T., 1982, American Delinquency, second edition. Home-wood, Ill.: Dorsey.

Eynon, Thomas G. and Jon E. Simpson, 1965, "The Boy's Perception of Himself in a State Training School for Delinquents." Social Service Review 39:31–37.

Foster, Jack D., Simon Dinitz, and Walter C. Reckless, 1972, "Perceptions of Stigma Following Public Intervention for Delinquent Behavior." Social Problems 20:202–209.

Gibbons, Don C., 1981, Delinquent Behavior, third edition. Englewood Cliffs, N.J.: Prentice-Hall.

Gibbs, Jack P., 1966, "Conceptions of Deviant Behavior: The Old and the New." Pacific Sociological Review 9:9–14.

Gibbs, Leonard E., 1974, "Effects of Juvenile Legal Procedures on Juvenile Offenders' Self-Attitudes." Journal of Research in Crime and Delinquency 11:51–55.

Giordano, Peggy C., 1976, "The Sense of Injustice? An Analysis of Juveniles' Reactions to the Justice System." Criminology 14:93–112.

Gould, Leroy C., 1969, "Who Defines Delinquency: A Comparison of Self-Reported and Officially Reported Indices of Delinquency for Three Racial Groups." Social Problems 16:325–336.

Gove, Walter R. (ed.), 1980a, The Labeling of Deviance, second edition. Beverly Hills, Calif.: SAGE.

——— , 1980b, "The Labeling Perspective: An Overview." Pp. 9–26 in Walter R. Gove (ed.), 1980a, q.v.

Hepburn, John R., 1977, "The Impact of Police Intervention Upon Juvenile Delinquents." Criminology 15:235–262.

Hindelang, Michael, Travis Hirschi, and Joseph G. Weis, 1981, Measuring Delinquency. Beverly Hills, Calif.: SAGE.

Hirschi, Travis, 1980, "Labeling Theory and Juvenile Delinquency: An Assessment of the Evidence: Postscript." Pp. 271–302 in Walter R. Gove (ed.), 1980a, q.v.

Jensen, Gary F., 1972, "Delinquency and Adolescent Self-Conceptions: A Study of the Personal Relevance of Infraction." Social Problems 20:84–103.

——— , 1980, "Labeling and Identity: Toward a Reconciliation of Divergent Findings." Criminology 18:121–129.

Jensen, Gary F. and Dean G. Rojek, 1980, Delinquency. Lexington, Mass.: D. C. Heath.

Kitsuse, John I., 1980, "The 'New Conception of Deviance' and Its Critics." Pp. 381–392 in Walter R. Gove (ed.), 1980a, q.v.

Klein, Malcolm W., 1974, "Labeling, Deterrence, and Recidivism: A Study of Police Dispositions of Juvenile Offenders." Social Problems 22:292–303.

Lemert, Edwin M., 1951, Social Pathology. New York: McGraw-Hill.

——— , 1974, "Beyond Mead: The Societal Reaction to Deviance." Social Problems 21:457–468.

Lipsitt, Paul, 1968, "The Juvenile Offender's Perception." Crime and Delinquency 14:49–62.

Mahoney, Anne R., 1974, "The Effect of Labeling upon Youths in the Juvenile Justice System: A Review of the Evidence." Law and Society Review 8:583–614.

McEachern, A. W. (ed.), 1968, "The Juvenile Probation System: Simulation for Research and Decision-Making." American Behavioral Scientist 11:1–48.

Meade, Anthony C., 1974, "The Labeling Approach to Delinquency: State of the Theory as a Function of Method." Social Forces 53:83–91.

Montanino, Fred, 1977, "Directions in the Study of Deviance: A Bibliographic Essay, 1960–1977." Pp. 277–304 in Edward Sagarin (ed.), Deviance and Social Change. Beverly Hills, Calif.: SAGE.

O'Connor, Gerald G., 1970, "The Impact of Initial Detention Upon Male Delinquents." Social Problems 18:194–199.

Ohlin, Lloyd E., Alden D. Miller, and Robert B. Coates, n.d., Juvenile Correctional Reform in Massachusetts. Washington, D.C.: U.S. Government Printing Office.

Sagarin, Edward, 1969, Odd Man In. Chicago: Quadrangle.

——— , 1975, Deviants and Deviance. New York: Prager.

Schur, Edwin M., 1971, Labeling Deviant Behavior. New York: Harper & Row.

Siegel, Larry J. and Joseph J. Senna, 1981, Juvenile Delinquency. St. Paul, Minn.: West.

Smith, Daniel D., Terrence Finnegan, and Howard N. Snyder, 1980, Delinquency 1977: United States Estimates of Cases Processed by Courts with Juvenile Jurisdiction. Pittsburgh, Pa.: National Center for Juvenile Justice.

Snyder, Eloise C., 1971, "The Impact of the Juvenile Court Hearing on the Child." Crime and Delinquency 17:180–190.

Street, David, Robert D. Vinter, and Charles Perrow, 1966, Organization for Treatment. New York: Free Press.

Tannenbaum, Frank, 1938, Crime and the Community. New York: Ginn and Company.

Thornton, William E., Jr., Jennifer A. James, and William G. Doerner, 1982, Delinquency and Justice. Glenview, Ill.: Scott, Foresman.

Thorsell, Bernard A. and Lloyd W. Klemke, 1972, "The Labeling Process: Reinforcement or Deterrent?" Law and Society Review 6:393–403.

Thrasher, Frederick M., 1936, The Gang, second, revised edition. Chicago: University of Chicago Press. First published in 1927.

Trice, Harrison M. and Paul Michael Roman, 1970, "Delabeling, Re-labeling, and Alcoholics Anonymous." Social Problems 17:538–546.

Werthman, Carl, 1970, "The Function of Social Definitions in the Development of Delinquent Careers." Pp. 9–44 in Peter G. Garabedian and Don C. Gibbons (eds.), Becoming Delinquent. Chicago: Aldine.

Williams, Jay R. and Martin Gold, 1972, "From Delinquent Behavior to Official Delinquency." Social Problems 20:209–229.

Wolfgang, Marvin E., Robert M. Figlio, and Thorsten Sellin, 1972, Delinquency in a Birth Cohort. Chicago: University of Chicago Press.

9

THE RADICAL THEORY
OF DELINQUENCY

HISTORICAL OVERVIEW

The radical theory of criminality argues that criminal behavior is a result of the repressive efforts of the ruling class to control the subject class. The effects of this repression are not only higher instances of crime and delinquency among the subjugated class (the lower class, generally), but also greater tendencies among the middle and upper classes to label the actions of the lower class as criminal in order to facilitate their control. Basically, this view is a more specific statement of a general conflict interpretation of criminality.

A conflict perspective of society stresses the existence of different value systems and norms that influence the efforts of people to establish rules and to regulate behavior. This perspective, as it relates to criminal and delinquent behavior, is implied or incorporated in the theories of Shaw and McKay, Merton, Sellin, and Sutherland (see Chapters 4 and 6). In addition to these contributions, others have developed theories of crime and delinquency that are conflict oriented. George Vold (1979), for example, notes that laws are passed in response to the struggles of competing interest groups. Furthermore, he contends that some criminal behaviors are committed in accordance with norms that were previously acceptable, but that have become illegal because of the successful efforts of competing interest groups.

Austin Turk (1969) contends that value conflicts can influence the eventual identification of one as a criminal or delinquent, particularly if the conflicts appear threatening to society's officials. This theory basically places the significance of value conflicts at the point of interaction between citizens and authority figures. Turk argues that among the groups most likely to be identified as delinquent are the juvenile gangs, because they are likely to be in open conflict with the police who often perceive the juveniles' behavior as threatening and hostile.

Another aspect of conflict theory is included in the assumptions of labeling theory (see Chapter 8). One part of labeling theory is conflict oriented—the aspect that examines the reasons why some individuals are labeled as criminals or delinquents and others are not, when both sets of people have committed essentially the same acts (see also Meier, 1980).

Most conflict theories of crime and delinquency assume that laws are developed and enforced because some people have a virtual monopoly on power and others are essentially powerless (Quinney, 1970; Chambliss, 1974). The nature of power conflicts is variously interpreted. The development of radical theory is seen by some as the culmination of thinking that views delinquency in terms of rule making and enforcement rather than as an individualistic tendency (Empey, 1982). Radical theory differs from other conflict theories in that it proposes that capitalism is the root cause of much criminal behavior, particularly that committed by the lower class. As such, the proper solution to the problem of crime is to eliminate capitalism and replace it with something more socialistic; to some, a radical solution indeed. The economic emphasis of radical theory is associated with Karl Marx and, accordingly, some argue that this approach should be called "Marxist" (a view which will be challenged later in this chapter).

The somewhat recent popularity of this perspective stems from the persistence of social ills, such as war, racism, poverty, social unrest, political and governmental corruption, and urban decay, which have plagued America and other Western societies for decades. The persistence and exacerbation of these problems, it is argued, have created a "crisis of legitimacy" in America that has promoted a fertile atmosphere for the growth of a radical perspective on crime and social problems in general (Sykes, 1974; Empey, 1978; Meier, 1980). But this does not mean that Marxist theories of crime are recent innovations; in fact, they were proposed in the early part of this century by Willem Bonger (1916).

BASIC ASSUMPTIONS[1]

The first and foremost assumption of the radical approach to delinquency is that most behavior is the product of a struggle among the classes within society, particularly between those who own the tools of production (the bourgeoisie) and those who do not (the proletariat).

Second, radical theory assumes that the economic system of capitalism is primarily responsible for the class divisions within society.

Third, it assumes that the bourgeoisie, either directly or through its agents, such as the State, controls the proletariat, economically, institutionally, or legally. For example, the occupational choices, educational opportunities, familial arrangements, and legality of customs and behavior among the proletariat are controlled by the bourgeoisie in order to protect the interests of the ruling class and to keep the proletariat in a subordinate position in society.

A fourth assumption of this theory is that most official crime and delinquency is committed by the lower and working classes as a form of accommodation to the restraints placed on them by the bourgeoisie. In addition, some "criminal" acts of the proletariat are artifactual judgments imposed by the agents of the bourgeoisie to keep certain people or certain situations under control.

Figure 14 schematically illustrates the assumptions of radical theory.

| The economic system of capitalism | → | Class divisions and struggles | → | Overt and covert attempts of the ruling class (bourgeoisie) to control the powerless class (proletariat) | → | Delinquency, either in the form of accommodations to bourgeois controls or the direct "criminalization" of certain norms and behavior |

FIGURE 14

KEY CONCEPTS

Class Conflict   While Marx and the radical criminologists indict capitalism as the root of most criminality, the major concept in this view of delinquency is class conflict, based on economic considerations. Without this conflict, and the attendant efforts of the bourgeois class to protect its interests, criminal behavior among the proletariat would not be necessary, either as a response of accommodation or as a mechanism of bourgeois control.

Surplus Labor   A second key concept in this perspective is surplus labor, the major instrument by which the ruling class in a capitalist society exploits the working, propertyless classes. Essentially, it is argued that a worker's labor produces a greater value in goods than the wage earned for work. The capitalist, or employer, can use the laborer to produce commodities whose value far exceeds the cost to the employer of the laborer's work (the wages). The capitalist can thus accumulate greater amounts of wealth with limited investment or risk. Laborers, if they are to work at all, must work the amount of hours assigned to them by their capitalist employers. Those hours employees are required to work over and above what is needed to replace their wages are called surplus labor. Surplus labor is one means by which the capitalist exploits the working class (Marx, 1950b; Hirst, 1975; Gintis, 1976).

DISCUSSION

Although the radical perspective draws heavily on the ideas of Karl Marx, it would be inaccurate to characterize all of the assumptions listed above as purely Marxist for the simple fact that Marx himself had little to say about the subjects of crime and delinquency. As a matter of fact, Marx classified most criminals as "lumpenproletarians," or the "dangerous class," the déclassé "scum" who had abdicated their class positions and could not be counted on for revolutionary purposes (Marx and Engels, 1950b; Marx, 1950a). Criminals, in other words, had little place in Marx's heart or in his visions of a just society. For this reason, it would be more appropriate to refer to radical theory as *neo-Marxist* (Friedrichs, 1980a).[2]

Borrowing, then, from some of the tenets of Marx, radical criminologists have built a number of theoretically important statements concerning the issue of criminality in capitalist societies. Notable among these efforts is the work of William Chambliss (1975), who lists a "Marxian paradigm" of propositions concerning crime and the law. The paradigm is divided into three sections: the nature of criminal law, the consequences of crime for society, and the causes of criminal behavior. Each section contains three propositions. An example of a proposition concerning the nature of criminal law is, "As capitalist societies industrialize and the gap between the bourgeoisie and the proletariat widens, penal law will expand in an effort to coerce the proletariat into submission." On the consequences of crime for society, Chambliss proposes that, "Crime diverts the lower class's attention from the exploitation they experience, and directs it toward other members of their own class rather than toward the capitalist class or the economic system." With regard to the causes of crime, Chambliss argues that "Criminal and non-criminal behavior stem from people acting rationally in ways that are compatible with their class position. Crime is a reaction to the life conditions of a person's social class" (1975:152-153).

Richard Quinney, well-known for his contributions to the radical perspective, discusses in *Class, State, and Crime* (1980) both the basic reasons for criminality among the oppressed and the injustices committed by, or in the name of, the capitalist (ruling) class against the noncapitalist classes.

Utilizing this framework, Quinney envisions two broad categories of criminality: crimes of domination and repression and crimes of accommodation and resistance. Crimes of domination and repression are committed by agents of the capitalist class to keep this class in a position of supremacy. Thus, crime control policies of the government serve to criminalize those of the working class who appear to threaten the existing order. These agencies may even break the law in order to obtain the more important goal of maintaining order (crimes of control and crimes of government). In addition, Quinney argues that the domination of the noncapitalist classes occurs through the manipulation of criminal values to the extent that those in the working class accept as legitimate the very laws and policies established to control *them*. Finally, under crimes of domination and repression, Quinney lists crimes of economic domination. Examples of these crimes include the white-collar offenses, environmental pollution, and organized crime, which is joined with the interests of the capitalists in preserving the capitalist system.

Crimes of accommodation and resistance are crimes committed mainly by the working class in order to survive the repressive and oppressive tactics of the capitalist class. Included in this category of crimes are predatory (economically oriented) crimes, such as burglary, robbery, and drug dealing. Second, there are the personal crimes of murder, assault, and rape, which are typically committed against members of the same class and not specifically against the capitalist system. In addition, Quinney lists crimes of clandestine assembly-line sabotage, political resistance, and open rebellion, committed by the working class as a means of resisting the control efforts of the capitalist class.

To Quinney and other Marxist criminologists (Spitzer, 1975), an inherent characteristic of capitalism is the existence of contradictions, stemming basically from the problem of surplus labor. Capitalism, it is argued, cannot create a situation in which the value of human labor is consonant with the needs of the capitalists. Consequently, "problem populations" emerge that must be continually guarded and controlled. This concern over problem populations creates among capitalists a greater dependence on the State and numerous social institutions to handle and control these people. Over time, the State assumes a major role in the criminalization of the working class and the management of those institutions established to control legally those of the working class (Gordon, 1973; Quinney, 1980). Quinney (1979) also argues that even criminologists have been co-opted by the State in the study and control of crime among lower-class people.

The contradictions of capitalism continue to grow as capitalism advances. Even the institutions designed to handle the problem populations for the ruling class begin to develop their own identities and functions, which are not always identical with the interests of capitalism and which further add to the problems and contradictions of capitalism (Spitzer, 1975). In addition, the growth of problem populations in advanced capitalism extends the oppressed or ruled classes to include even the petty bourgeoisie, such as professionals and middle-management bureaucrats (Quinney, 1980).

Not all spokespersons for the radical perspective, of course, agree on every point regarding crime and delinquency (Friedrichs, 1980). David Gordon (1973), for example, argues that basic institutions within capitalist societies must be altered substantially if crime is to be prevented. While he contends that capitalism is the fundamental cause of crime, the system is so entrenched in society that its abolition cannot be a realistic mechanism of crime prevention. Instead, the institutions that serve capitalism must be changed to serve the needs of all the people. Gordon suggests that a "Family Model of the Criminal Process" (1973:185) be considered in which the criminal is viewed as a transgressor of family rules and trust. The proper response would be a loving, supportive concern for the well-being of the transgressor, a response designed not only to admonish and correct the offender, but also to examine the family's contribution to his misdeeds.

Steven Spitzer (1975) contends that the transformation of a "bothersome population" into a group deemed in need of control is neither a simple nor an automatic process. Instead, the transformation depends on a variety of situations and circumstances that involve both the control system and the potential target population, such as the relative power of the State in the control system, the perceived size and degree of threat of the population, the degree of organization of this population, the availability and effectiveness of alternatives to control and domination, and the utility of the problem population to the capitalist system.

EVALUATION

As Ronald Akers suggests (1979), the evaluation of the radical perspective must carefully distinguish between the *theory* of Marx and the *ideology* of Marxist philosophy. It is sometimes difficult to distinguish between what is thought to be an observation of the societal contributions to crime and a description of what societal conditions *ought* to be relative to crime. Moreover, in some treatises, the topic of crime becomes secondary to the issues of humanitarianism and human rights and how these relate to capitalism and socialism (Taylor et al., 1973). In an earlier edition of *Class, State, and Crime*, for example, Quinney (1977) concludes his discussion with the statement, "We are engaged in socialist revolution" (1977:165). In other words, capitalism must be destroyed and the contradictory and unjust way in which criminality is handled in capitalist societies is just another reason why capitalism should be eliminated.

If one concentrates on the social theory of Marx as it pertains to criminality, two fairly distinct issues emerge: (1) how capitalism contributes to criminality, especially among the lower classes, and (2) how capitalist interests are served by the identification and legel control of individuals, groups, or social categories of people.

The influence of capitalism and the capitalist class on crime and delinquency rests largely on the assumption that delinquency is a lower-class phenomenon (Klockars, 1979). In recent years, a debate has emerged concerning just how "delinquent" or "criminal" the members of various social classes really are (Tittle et al., 1978; Hindelang et al., 1979; Clelland and Carter, 1980; Elliott and Ageton, 1980; Krohn et al., 1980; Akers et al., 1981; Braithwaite, 1981; Thornberry and Farnworth, 1982). To reiterate a point made in Chapter 5, evidence points to a significant amount of delinquency among youth from lower *and* middle social classes (see also Schwendinger and Schwendinger, 1976), although delinquency among lower-class youth seems to be relatively more violent, and probably committed by a small segment of young males. The existence of middle- or upper-middle-class delinquency creates a problem for the argument that class-based conflicts and oppressions generate criminality within the subordinate or powerless class. If the ruling class creates the rules and determines the economic course of society, how is it that some (perhaps many) of those in the ruling class themselves resort to crime and delinquency? If it is assumed that greed and conflict among the bourgeoisie contribute to their criminality, then the same *intraclass* factors may be presumed to operate on the proletariat as well. Attempts to expand the definition of the oppressed class to include all but a very few members of society in effect explain nothing from a class standpoint, because the variation among classes has been virtually eliminated.[3]

The focus of the radical perspective on the economic domination of the lower class has been previously discussed under the topic of delinquency and opportunity (Chapter 5). To restate the general conclusion of that discussion, evidence demonstrating the influence of economic issues and concerns on *delinquent* behavior is at best inconsistent and often weak. Juveniles are concerned with many other things, besides their economic position in society, including personal status among peers, school status, and parental relationships. It may be the case that modern youth are becoming more pragmatic and economically motivated than their counterparts in previous generations. This possibility is in need of further investigation. If children and adolescents are becoming more economically oriented, however, the relationship between delinquency and social class position would not necessarily be better interpreted from a radical perspective. It might be, for example, that strain theories, such as Cloward and Ohlin's differential opportunity thesis, would best explain delinquency. Perhaps new theories would have to be formulated if it were found that pragmatism and economic concerns characterized youth from all social class levels.

Not all of the advocates of the radical perspective feel that capitalism has a direct economic effect on delinquency. Some find that capitalism exerts numerous indirect effects on delinquency by directly affecting the social institutions that influence the lives of juveniles (Schwendinger and Schwendinger, 1976; Liazos, 1979). David Greenberg (1977) suggests that the age structure of capitalist societies results in depressed economic opportunities for juveniles. At the same time, the period of adolescence is stressful on peer relations and the inability in essence to "buy" friends and good times forces many juveniles to steal. In addition, stigmatizing school experiences and degrading work opportunities (among the few jobs which are available) are particularly focused on working- and lower-class youth, creating even greater incentives for delinquency among these adolescents in capitalist societies.

The importance of institutional factors in the explanation of delinquency has already been examined (see Chapter 8). Indeed, such factors do have considerable influence on delinquency and their incorporation into radical theory is laudable. The contention that adolescence is a period of status anxiety and peer concern, however, is hardly novel, nor is it *necessarily* linked to capitalism (a point which Greenberg himself makes; Greenberg, 1977). Similarly, the connection between capitalism and degrading school experiences, mentioned earlier, has neither been logically nor empirically demonstrated. Thus, Greenberg's ideas are somewhat accurate, but their connection with capitalism is tenuous at best.

In summary, the connection between capitalism and delinquency is questionable because of several factors: (1) the existence of widespread delinquency among middle- and upper-middle-class juveniles; (2) the relative lack of concern for economic and work force status among juveniles; and (3) the lack of a necessary connection between capitalism per se and institutional or demographic conditions within a society.

The second point raised in radical theory is the influence of the capitalist, ruling, upper class (the exact composition of this class is not universally accepted) on the identification or handling of the lower or oppressed classes.[4] This topic has been investigated from two general approaches: historical analysis and contemporary investigations of juvenile justice decisions. Historically, several observations have indicated the influence of middle-class values and capitalistic interests in the establishment of the juvenile court and the philosophy of juvenile justice in eighteenth- and nineteenth-century America (Platt, 1974; Schwendinger and Schwendinger, 1976; Platt, 1977; Krisberg and Austin, 1978). Anthony Platt (1977) further indicates that the values of middle-class housewives heavily influenced policies and legislation affecting juvenile delinquents in the nineteenth century.

The accounts of these developments, however, do not demonstrate that ruling class interests were the only considerations involved in the development of a juvenile justice system. A term often applied to mid-nineteenth-century juvenile reform efforts is the "Child-Saving Movement" (Platt, 1977; Krisberg and Austin, 1978). Although Platt and others debate the issue, it seems reasonable that some of the motivations of these reforms were aimed at humanitarian accomplishments in addition to, or apart from, the protection of middle- and upper-class interests (see also Mennel, 1973).

Lamar Empey (1982) asserts that the concept of childhood preceded the invention of delinquency (see also Ariès, 1962). The modern concept of childhood embodies sentiments of fragility and innocence, yet arrogance and susceptibility. This view of the child, according to Empey, gradually emerged over many centuries and was influenced by the events of "the Rennaissance, the Protestant Reformation, the colonization of the New World, and eventually the Industrial Revolution" (Empey, 1982:38). Moreover, the specific influences that led to the creation of the legal concept of delinquency in 1899 included a host of factors besides those of economics and social class. Empey indicates that religious (particularly Puritan) influences were most important in nineteenth-century reform efforts, which eventually led to the development of separate confinement facilities and legal proceedings for children (see also Rothman, 1971). Furthermore, changes in attitudes and in family and community structures in the aftermath of the Declaration of Independence also contributed heavily to the separate confinement of juveniles and to the creation of juvenile court.

While Empey accepts the validity of some of the Marxist interpretations of the development of delinquency in nineteenth-century America, he ultimately concludes that emphasizing economic and class factors does not do justice to an historical interpretation of this development (1978).

Moreover, an examination of the development of delinquency legislation in Canada concluded that the emergence of probation agencies was more responsible for this legislation than the contradictions of capitalism or the political maneuverings of a ruling class (Hagan and Leon, 1977).

At best, therefore, it would seem that a neo-Marxist historical view of delinquency is incomplete and only partially valid. Of course, class divisions exist in society. It is also certain that some laws are enacted to protect interests that may be identified with certain social class positions. To contend that class factors influence the making of all laws, or even the bulk of them, however, is assuming something that has yet to be conclusively demonstrated.

Contemporary studies of the processing of delinquents by police and court officials also yield limited support for the neo-Marxist approach. The significance of social class in the decisions of these officials is very questionable. There is some evidence that social class does indeed exert an influence on the official handling of juveniles (Thornberry, 1973), particularly when social class is measured according to the *perceptions* of juvenile justice officials (Carter, 1979) or when the type of delinquency under consideration involved moral or status offenses (Carter and Clelland, 1979).

Many studies, however, have found that social class has little significance on the official handling of juveniles, especially in comparison to variables such as offense severity and number of prior offenses (Arnold, 1971; Scarpitti and Stephenson, 1971; Thomas and Sieverdes, 1975; Cohen and Kluegel, 1978; Hindelang et al., 1979; Sieverdes et al., 1979; Horwitz and Wasserman, 1980).

Besides the importance of offense-related variables in the handling of juveniles, some investigations have pointed to the influence of other non-offense-related factors besides social class. Studies of police decisions have often indicated that situational, "curbside" considerations and departmental norms and regulations have an influence on the processing of juveniles (Piliavin and Briar, 1964; Black and Reiss, 1970; Weiner and Willie, 1971; Lundman et al., 1978). Donald Black and Albert Reiss (1970) maintain that what might appear to be racial (and to some extent class) discrimination on the part of the police is actually a reflection of the complainant's visible preference for the police to make an arrest. The preference for police action, furthermore, is greater among black complainants, who are more often victimized by black juveniles than by white youth. This study was replicated several years later in another location, and the results were the same (Lundman et al., 1978).

The importance of juvenile court norms and organizational procedures on the processing of youth was mentioned in the previous chapter. Additional research indicates that juvenile court judges are strongly influenced by the recommendations of the caseworkers working with the court (Kraus, 1975; Warner, 1981), and the recommendations of these officers are not necessarily associated with the social class of the juveniles referred to court.

The empirical support for the assumption that social control officials discriminate against lower-class (and often nonwhite) juveniles is inconsistent. While it is obviously true that such discrimination does exist, its extent and overall significance in the processing of juveniles are variable. The data suggest that social class exerts an influence in the making and enforcing of some laws, at various times, in different locations, and in connection with other factors. The specification of all of these conditions, however, has not been systematically identified, nor have these qualifiers been formally incorporated into radical theory.

SUMMARY

The neo-Marxist or radical approach to delinquency is based on broad conceptualizations of juvenile behavior and societal responses. Perhaps because of the generalizations which often accompany such an approach, efforts to assess the validity of its assumptions have yielded inconclusive results. Some feel that radical criminologists find unacceptable any attempt to quantify the decisions of police and court officials and the behavior of juveniles (Jensen, 1981). This type of approach to criminology is thought to serve only the ruling class and the State, at the expense of the oppressed masses. From this perspective, no amount of empirical evidence could dissuade one from Marxist assumptions. To become a viable theoretical perspective, however, the radical approach must begin to adopt the usual tenets of the scientific, or at least empirical, approach to discovery. To deny the value of empirical assessments of a perspective is to deny the theoretical process altogether. One is left having to decide what is acceptable on the subjective grounds of faith and belief.

In some ways the subjective nature of the radical position is its most appealing characteristic. The assumption that delinquency and its treatment (or punishment) are influenced by class considerations is based on traditional sociological conceptions (see Chapters 4 and 5) and is, therefore, certainly not without precedent. Calls for changes in the processing of delinquents based on their social class position are praiseworthy, even if such reforms are not solidly based on empirical findings. It is precisely this distinction between theory and action that must be maintained in the overall evaluation of radical theory. The assumptions of this perspective are questionable, considering research findings. The stronger value of this approach would appear to lie with its attention to social injustices and the need to correct them.

As an *explanation* of delinquency, radical theory has several deficiencies: (1) the existence of crime and delinquency, in varying degrees, in socialist countries, such as the U.S.S.R., Cuba, and China (Connor, 1970; 1972; Hinners, 1973; Liazos, 1979); (2) the presence of middle-class delinquency; (3) the relative strength of other factors, besides social class and economics, in the explanation of delinquency and reactions to it; and (4) the problem of documenting *class-linked* motives for behavior, both on the part of juveniles and social control officials, such as the police and judges. Until these issues are resolved within the framework of the radical perspective, the importance of radical theory will likely remain within the realm of identifying and correcting social injustices rather than within the category of explanations of delinquency.

NOTES

1. The following discussion is based on a number of sources, including Marx and Engels (1950a), Bottomore (1956), Gordon (1973), Chambliss (1975), Spitzer (1975), and Quinney (1980).
2. To be sure, Marx advocated political revolution throughout much of his writing. In this sense, one could argue that he actually championed criminality. By and large, however, Marx did not envision himself as a

criminal and he certainly did not categorize himself with street criminals, the scum he so derisively excluded from his revolutionary plans.

3. It is certainly plausible to assume that social and economic conditions may have adverse consequences for members of all social classes. The point here is that the economic frustrations and related criminal accommodations thought to be generated by capitalism are likely to be relatively more pronounced for those in the lower classes. Nonetheless, radical theory is placed in the position of having to account both for the existence of crime among all social classes and for the relative ability of those in higher social classes to handle the negative economic effects of capitalism in noncriminal ways.

4. A general issue here is the question of who *rules* versus who controls or manages wealth and corporate power. It is begging the question to assume the two are one and the same. At any level of society, decisions, policies, and laws are made that may reflect various interests or class positions. The important task is to determine more precisely which interests are involved in which decisions or laws and the processes whereby one set of interests prevails over another. Such concerns as these are beyond the topic of juvenile delinquency, but their investigation is central to the conflict and radical positions.

REFERENCES

Akers, Ronald L., 1979, "Theory and Ideology in Marxist Criminology: Comments on Turk, Quinney, Toby, and Klockars." Criminology 16:527–544.

Akers, Ronald L., Marvin D. Krohn, Marcia Radosevich, and Lonn Lanza-Kaduce, 1981, "Social Characteristics and Self-Reported Delinquency: Differences in Extreme Types." Pp. 48–62 in Gary F. Jensen (ed.), Sociology of Delinquency. Beverly Hills, Calif. SAGE.

Ariès, Philippe, 1962, Centuries of Childhood. New York: Knopf.

Arnold, William R., 1971, "Race and Ethnicity Relative to Other Factors in Juvenile Court Dispositions." American Journal of Sociology 77:221–227.

Black, Donald J. and Albert J. Reiss, Jr., 1970, "Police Control of Juveniles." American Sociological Review 35:63–77.

Bonger, Willem, 1916, Criminality and Economic Conditions. Reprinted, Bloomington, Ind.: University of Indiana Press, 1969.

Bottomore, T. B., translator, 1956, Karl Marx. New York: McGraw-Hill.

Braithwaite, John, 1981, "The Myth of Social Class and Criminality Reconsidered." American Sociological Review 46:36–57.

Carter, Timothy J., 1979, "Juvenile Court Dispositions: A Comparison of Status and Nonstatus Offenders." Criminology 17:341–359.

Carter, Timothy J. and Donald Clelland, 1979, "A Neo-Marxian Critique, Formulation, and Test of Juvenile Dispositions as a Function of Social Class." Social Problems 27:96–108.

Chambliss, William J., 1974, "Functional and Conflict Theories of Crime." MSS Modular Publications 17:1–23.

———, 1975, "Toward a Political Economy of Crime." Theory and Society 2:149–170.

Clelland, Donald and Timothy J. Carter, 1980, "The New Myth of Class and Crime." Criminology 18:319–336.

Cohen, Lawrence E. and James R. Kluegel, 1978, "Determinants of Juvenile Court Dispositions: Ascriptive and Achieved Factors in Two Metropolitan Courts." American Sociological Review 43:162–176.

Connor, Walter D., 1970, "Juvenile Delinquency in the U.S.S.R.: Some Quantitative and Qualitative Indicators." American Sociological Review 35:283–297.

———, 1972, Deviance in Soviet Society. New York: Columbia University Press.

Elliott, Delbert S. and Suzanne S. Ageton, 1980, "Reconciling Race and Class Differences in Self-Reported and Official Estimates of Delinquency." American Sociological Review 45:95–110.

Empey, Lamar T., 1978, American Delinquency. Homewood, Ill.: Dorsey.

———, 1982, American Delinquency, revised edition. Homewood, Ill.: Dorsey.

Friedrichs, David O., 1980a, "Radical Criminology in the United States: An Interpretive Understanding." Pp. 35–60 in James A. Inciardi (ed.), Radical Criminology. Beverly Hills, Calif.: SAGE.

———, 1980b, "Carl Klockars vs. the 'Heavy Hitters': A Preliminary Critique." Pp. 149–160 in James A. Inciardi (ed.), q.v.

Gintis, Herbert, 1976, "The Nature of Labor Exchange and the Theory of Capitalist Production." Review of Radical Political Economics 8:36–54.

Gordon, David M., 1973, "Capitalism, Class, and Crime in America." Crime and Delinquency 19:163–186.

Greenberg, David F., 1977, "Delinquency and the Age Structure of Society." Contemporary Crisis 1:189–223.

Hagan, John and Jeffrey Leon, 1977, "Rediscovering Delinquency: Social History, Political Ideology, and the Sociology of Law." American Sociological Review 42:587–598.

Hindelang, Michael J., Travis Hirschi, and Joseph G. Weis, 1979, "Correlates of Delinquency." American Sociological Review 44:995–1014.

Hinners, James E., 1973, "Soviet Correctional Measures for Juvenile Delinquency." British Journal of Criminology 13:218–226.

Hirst, Paul Q., 1975, "Marx and Engels on Law, Crime and Morality." Pp. 203–232 in Ian Taylor, Paul Walton, and Jock Young (eds.), Critical Criminology. London: Routledge & Kegan Paul.

Horwitz, Allan and Michael Wasserman, 1980, "Some Misleading Conceptions in Sentencing Research: An Example and a Reformulation in the Juvenile Court." Criminology 18:411–424.

Jensen, Gary F., 1981, "The Sociology of Delinquency: Current Issues." Pp. 7–19 in Gary F. Jensen (ed.), Sociology of Delinquency, q.v.

Klockars, Carl B., 1979, "The Contemporary Crises of Marxist Criminology." Criminology 16:477–515.

Kraus, Jonathan, 1975, "Decision Process in the Children's Court and the Social Background Report." Journal of Research in Crime and Delinquency 12:17–29.

Krisberg, Barry and James Austin (eds.), 1978, The Children of Ishmael. Palo Alto, Calif.: Mayfield.

Krohn, Marvin D., Ronald L. Akers, Marcia J. Radosevich, and Lonn Lanza-Kaduce, 1980, "Social Status and Deviance: Class Context of School, Social Status, and Delinquent Behavior." Criminology 18: 303–318.

Liazos, Alexander, 1979, "Capitalism, Socialism, and Delinquency." Pp. 336–379 in Lamar T. Empey (ed.), The Future of Childhood and Juvenile Justice. Charlottesville, Va.: University Press of Virginia.

Lundman, Richard J., Richard E. Sykes, and John P. Clark, 1978, "Police Control of Juveniles: A Replication." Journal of Research in Crime and Delinquency 15:74–91.

Marx, Karl, 1950a, "The Eighteenth Brumaire of Louis Bonaparte." Pp. 225–311 in Karl Marx and Frederick Engels, Selected Works, Volume 1. London: Lawrence and Wishart Ltd.

———, 1950b, "Wages, Price and Profit." Pp. 361–405 in Karl Marx and Frederick Engels, q.v.

Marx, Karl and Frederick Engels, 1950a, Selected Works, Volume 1. London: Lawrence and Wishart Ltd.

———, 1950b, "Manifesto of the Communist Party." Pp. 21–61 in Karl Marx and Frederick Engels, q.v.

Meier, Robert F., 1980, "The New Criminology: Continuity in Criminological Theory." Pp. 372–387 in Stuart H. Traub and Craig B. Little (eds.), Theories of Deviance, second edition. Itasca, Ill.: F. E. Peacock.

Mennel, Robert M., 1973, Thorns and Thistles. Hanover, N.H.: University Press of New England.

Piliavin, Irving and Scott Briar, 1964, "Police Encounters with Juveniles." American Journal of Sociology 70:206-214.

Platt, Anthony, 1974, "The Triumph of Benevolence: The Origins of the Juvenile Justice System in the United States." Pp. 356-389 in Richard Quinney (ed.), Criminal Justice in America. Boston: Little, Brown.

——, 1977, The Child Savers, second, enlarged edition. Chicago: University of Chicago Press.

Quinney, Richard, 1970, The Social Reality of Crime. Boston: Little, Brown.

——, 1977, Class, State, and Crime. New York: David McKay.

——, 1979, "The Production of Criminology." Criminology 16:445-457.

——, 1980, Class, State, and Crime, second edition. New York: Longman.

Rothman, David J., 1971, The Discovery of the Asylum. Boston: Little, Brown.

Scarpitti, Frank R. and Richard M. Stephenson, 1971, "Juvenile Court Dispositions: Factors in the Decision-Making Process." Crime and Delinquency 17:142-151.

Schwendinger, Herman and Julia R. Schwendinger, 1976, "Delinquency and the Collective Varieties of Youth." Crime and Social Justice 5:7-25.

Sieverdes, Christopher M., Donald J. Shoemaker, and Orville Cunningham, 1979, "Disposition Decisions by Juvenile Court Probation Officers and Judges: A Multivariate Analysis." Criminal Justice Review 4:121-132.

Spitzer, Steven, 1975, "Toward a Marxian Theory of Deviance." Social Problems 22:638-651.

Sykes, Gresham M., 1974, "The Rise of Critical Criminology." Journal of Criminal Law and Criminology 65:206-213.

Taylor, Ian, Paul Walton, and Jock Young, 1973, The New Criminology. New York: Harper & Row.

Thomas, Charles and Christopher M. Sieverdes, 1975, "Juvenile Court Intake: An Analysis of Discretionary Decision-Making." Criminology 12:413-434.

Thornberry, Terence P., 1973, "Race, Socioeconomic Status and Sentencing in the Juvenile Justice System." Journal of Criminal Law and Criminology 64:90-98.

Thornberry, Terence P. and Margaret Farnworth, 1982, "Social Correlates of Criminal Involvement: Further Evidence on the Relationship Between Social Status and Criminal Behavior." American Sociological Review 47:505-518.

Tittle, Charles R., Wayne J. Villemez, and Douglas A. Smith, 1978, "The

Myth of Social Class and Criminality: An Empirical Assessment of the Empirical Evidence." American Sociological Review 43:643–656.

Turk, Austin T., 1969, Criminality and Legal Order. Chicago: Rand McNally.

Vold, George, 1979, Theoretical Criminology, second edition, prepared by Thomas J. Bernard. New York: Oxford University Press.

Warner, Jerry T., 1981, "Disposition Decisions by Court Officials in a Rural Setting." Unpublished Master's Thesis. Blacksburg, Va.: Virginia Polytechnic Institute and State University.

Weiner, Norman L. and Charles V. Willie, 1971, "Decisions by Juvenile Officers." American Journal of Sociology 77:199–210.

10

FEMALE DELINQUENCY

HISTORICAL OVERVIEW

The subject of female involvement in crime, delinquency, and deviant behavior has been relegated to secondary importance, although special attention was given to it by Cesare Lombroso (Lombroso and Ferrero, 1895), W. I. Thomas (1925), Sheldon and Eleanor Glueck (1934), and Otto Pollak (1950), in the period from the turn of the century to World War II. With the advent of the new feminism, that informed the activism of the 1970s and continues to play an important part in societies in the 1980s, a new focus on this subject was made by Freda Adler (1975), Rita Simon (1975), and others, and a controversy was ignited that has not abated. Virtually all of the theories discussed thus far have focused on male participation in delinquent acts. This inattention to women is partly attributed to their perceived limited involvement in crime and delinquency. In addition, some feel that males have controlled the accumulation and dissemination of information concerning crime and have collectively perpetuated the myth of low female involvement in crime as one means of dominating women (Pollak, 1950), while others feel that the relatively greater male criminality is far from mythical, whether it be rooted in biological or sociocultural factors (Sutherland and Cressey, 1978).

Three categories of explanations for female criminality are discussed in this chapter: (1) innate, or basic, sexual characteristics; (2) sex roles; and (3) the women's movement, or female emancipation.

For the most part, these explanations of female criminality have tended to ignore demographic differences, such as age, and to account for criminal behavior among females in general. Accordingly, the following discussions concentrate on the theories themselves, with special reference to adolescent behavior where possible.

BASIC BIOLOGICAL AND PSYCHOLOGICAL APPROACHES

Many students of human behavior, deviant or conforming, contend that behavior is at least partially a product of natural, inborn traits or tendencies—that is, predispositions. This applies to all human behavior, acts of males and females, and to people of different races, nationalities, or other sociological divisions. As discussed in Chapter 2, a proponent of this point of view, with respect to criminality, was Cesare Lombroso.

Although Lombroso's analyses of criminals were largely confined to the male sex, he did produce one volume reflecting on female criminality (Lombroso and Ferrero, 1895). In this work, Lombroso maintained that females, as a category, were lacking in sensitivity, compared to men; he also found females more childlike, morally deficient, jealous, and vengeful. Ordinarily, Lombroso reasoned, these traits of vengeance and cruelty are balanced by maternity, lack of passion, and low intelligence. In some women, however, these neutralizers are absent, for a variety of reasons, and the innate cruel tendencies of such women are released to yield a "born criminal more terrible than any man," a "double exception" to civilized behavior (Lombroso and Ferrero, 1895: 151).

Like males, however, Lombroso reasoned that the majority of female delinquents could be classified as "occasional criminals" whose physical features contain no signs of degeneration and whose moral character is similar to that of their "normal sisters" (Lombroso and Ferrero, 1895: 193–195). In addition, he argued that occasional female criminals could be encouraged to commit crime because of the increased frustrations they would meet in life upon the broadening of their education. Lombroso, therefore, recognized the influences of female criminality that have gained popularity in recent years.

Another explanation of female criminality was given by Sigmund Freud, who suggested that females have a natural tendency to envy the symbol of male dominance in society (penis envy). This situation becomes a type of "castration complex" for girls. Penis envy is present in young children of both sexes, but Freud felt that it is of more importance for females than males (Freud, 1933). As with other significant events in the psychosexual development of children, Freud proposed that penis envy does not necessarily lead to problems of adjustment and deviant behavior. Sometimes the girl becomes sexually normal and passes through the self-doubt and mother rejection that accompany the castration complex. Some girls, however, become sexually inhibited or neurotic, while still others develop a masculinity complex, an identity with maleness, so to speak, in which the girl refuses to recognize her feminine sexuality. Both sexual inhibition and masculine identity can create behavioral problems for females. Freud suggested that the masculinity complex can lead to homosexuality, and presumably to patterns of delinquency, among girls. Furthermore, he maintained that the development of a masculinity complex was probably related to a biological cause, thus linking female criminality with some type of natural condition.

Freud, however, had little to say about female criminality, adolescent or adult. He acknowledged the small amount of information that existed on female personality characteristics in general and suggested that his ideas were rather speculative (Freud, 1933).

The views of W. I. Thomas on the female personality and female delinquency represent a combination and extension of the ideas of Lombroso and Freud. In *Sex and Society* (1907), Thomas proposed that women were basically *anabolic* in constitution, while men were essentially *katabolic*. By this, he meant that women tended to accumulate body fat and fluid, while men tended to release such bodily products. Consequently, women were seen as more passive and more capable of constitutionally adapting to stresses and strains than men, who were considered more energetic and less able to resist the biological complications of environmental stress. By extension, Thomas further suggested that the inherent nature of the male is to be both "the hero and the criminal" (Thomas, 1907: 168), while the female is destined to be concerned about morality and stability and behavioral acquiescence to the rules of men.

In *The Unadjusted Girl* (1925), Thomas argued that people behave according to four basic wishes: new experience, security, response, and recognition. With respect to female delinquency, Thomas felt that it basically starts with the wish for new experience and excitement, which girls ultimately learn they can achieve by manipulating their "capital"—that is, their sexuality. Thomas argued that the concern with excitement and amusement in delinquent girls largely occurred among lower-class girls, who he characterized as "amoral"—in other words, neither immoral nor moral—who manipulate their sexual capital for personal excitement and perceived gain. In this way, also, Thomas argued that female delinquency was a result of "adjustment" problems, similar to the Freudian view but without the concept of castration complex. At the same time, it appears that Thomas foreshadowed the later explanations of female crime and delinquency, which have stressed the importance of sex roles on such behavior.

Later, theorists sought to explain biological and psychological properties of female offenders in a variety of ways. Thus, female delinquency has been related to abnormal chromosomal configurations (Cowie et al., 1968), overweight and physical overdevelopment problems (Healy, 1915; Pollak, 1950), and biopsychological problems associated with menstruation and puberty (Konopka, 1966). The relationship of menstruation to delinquency has also been considered by Otto Pollak (1950), who used a Freudian framework. Essentially, Pollak argues that menstruation adds to the anxiety girls experience over their sexual identities. If they are going through a castration complex and are attempting to resolve it through male identification, the event of menstruation destroys this type of resolution. Thus, menstruation heightens female adolescent problems of identity (stemming from the castration complex), apart from the other biological and psychological complications it may produce.[1]

These other biological and psychological factors, however, represent relatively minor modifications of the basic themes of female criminality which were proposed at the turn of the century. The dominant image from this perspective remains that of inherent differences between males and females that influence the degree and type of female involvement in crime and delinquency.

SEX ROLES AND DELINQUENCY

According to some, the major explanation of female deviance up to the 1960s was the Freudian perspective (Simon, 1975), although the specific concept of castration complex was not always given as the major underlying cause of such behavior. Actually, beginning in the 1950s, another explanation of female offenses began to appear—the influence of sex roles. Essentially, this explanation argues that women act and think in accordance with the roles in society they have been taught and are expected to play. From this perspective it is reasoned that women are expected to be passive, orderly, motherly, and, if ambitious, wily and cunning, inasmuch as women are not likely to be freely given occupational responsibilities and social power outside of the home and family.

In some discussions, it is hard to distinguish between sex roles considered *natural* and sex roles that are *learned* or acquired. The importance of this perspective, however, lies in its contention that sex roles are taught and learned, not biologically influenced. While it is certainly true that biological differences between males and females exist, this approach maintains that acting as a male or female is *expected* to behave is not necessarily inborn or biologically predisposed but, instead, is influenced by cultural and social definitions that one learns from early childhood. In other words, traits such as *maleness* and *femaleness* are biological, whereas the concepts of *masculinity* and *femininity* are socially learned roles (Smart, 1976; Klein, 1979).

An earlier example of this approach to female criminality was offered by Otto Pollak (1950) who argued that female involvement in crime was greater than official estimates indicate because female criminality is essentially masked or hidden. Besides being accorded a more chivalrous or protective attitude by criminal justice officials, females are given roles in society that tend to isolate them from public view. In some cases, the criminal behavior of women is private indeed, such as with illegal abortions. In addition, Pollak argued that women participate in crimes as accomplices, particularly with respect to property offenses. Violent crimes by females, he maintained, are often committed within the privacy of the home and involve methods that are hard to detect, such as poisoning.

Ruth Cavan and Theodore Ferdinand (1975) assert that delinquent behavior among girls is associated with cultural values and social roles. These values and roles, moreover, are influenced by social class and ethnic background. The authors suggest that among middle-class girls the previously taught values of sexual chastity and domestic happiness are being challenged, thus giving these girls and their parents confusing ideas about what constitutes proper supervision and appropriate behavior. Should the girl be allowed to spend the night with a boy, with or without the company of peers? Is it alright to let the juvenile experiment with drugs, especially with other youth? Such issues as these may not allow the middle-class female adolescent to entertain new role expectations and social norms, but they may also serve to generate conflicts between her and her parents, teachers, and more "conventional" peers. These conflicts may lead or further push the teenage female into delinquency.

According to Cavan and Ferdinand, deviations from social expectations of sexual and moral conformity are more accepted among lower-class female juveniles than among middle-class girls. Delinquent acts such as running away, sexual promiscuity, and ungovernability are thus somewhat expected of lower-class girls. However, they assert that among some ethnic groups, such as Italians, sexual standards and morals are rigidly enforced, even among those in the lower class, and sexual delinquencies among girls in Italian-American neighborhoods are relatively rare.

These two examples of a sex-role perspective of female criminality are tinged with various considerations that tend to merge them with other explanations. Pollak's analysis suggests that some of the characteristics of female crime are biologically influenced. Cavan and Ferdinand essentially describe female delinquency in terms of sexual and moral behavior, similar to the "adjustment" problems seen by Freud, Thomas, and others to be so predominant among delinquent girls.

More sociological sex-role explanations of female delinquency have been offered by George Grosser (cited by Gibbons, 1981: 239–241) and Albert J. Reiss (1960). According to Grosser, delinquent boys are predominantly involved in theft because stealing is daring and risky, masculine, as it were, and that is what males are supposed to be. In addition, stolen goods can be used to help support the masculine role of provider, such as paying the way on dates. Females, on the other hand, tend to steal less often than males because stealing does not directly express the qualities of femininity (although the incidence of theft among adolescent females is increasing, as will be discussed later in this chapter). Some girls may steal, however, because stolen property may help them to maintain female appeal.

Sexually promiscuous behavior among female adolescents was not explained by Grosser in role terms. However, Reiss contends that sexual offenses among females and males (particularly in the lower class) are a means of expressing approved social roles with peers in the peer-oriented adolescent society. Males engage in (consensual) sex acts with females because they gain status and prestige by so doing. Females engage in sex because relationships with males are the primary source of status and prestige among girls, and to develop relationships with boys, girls have to often "give in" to the sexual demands of boys. The sexual behavior of girls becomes a problem when complications result, such as pregnancy or venereal disease, or when the behavior becomes too visible in other ways. At that point, the girl risks losing her status and reputation among both male and female peers, and additional involvement in delinquency may result. In essence, sexual promiscuity is generally seen as a problem or an instance of delinquency when it is committed by females more than when it pertains to males. While this last scenario is reminiscent of Thomas' unadjusted girl syndrome, the role implications of Reiss' explanation are clear.

WOMEN'S EMANCIPATION

During the 1970s, a number of books and articles appeared that attributed an increase in female crime in the United States to the increased participation of women in the labor force, as well as to the general emancipation and liberation of women from traditional domestic and sexual behavior roles (Adler, 1975; Simon, 1975; Smart, 1976; Klein and Kress, 1979). The argument in essence has been that, as women become freer to develop their individual potentials and to achieve their goals in life, they simultaneously become exposed to the crime-inducing frustrations and stresses of life that have characterized the male experience for years, as well as to increased opportunities to commit crime. The current "women's movement," as such, is generally regarded as having started in the early to mid-1960s, contemporaneously with civil rights and anti-war demonstrations (Adler, 1975; Simon, 1975), although most accounts recognize earlier efforts to allow women greater economic and political involvement, such as the suffrage movement of the late nineteenth and early twentieth centuries.

Indeed, the recognition of the effects of increased freedom for women on female crime rates is evident in the work of Lombroso, as mentioned above, as well as others writing around that time (Bonger, 1916). In addition, the previously discussed work of Pollak directed considerable attention to the criminological effects of increased participation of women in the labor force. In fact,

Pollak asserts that a rise in female crime because of the emancipation of women has been predicted by criminologists since at least the 1870s.

Discussions of the connection between increased freedom for women and a subsequent rise in crime rates have often suggested that the increase will largely occur with property crimes, although some contend that an increase in other crimes, by females, including drug offenses and violence, can be expected to occur as the women's liberation movement continues (Adler, 1975; Smart, 1976).

For the most part, these accounts of the relationship between female criminality and the emancipation of women leave out the connection with juvenile delinquency. Freda Adler (1975), however, maintains that the results of increased freedom and changing sex roles for women can be seen among girls as well. To a large extent, Adler suggests that younger females emulate their mothers or older sisters in their quest for increased freedom. Thus, all of the different types of crime that may be expected of adult women may be expected of girls as well.

While she argues that one of the changes the liberation movement has created for adolescent girls is in the area of sexual behavior (recall the previous discussion of Cavan and Ferdinand's analysis of middle-class female delinquency), Adler claims that the effects have been most notable in two areas: (1) a general imitation of masculine behavior, as evidenced in greater involvement in fighting and gang behavior, and (2) an increased rate of delinquency in general, as the confusion accompanying liberation adds to the turmoil and uncertainty of an already troubled period of life—adolescence. In connection with violent crime and delinquent behavior changes, Adler indicates an increase in gang involvement among girls, both in their traditional role as accomplices to male gangs and as members of exclusive female gangs or cliques. In addition, she points to numerous and varied violent episodes among girls in general, such as reformatory rioting and aggressive political protesting.

In summary, whether or not girls are seen as becoming more violent, the general hypotheses of the emancipation explanation of female delinquency are that rates of female delinquency will be greater in more industrialized and technologically "advanced" societies and that increases in these rates can be traced to the rise of the women's liberation movement, especially as this movement has blurred the traditional distinctions between masculine and feminine roles.

EVALUATION

The idea that females and males behave according to innate characteristics has been challenged for some time. That females are innately passive, naive, cunning, or anything else is arguable with respect to the various learning theories of the social and behavioral sciences. Of course, modern biological theories stress that an interaction between physical predispositions and socio-cultural conditions produce behavior. Even this position, how-ever, is not totally accepted by those who emphasize the importance of environmental factors in the explanation of behavior.

A common notion of the naturalistic explanation of female delinquency is that such behavior is caused, or associated with, adjustment problems, particularly those stemming from the home environment. To some extent, the literature supports this view. Numerous accounts of female delinquency have stressed what may be called a "wayward girl" syndrome, in which the delinquent girl is characterized as having difficulties at home, becoming incorrigible or "ungovernable," running away from home, becoming or suspected of becoming sexually promiscuous, and perhaps ultimately becoming involved in various acts of criminal behavior (Glueck and Glueck, 1934; Konopka, 1966; Vedder and Somerville, 1975). In addition, several studies have noted that there is a stronger relationship between broken homes and family relationships and official measures of delinquency among females than males (Gibbons and Griswold, 1957; Monahan, 1957; Toby, 1957). Other investigations have found that female delinquency (as measured by self-reports) is more strongly related to family factors than is male delinquency, especially for status offenses, such as ungovernability and running away (Nye, 1958; Datesman and Scarpitti, 1975; Norland et al., 1979).

The validity of the wayward girl syndrome ultimately rests on the extent to which girls actually do commit status offenses. Official estimates of female delinquency have consistently associated the delinquent girl with such offenses as running away and incorrigibility, offenses which fit the pattern of being wayward (Barton, 1976; Cernkovich and Giordano, 1979a; Gibbons, 1981; Richards, 1981; Empey, 1982; Weis, 1982). While the results of self-report surveys indicate that, overall, males are more delinquent than females, the difference is mostly attributable to the greater involvement of males in property and violent offenses. Differences between males and females with respect to status offenses are negligible or indicate greater involvement among males than females. In a study of delinquency among a sample of nearly 600 middle-class high school students in Connecticut, for example, Nancy Wise (1967) found that the proportion of males admitting to sex and alcohol offenses was about the same as for females, one-third and between 50 and 60 percent, respectively. The percentage of males who admitted to being ungovernable, however, was nearly twice the figure for females, 26.6 to 13.7 percent. The percentages of boys involved in theft and violent offenses were greater than for females, which yielded a higher overall rate of delinquency for males than for females (see also Hindelang, 1971). A comparative analysis by Rachelle Canter (1982b) suggests that the findings of Wise and others have been replicated in different parts of the country and over a period of at least 10 years.

The results of these self-report surveys suggest that the official data concerning female delinquency are correct, but incomplete. Female delinquents do often commit status offenses, but no more than do males. Certainly, many female delinquents have difficulties at home and become involved in numerous status offenses in connection with those problems. The high proportions of female status offenders in juvenile courts and institutions, however, must be accounted for in terms of societal reactions to the behavior, as well as the behavior itself. It could well be that a stereotype of the delinquent girl as wayward and promiscuous is associated not only with the theoretical explanation of psychological and biological problems of adjustment but, also, with official decisions concerning what to do with disobedient or runaway girls. Clearly, the data suggest that additional theories and information are needed for a fuller understanding of female delinquency.

To some extent, the sex-role explanation of female delinquency has been supported with research that investigates social expectations of behavior as these are differentiated by sexual status. Ruth Morris (1965), for example, studied the connection between social role expectations and delinquency among males and females. Overall, Morris found that girls expressed more shame and guilt than boys over having been in trouble with the police. In addition, she found that girls were more critical of delinquency than boys, especially delinquency committed by boys. These findings suggest that females are socialized into greater conformity and less delinquency than males. When females commit acts of delinquency, they are essentially violating their social role expectations.

A more specific test of female delinquency from a social role perspective is provided by a test of the "masculinity hypothesis," which suggests that females who commit delinquent acts are conforming to the masculine role more than are nondelinquent girls (Cullen et al., 1979). Numerous tests of the masculinity hypothesis have provided conflicting results. A study of self-reported delinquency among male and female midwestern university students, for example, found that those who scored high on such "masculine" traits as aggressiveness, dominance, competition, and independence tended to have high levels of delinquency (Cullen et al., 1979). The relationship between delinquency and masculine traits, moreover, was stronger for males than for females. Being male and having relatively high levels of masculinity were more likely to coincide with delinquent behavior than were being female and having masculine expectations. A similar conclusion was reached in another self-report study of delinquency in Nashville (Thornton and James, 1979). Additional analysis of these data indicated, however, that masculine views (including such items as who will pay the way on dates and who will provide the most income and make "major" family decisions in marriage) were less related to delinquency than the possession of feminine characteristics (such as expecting to do housework and caring for a family, telling parents about one's whereabouts on dates, and relocating according to a spouse's work). Accepting feminine expectations was associated with low rates of self-admitted property offenses for both males and females and with lower rates of aggressive offenses for females. Masculine role attitudes were not significantly related to delinquency for either sex (Shover et al., 1979).

While the masculinity hypothesis as such has not been verified in the literature, the data do indicate that, as females reject traditional feminine roles, their rates of delinquency increase. One of the difficulties of the sex-role explanation of delinquency, however, is that it cannot account for the *changes* in sex-role orientations and expectations and, thus, for changes in patterns of delinquency. Basically, it is the attempt to account for such variations that separates the sex-role explanation of female delinquency from the emancipation theory.

A central issue of the emancipation argument is whether or not female crime rates have increased during the years the contemporary women's liberation movement is thought to have occurred (1960s to the present). Assessments of both official and self-report measures of crime and delinquency support the contention that female involvement in criminality has increased during the last twenty years or so (Adler, 1975; Simon, 1975; Steffensmeier and Steffensmeier, 1980; Empey, 1982; Leonard, 1982). Most of this increase has occurred in the areas of theft and drug use, contrary to Adler's prediction that female crime rates would rise for several different types of crime. Furthermore, reports of widespread increases in female participation in violent *gang* behavior are unconfirmed by studies that have attempted to document this type of delinquent activity (Miller, 1975).

To attribute this increase in female crime and delinquency to the women's movement, however, is debatable for several reasons.

First, the increase occurred largely before the 1970s, when the effects of the movement would not have been at their height, and leveled off in subsequent years, when the impact of the movement would be expected to have increased (Steffensmeier and Steffensmeier, 1980).

Second, no consistent evidence has appeared that connects rising female crime rates with rising levels of industrialization and socioeconomic development (Simon, 1975), which is one of the hypotheses of the emancipation explanation.

Third, the unique connection between liberation attitudes toward the feminine role and female delinquency has not been established (Smart, 1976). In order to establish a specific connection between a social movement and behavior changes, it is important, although not necessary, to document the influence of the movement's ideas and goals on those whose behavior is thought to be associated with them. With respect to the women's movement and female delinquency, it has been pointed out that some indices of female liberation, such as employment opportunities, may have relatively little relevance for girls (Giordano and Cernkovich, 1979). In addition, the association between self-reported delinquency and liberated attitudes toward female roles has not been consistently documented. In fact, in some instances, those girls who express traditional female sex-role views are *more* delinquent than females who espouse liberated opinions (Giordano and Cernkovich, 1979; see also, Giordano, 1978). Of course, it is possible for a movement to influence general behavior patterns without affecting any particular individual. In the present case, however, a presumed consequence of the women's movement—liberated attitudes among females—is found not to be associated with relatively high rates of female delinquency.[2]

Thus, while the women's liberation movement offers a general explanation of changing female sex roles and increases of crime and delinquency among women, a documented connection between the two has not been established. In the course of sorting out the influence of sex-role changes on female criminality, several commentators have suggested the importance of other factors that have traditionally been associated with male delinquency. The previously discussed study by Peggy Giordano and Stephen Cernkovich, for example, indicated that peer relations, especially in mixed-sex group contexts, play a more important part in the explanation of female delinquency than do liberated attitudes (1979).[3] In another study of female delinquency, Cernkovich and Giordano indicate that the perception that there are less general opportunities for advancement is more related to delinquency than are blocked opportunities that result from sex discrimination (1979b; see also Datesman et al., 1975).

Beyond these inquiries, evidence is still accumulating in support of social control factors that play an important part in the explanation of female delinquency. Besides the influence of family factors, some research suggests that other control variables, such as lack of commitment to conventional goals and attachment to school, contribute significantly to delinquency among females (Duke and Duke, 1978; Thornton and James, 1979).

Since adjustment problems stemming from family situations have been associated with female delinquency for a long time, it is logical that control variables in general are presumed to be strongly related to delinquency among girls, especially since social control theory has become the subject of considerable interest (see Chapter 7). The specific effect of control variables on female delinquency, however, may still not account for differences in rates of delinquency between males and females. For example, Gary Jensen and Raymond Eve (1976) utilized the same data set on which Hirschi developed his social control theory of delinquency among males and analyzed the data for females. While their analysis supported control theory hypotheses (that is, girls who are more attached to family and school admitted to less acts of delinquency), males were more involved in delinquency than females *regardless* of the degree of attachment to families, schools, and so on. Obviously, many other factors, certainly including those previously discussed in this chapter, must be considered if an adequate understanding of the etiology of female delinquency is to be obtained.

SUMMARY

With the accumulation of evidence on the contributing factors to female criminality, it becomes increasingly clear that no simple answers are to be found any more for the explanation of female delinquency than for an understanding of male offenses. Certainly it would appear that we have come a long way from the simple, often paternalistic view of women and their transgressions which prevailed less than a century ago.

In the search to understand the delinquent behavior of people, theories that have been developed to explain male criminality are now being applied to female deviance as well. Because these theories seem to be appropriate for both sexes, some have called for the discontinuation of lines of inquiry that posit explanations of crime or delinquency among males as separate from females (Harris, 1977; Smith, 1979).

While the investigation of factors that contribute to a *general* understanding of crime and delinquency is defensible, it may be too early to abandon the search for unique clues to an understanding of male behavior as distinct from female behavior. Not only are males and females biologically different but, even now, boys are socialized differently from girls. The influence of sex roles on behavior, for example, may be an important link between biological factors and a host of environmental factors that have been offered as explanations of behavior, and yet research on this topic is only just beginning to expand. In discussing sex-related behavior, both biologically and psychologically oriented accounts acknowledge the influence of environmental factors, such as parent-child interactions, on sexual identities and sex-role behavior (Money and Ehrhardt, 1972; Maccoby and Jacklin, 1974). Gender identification and sex-related behavior are very complex phenomena. It would thus be a mistake to ignore the investigation of sex-role perceptions and identifications in female (and male) delinquency, regardless of whether these are associated with the emancipation of women, *in favor* of continued explorations into general patterns of delinquency.

234   THEORIES OF DELINQUENCY

NOTES

1. Pollak discusses the biological sources of female criminal behavior according to three major events: menstruation, pregnancy, and menopause (1950). Clearly, menopause lies outside the realm of adolescence and, for the most part, Pollak's discussion is focused on adult women more than adolescent girls. For additional information concerning the connection between menstruation and crime, see Shah and Roth, 1974.
2. Roy Austin (1982) argues that female liberation in America, as measured by changes in divorce rates and female labor force participation rates, cannot be overlooked as a possible cause of increased female crime rates (juvenile and adult) that started in the mid-1960s, especially for the crimes of robbery and auto theft. However, he acknowledges that other factors besides female emancipation may be responsible for this increased crime, such as an increase in self-service businesses and increased female exposure to television advertising and programming. Furthermore, although his crime data did include juveniles, his measures of emancipation (divorce and employment statistics) would appear to be more relevant for adults than for adolescents.
3. Canter (1982a) argues that family factors may be more significant as an explanation of male delinquency than female delinquency, especially for serious offenses. She also contends, however, that peer influences may be more important than family bonds in the etiology of female delinquency.

REFERENCES

Adler, Freda, 1975, Sisters in Crime. New York: McGraw-Hill.

Austin, Roy L., 1982, "Women's Liberation and Increases in Minor, Major, and Occupational Offenses." Criminology 20:407–430.

Barton, William H., 1976, "Youth in Correctional Programs." Pp. 20–53 in Robert Vinter (ed.), with Theodore M. Newcomb and Rhea Kish, Time Out. Ann Arbor, Mich.: National Assessment of Juvenile Corrections.

Bonger, William, 1916, Criminality and Economic Conditions. Reprinted, Bloomington, Ind.: University of Indiana Press, 1969.

Canter, Rachelle J., 1982a, "Family Correlates of Male and Female Delinquency." Criminology 20: 149–167.

———, 1982b, "Sex Differences in Self-Report Delinquency." Criminology 20:373–393.

Cavan, Ruth Shonle and Theodore N. Ferdinand, 1975, Juvenile Delinquency, third edition. Philadelphia: Lippincott.

Cernkovich, Stephen A. and Peggy C. Giordano, 1979a, "A Comparative Analysis of Male and Female Delinquency." Sociological Quarterly 20:131-145.

———, 1979b, "Delinquency, Opportunity, and Gender." Journal of Criminal Law and Criminology 70:145-151.

Cowie, John, Valerie Cowie, and Eliot Slater, 1968, Delinquency in Girls. London: Heinemann.

Cullen, Francis T., Kathryn M. Golden, and John B. Cullen, 1979, "Sex and Delinquency: A Partial Test of the Masculinity Hypothesis." Criminology 17:301-310.

Datesman, Susan K. and Frank R. Scarpitti, 1975, "Female Delinquency and Broken Homes: A Reassessment." Criminology 13:33-55.

Datesman, Susan K., Frank R. Scarpitti, and Richard M. Stephenson, 1975, "Female Delinquency: An Application of Self and Opportunity Theories." Journal of Research in Crime and Delinquency 12: 107-123.

Duke, Daniel Linden and Paula Maquire Duke, 1978, "The Prediction of Delinquency in Girls." Journal of Research and Development in Education 11:18-33.

Empey, Lamar T., 1982, American Delinquency, revised edition. Homewood, Ill.: Dorsey.

Freud, Sigmund, 1933, New Introductory Lectures on Psychoanalysis, translated and edited by James Strachey. New York: Norton.

Gibbons, Don C., 1981, Delinquent Behavior, third edition. Englewood Cliffs, N.J.: Prentice-Hall.

Gibbons, Don C. and Manser Griswold, 1957, "Sex Differences among Juvenile Court Referrals." Sociology and Social Research 42:106-110.

Giordano, Peggy C., 1978, "Guys, Girls, and Gangs: The Changing Social Context of Female Delinquency." Journal of Criminal Law and Criminology 69:126-132.

Giordano, Peggy C. and Stephen A. Cernkovich, 1979, "On Complicating the Relationship Between Liberation and Delinquency." Social Problems 26:467-481.

Glueck, Sheldon and Eleanor Glueck, 1934, Five Hundred Delinquent Women. New York: Knopf.

Harris, Anthony R., 1977, "Sex and Theories of Deviance: Toward a Functional Theory of Deviant Type-Scripts." American Sociological Review 42:3-16.

Healy, William, 1915, The Individual Delinquent. Boston: Little, Brown.

Hindelang, Michael J., 1971, "Age, Sex and the Versatility of Delinquent Involvements." Social Problems 18:522-535.

Jensen, Gary J. and Raymond Eve, 1976, "Sex Differences and Delinquency: An Examination of Popular Sociological Explanations." Criminology 13:427–448.

Klein, Dorie, 1979, "The Etiology of Female Crime." Pp. 58–81 in Freda Adler and Rita James Simon (eds.), The Criminology of Deviant Women. Boston: Houghton Mifflin.

Klein, Dorie and June Kress, 1979, "Any Woman's Blues." Pp. 82–90 in Freda Adler and Rita James Simon (eds.), The Criminology of Deviant Women, q.v.

Konopka, Gisela, 1966, The Adolescent Girl in Conflict. Englewood Cliffs, N.J.: Prentice-Hall.

Leonard, Eileen B., 1982, Women, Crime, and Society. New York: Longman.

Lombroso, Cesare and Guglielmo Ferrero, 1895, The Female Offender. New York: Appleton.

Maccoby, Eleanor Emmons and Cary Nagy Jacklin, 1974, The Psychology of Sex Differences. Stanford, Calif.: Stanford University Press.

Miller, Walter B., 1975, Violence by Youth Gangs and Youth Groups as a Crime Problem in Major American Cities. Washington, D.C.: U.S. Government Printing Office.

Monahan, Thomas P., 1957, "Family Status and the Delinquent Child: A Reappraisal and Some New Findings." Social Forces 35:250–258.

Money, John and Anke A. Ehrhardt, 1972, Man and Woman: Boy and Girl. Baltimore: Johns Hopkins University Press.

Morris, Ruth R., 1965, "Attitudes Toward Delinquency by Delinquents, Non-Delinquents and Their Friends." British Journal of Criminology 5:249–265.

Norland, Stephen, Neal Shover, William E. Thornton, and Jennifer James, 1979, "Intrafamily Conflict and Delinquency." Pacific Sociological Review 22:223–240.

Nye, F. Ivan, 1958, Family Relationships and Delinquent Behavior. New York: Wiley.

Pollak, Otto, 1950, The Criminality of Women. Philadelphia: University of Pennsylvania Press.

Reiss, Albert J., 1960, "Sex Offenses: The Marginal Status of the Adolescent." Law and Contemporary Problems 25:309–333.

Richards, Pamela, 1981, "Quantitative and Qualitative Sex Differences in Middle-Class Delinquency." Criminology 18:453–470.

Shah, Saleem, A. and Loren H. Roth, 1974, "Biological and Psychophysiological Factors in Criminality." Pp. 101–173 in Daniel Glaser (ed.), Handbook of Criminology. Chicago: Rand McNally.

Shover, Neal, Stephen Norland, Jennifer James, and William E. Thornton, 1979, "Gender Roles and Delinquency." Social Forces 58:162–175.

Simon, Rita James, 1975, The Contemporary Woman and Crime. Washington, D.C.: U.S. Government Printing Office.

Smart, Carol, 1976, Women, Crime and Criminology. London: Routledge & Kegan Paul.

Smith, Douglas A., 1979, "Sex and Deviance: An Assessment of Major Sociological Variables." Sociological Quarterly 20:183–195.

Steffensmeier, Darrell J. and Renee Hoffman Steffensmeier, 1980, "Trends in Female Delinquency: An Examination of Arrest, Juvenile Court, Self-Report, and Field Data." Criminology 18:62–85.

Sutherland, Edwin H. and Donald R. Cressey, 1978, Criminology, tenth edition. New York: Lippincott.

Thomas, William I., 1907, Sex and Society. Chicago: University of Chicago Press.

——, 1925, The Unadjusted Girl. Boston: Little, Brown.

Thornton, William E. and Jennifer James, 1979, "Masculinity and Delinquency Revisited." British Journal of Criminology 19:225–241.

Toby, Jackson, 1957, "The Differential Impact of Family Disorganization." American Sociological Review 22:505–512.

Vedder, Clyde B. and Dora B. Somerville, 1975, The Delinquent Girl, second edition. Springfield, Ill.: Charles C. Thomas.

Weis, Joseph G., 1982, "The Invention of the New Female Criminal." Pp. 152–167 in Leonard D. Savitz and Norman Johnston (eds.), Contemporary Criminology. New York: Wiley.

Wise, Nancy Barton, 1967, "Juvenile Delinquency among Middle-Class Girls." Pp. 179–188 in Edmund W. Vaz (ed.), Middle-Class Juvenile Delinquency. New York: Harper & Row.

11

MIDDLE-CLASS DELINQUENCY

HISTORICAL OVERVIEW

Interest in middle-class delinquency grew during the 1960s when drug use, particularly marijuana smoking, and student unrest were apparently becoming widespread among all youth. Such behavior was not only considered deviant, but it was seen as a sign of other, hidden forms of delinquency among middle-class juveniles. This suspicion was confirmed by numerous self-report studies, which detailed the widespread existence of delinquency among middle-class, as well as lower-class, youngsters (Flacks, 1971; Gibbons, 1981; Empey, 1982). While middle-class delinquents were not often recorded in the official records of the police and juvenile courts, they were certainly not young innocents who never violated the law (giving greater credence to charges of class discrimination on the part of the juvenile justice officials).

The eventual acceptance of middle-class delinquency as a fact led to many doubts concerning the total validity of those theories that had been developed to explain lower-class delinquency (such as those discussed in Chapter 5). The sons and the daughters of the well-to-do could hardly be committing acts of theft because they *needed* money, or because they had been taught to steal for money by their parents. Some contended that the typical form of delinquency committed by middle-class youth involved illicit drug use, condemned sexual behavior, and vandalism (Vaz, 1976b). These youngsters, it could be argued, were not accepting the socialization that their parents and teachers had been trying to instill in them; they were, in effect, rebelling against authority and the basic institutions and values of society.

To some, this element of rebellion required specific explanations, reasons which applied to the particular experiences of middle-class youth. If, it could be reasoned, special theories of delinquency in general were needed, as opposed to theories of adult criminality, then particular theories of specific kinds of delinquency, such as that committed by youth or different social classes, were needed as well. Not everyone, of course, agrees with this view and, as a result, the explanations of middle-class delinquency cover a range of topics and issues rather than a coherent set of ideas and concepts.

Thus, Fred Shanley (1967) finds several explanations of middle-class delinquency, including a youth culture argument, the existence of masculine identity problems among middle-class boys, general rebelliousness among middle-class youth, inadequate or ineffective parental or school socialization and control efforts, and general inquisitiveness and mischievousness which can sometimes develop into delinquency.

Don Gibbons (1981) discusses six middle-class theories of delinquency: the contributory effects of a youth culture, masculine (identity) anxiety, status inconsistency and social mobility, lower-class value diffusion, lack of commitment, and subterranean values. The orientations and emphases of Shanley and Gibbons do not clash, and their views are reflected in the work of Edmund Vaz, *Middle-Class Juvenile Delinquency* (1967a), one of the first books devoted to this theme.

The youth culture and the masculine identity explanations of middle-class delinquency appear to have been most seriously studied. In addition, lower-class value diffusion, status inconsistency, and social mobility are worthy of attention, but mainly as a means of demonstrating the range of explanations that exist. Finally, more general explanations of middle-class delinquency have emerged, which can be used to explain other forms of difficulty between the youth of society and the surrounding environment and its people.

YOUTH CULTURE AND MIDDLE-CLASS DELINQUENCY

The dominant explanation of illegal behavior among well-to-do juveniles is the youth culture argument. Gibbons (1981) notes that a key component of this explanation is that juveniles, particularly middle-class ones, have become more and more separated from their parents and from adults in general. This separation has occurred not only physically but also in terms of values and culture; in other words, it can take on the form of alienation from the adult world. In essence, it is argued that a separate youth culture has developed, a culture which can sometimes lead its adherents directly into delinquent behavior.

Lamar Empey (1982) has summarized this view of delinquency into four propositions: (1) the position of middle-class adolescents in society (Western society, that is) is uncertain; (2) this lack of clarity of status in society separates youth from the adult world of work and responsibility; (3) the separation of youth from adults in society generates a "middle-class youth subculture"; (4) the middle-class youth subculture contributes directly to delinquency by spreading a sense of "hedonism and irresponsibility" among youth in society (Empey, 1982:200–202).

According to Ralph England (1967) the beginnings of a youth culture took root in the nineteenth-century effects of industrialization and urbanization. In essence, these developments led to a decrease in the importance youth played in the work and economy of society. The status of youth has become confused and uncertain—neither child nor adult, but something in between, yet unspecified. England further links this unproductive and uncertain status primarily to middle-class youth who, he argues, are faced with a number of contradictions: they are not allowed to vote or hold public office but are expected to be civic-minded; they are not supposed to be actively involved in productive, full-time employment but are still expected to be active and energetic; they are discouraged from marrying early, but courtship behavior is encouraged.

The present national status of the middle-class youth culture, according to England, is based on several post-World War II developments that have collectively contributed to the earlier effects of industrialization and urbanization. (1) The use and even exploitation of a large market of goods and services aimed at adolescents. This market condition is related not only to an accumulation of spending money in the hands of youth but also to the rise of a national youth culture based on material possessions. (2) The rise of mass media communication influences, especially the popularization of rock music and disc jockeys through radio and television broadcasts. (3) The increase in magazine publications that focus on youth issues and concerns. Rather than portraying the solutions to youth problems in moralistic tones, England maintains that these magazines urge the hedonistic values of play and diversion on youth. (4) The emergence of a general national concern over the emotional and behavioral problems of youth.

The result of all of these factors is not only a national youth culture separated from adults and children, but a culture dominated by hedonistic and materialistic values combined with an abundance of money with which to exercise those values. While the pursuit of pleasure for its own sake does not directly lead to delinquency, England argues that this activity, at the expense of such concerns as thrift and hard work, can influence juveniles to pick and choose those options in life that most satisfy their own wishes and desires. When adolescent activity goes against the wishes of adults, delinquency (in the form of *inappropriate* behavior) occurs; Talcott Parsons explores this idea in an essay on the significance of parent-child relationships as a source for youthful rebellion (1942). For example, the accepted adult use of an automobile for transportation to work is transformed by youth into a vehicle for the pursuit of pleasure (joy-riding, cruising, playing "chicken," and so on). Thus, youth may be involved in delinquency through stealing a car, driving recklessly, creating a public disturbance, vandalism, or in other ways, because they use an accepted item of culture, the automobile, in ways unacceptable to adults. The car, in other words, becomes significant in the lives of juveniles, yet they may use unacceptable methods to obtain it and may use it in unapproved ways once it is in their possession.

Another account of the development of a middle-class youth culture has been presented by Richard Flacks (1971). For Flacks, the concept of "youth" as a separate social category may be traced back to the effects of industrialization and urbanization, a notion that can be related to the idea that historians, particularly Philip Ariès (1962), had brought forth, that childhood was a "discovery" rather than a natural and inevitable status. As societies have become larger, more complex, and more industrialized, the segregation of youth has become planned as progressive and functional to society, Flacks contends. However, his argument continues, economic and occupational changes occurred during the twentieth century in America that helped to transform the category of youth into a youth subculture, particularly among middle-class youth. In essence, the American economic system has changed from individual ownership of business to corporate organization of business, from free market enterprise to bureaucratic distribution of goods and services, and from a system based on the production and accumulation of material to the marketing and consumption of products.

These changes in the economic structure of American life have also been related to changes in those institutions that have traditionally been responsible for the socialization of children and youth in society—the family and schools. Flacks discusses twentieth-century changes in the American educational system at length, but he concentrates on the system of higher mass education and its relationship to the rebelliousness of college students.

The connection between youth culture and delinquency is more strongly made through the family. Essentially, Flacks argues that in the twentieth century the dominant family structure has shifted from extended (including grandparents, aunts and uncles, parents, and children) to nuclear (including parents and children only) family units. This change has shifted a greater burden of child-rearing on parents who are asked to teach basic values to their children without the aid of relatives.

On the assumption that value changes in society are first reflected in the higher social classes, Flacks suggests that the demanding role of child-rearing facing parents today is made more difficult by the proliferation of enlightened child-rearing philosophies suggested to middle-class parents by educated experts. These suggestions are not only sometimes internally contradictory, but they may also conflict with the parent's own upbringing techniques. The progressive child is to be encouraged to explore and express him or herself as part of the educational process. At the same time, the role of the parent has changed from authoritative disciplinarian to confidant and guide, which requires more time and energy than some parents are willing or able to give.

Added to this parental role confusion is the guilt and frustration many middle-class fathers, and now mothers, feel toward their children because of their own perceived inadequacies at work or their failure to provide an acceptable home life because of the demands of their work. This situation may result in the showering of gifts and presents on the children (easily accomplished in affluent, middle-class homes) as a way of making up for perceived failures in other areas. It is also suggested that mothers in middle-class homes may attempt to compensate for the absence of the father, or their own job-related absences or frustrations, by "seducing" their children through strong emotional ties and overprotective attitudes. When this situation occurs with a son, one consequence may be masculine identity problems for the boy.

While none of these connections is related by Flacks to delinquency in any empirical sense, the implications are clear. Children reared in atmospheres such as those described above are suspected of being controlled by their own wishes rather than those of parents or other adults and are likely to adopt the attitude that material possessions and gifts represent real expressions of love and acceptance in this world. Such attitudes, moreover, may be expected to contribute to rebellious and radical behavior among college students, as Flack maintains, but also to acts of delinquency among middle-class youth before they reach college age.

Others have searched for the roots of delinquency, particularly as it manifests itself in the sons and daughters of the economically and socially successful, in family- and school-related factors. Albert Cohen (1967; 1972) speaks of the inability of parents and school officials to control middle-class juveniles because they are increasingly unable to demonstrate future tangible rewards for present conforming behavior. In effect, Cohen argues that the pattern of *deferred gratification*, once thought to be highly characteristic of the middle-class style of life, has given way to a new spirit of permissiveness and immediate satisfaction of wishes (Cohen, 1967). While Cohen's argument is similar to the youth culture explanation of middle-class delinquency, he does not specifically relate the decline of deferred gratification to a youth culture. Instead, the condition is linked to middle-class delinquency irrespective of a separate set of values for youth.

MALE ANXIETY AND THE MIDDLE-CLASS DELINQUENT

To some theorists, middle-class life-styles contribute to sex-role confusion and identity problems, especially for males. It is often recognized that anxieties and uncertainties concerning sexual identification occur among all youth (as a study of the psycho-analytic approach to delinquency reveals). The specific connection between male anxiety and middle-class delinquency, however, lies in the assumption that it is typically in the middle-class home that the father is regularly absent for a major portion of the day. This point was brought out above in the discussion of Flacks' explanation of middle-class delinquency.

Talcott Parsons (1942; 1954) was an earlier observer of this situation and he is often given credit for first offering male identity problems as factors specifically related to middle-class male youth. According to Parsons, sexual identities are acquired through the learning and assimilation of roles appropriate to one's sexual status. Such roles are perceived in early socialization patterns, particularly in the family. Thus, while the daughter may easily, and perhaps comfortably, learn the appropriate roles of girls and women in the home, no such opportunities exist for the youthful male in the home. The boy has no visible male role model to copy and learn from because his father is away at work most of the time (1942; 1954).

Albert Cohen (1955) picked up on this theme and specifically related it to delinquency. It will be recalled from previous discussion (see Chapter 5) that Cohen basically explained lower-class male delinquency in terms of conflicts in social class values, which are heightened within the school context. Recognizing that such an interpretation of middle-class delinquency would be difficult to maintain, Cohen speculated that middle-class delinquency was related to the sex-role anxieties that developed in middle-class males because of the absence of a strong father figure in the home. Such anxieties could specifically translate into delinquent conduct because this activity would help repudiate any tendencies of a boy to identify with the feminine role. Anything associated with the wishes of a mother, which would presumably be connected with conformity to rules, is to be rejected. Thus, to be "bad" is to be a male; to be "good" is to be a female.

This line of reasoning may be questioned on two counts: (1) the father absence given as an important facet in the lives of middle-class youth may be just as important in the lives of lower-class youth, whose fathers may also be absent from the home because of job constraints; (2) sex roles (and related work roles) are changing such that it is becoming more difficult to assign a particular task as being primarily male or female, thus making it less certain that a young person would have sexual identity problems (of whatever nature) based on job expectations, in or out of the home.

DIFFUSION OF LOWER-CLASS CULTURE

Some commentators have suggested that middle-class delinquency is connected with the same factors that contribute to lower-class delinquency. One such explanation has been offered by William Kvaraceus and Walter Miller (1967). Miller developed a theory of lower-class delinquency based on a number of lower-class values or focal concerns (see Chapter 5). With Kvaraceus, he extends this argument to middle-class delinquency by suggesting that such behavior is a result of the "diffusion" of lower-class values into middle-class culture. Such diffusion, it is claimed, has primarily occurred through the music industry, from the initial acceptance of jazz music to the more recent popularity of rock-and-roll music. All of these musical forms have lower-class origins and address issues and concerns of relevance to the lower-class style of life, concerns such as toughness, fate, excitement, and present-centered need satisfaction. The adoption of the musical expression of these themes among middle-class youth is thought by Kvaraceus and Miller to contribute to middle-class delinquency, in the same manner that these values contribute to lower-class delinquency. That is, it is assumed that this music encourages independence from authority, rebellion, and a commonality among youth who share similar problems, all of which contribute to the questioning of adult values and rules, and thus to delinquent behavior.

Lower-class focal concerns tend to be more permanent for those in the lower class. The adoption of these concerns by the middle class tends, however, to be faddish. Kvaraceus and Miller conclude their discussion with an uncertain assessment of how much middle-class delinquency represents a temporary acceptance of another life-style as a means of rebelling against parental and school authority, as opposed to a more permanent adoption of a set of values which is opposed to middle-class norms and values. Whether such behavior is a temporary or more permanent phenomenon, the explanation of lower-class value diffusion is still offered by Kvaraceus and Miller as the basic explanation of this behavior.

STATUS INCONSISTENCY AND SOCIAL MOBILITY

Another explanation of middle-class delinquency is that it represents a form of behavior that is committed by youngsters who are defined as middle class, but whose major value orientations are of the lower class. This explanation is related to the notion that inconsistencies in social status are important (Bohlke, 1967; see also Cohen, 1955). It is recognized by proponents of this view that Americans have constituted a mobile population for years. They tend to move not only from one geographical location to another, but also from one type of job and occupational status to another. These moves require the usual adjustment patterns of making new friends and learning new procedures, for youths and adults alike. In addition, movement from one occupational status to another may be accompanied by conflicts in value orientations, from lower- or working-class to middle-class orientations, for example.

Robert Bohlke (1967) has taken these ideas and applied them to middle-class delinquency. Bohlke argues that mobility patterns in the United States have increased to the point that we now have a collection of people he refers to as "nouvelle bourgeoisie," that is, people who have moved from working-class, blue-collar jobs to middle-class, white-collar occupations. As these individuals accept new, higher status positions in new towns or cities, their children are exposed to the stressful conditions that accompany moves. Bohlke also suggests that some middle-class delinquency results from the fact that these newly arrived middle-class juveniles still retain, and are influenced by, working-class values. Rather than experiencing lower-class value diffusion, as Kvaraceus and Miller suggest, some middle-class youngsters, Bohlke argues, never give up these lower-class values; coupled with the stresses and strains of moving, they engage in delinquent acts. Another aspect of middle-class delinquency, according to Bohlke, is the decline of status and income in some families still perceived as middle class (the "old middle class"), which makes it difficult for the children in these families to maintain old friends and social contacts. These juveniles may engage in delinquency to gain acceptance among newfound working-class acquaintances, or as a means of rejecting middle-class values and norms that seem to have failed them and their parents.

In general terms, Bohlke is suggesting that the middle-class delinquent is a "marginal youth" who does not seem to fit neatly into the patterns of either the working or the middle class. This marginality is specifically related to the mobility patterns of the juvenile's parents, whether they seem to be moving up or down the occupational ladder.

EVALUATION

Perhaps more than with any other explanation, or set of explanations, of delinquency, theories of middle-class delinquency have been the least researched. This statement is true even for the youth culture theory, even though it is much discussed among students of the subject. It would appear preferable, therefore, to evaluate the theories of middle-class delinquency according to their logical properties rather than on the basis of some empirical validation.

Although the youth culture argument seems plausible, there are some problems that render its wholesale acceptance questionable. For one thing, the dominance of a youth culture that is superimposed on all youth, to the exclusion of competing factors in a person's life, is highly debatable. Young people may share many things in common, particularly through such influences as the mass media, clothing fashions, and the music industry. It is debatable, however, whether such commonalities represent a youth culture. Even if such an overriding culture could be identified, its significant effect on the attitudes and behavior of youth would be doubtful, when it is recognized that youth still interact with and are influenced by adults, such as parents and school officials.

To the extent that cultural conditions influence behavior, it may be, as Gibbons suggests (1981), advisable to focus on the existence and influence of a variety of youth subcultures. It is quite conceivable that local youth subcultures continually develop, perhaps generally influenced by a vaguely identified, common set of norms, fashions, language, and the like, yet differentiated according to local traditions and circumstances, religious affiliations, minority statuses, and other types of distinguishing characteristics. Another issue in the delineation of youth subcultures is their distribution by social class. Why are lower-class youth not influenced by these subcultures (see, for example,

Tanner, 1978), and yet all middle-class youth similarly are affected? Those often designated as being in the middle class can be further segmented into upper and lower middle-class ranks, and it would seem logical that such differences would contribute to the nature of a youth subculture.

In general, the existence of an all-powerful cultural set of norms and attitudes does not exist any more certainly for middle-class youngsters than it does for lower-class juveniles. Certainly, youth subcultures exist and they most likely do have an influence on adolescent behavior. At this point, however, it seems more likely that the influence of a youth subculture on juvenile behavior exists in the form of a general set of guidelines that are modified by local community, institutional, and peer group norms and values.

The sexual identity explanation of middle-class delinquency is largely based on the assumption that middle-class adolescents experience father absences from the home. Yet, such a situation is also characteristic of lower-class homes. In the case of lower-class families, however, the father absence is considered to be more permanent than daily occupational duties would dictate. It would seem that masculine anxiety would be more of a contributory factor for lower-class than for middle-class delinquency, according to this line of thought. While some studies have found a relationship between masculinity anxiety (as often operationalized by father absence) and delinquency (Silverman and Dinitz, 1974), such a relationship is not necessarily associated with social class (Linden, 1978). Even when distinct differences have been noted between lower- and middle-class delinquents concerning male identities, the differences have not been pronounced and they do not point to the existence of class-based male identity *problems* (Fannin and Clinard, 1967).

Aside from the empirical evidence for this explanation, which is both meager and contradictory, there are several logical inconsistencies that question its validity (see, for example, England, 1967). For instance, why are uncertainties about masculine identity selective in their results, contributing to aggressiveness and destructiveness but not responsibility, which is also thought to be a male "trait"? In addition, how does a *masculine* identity crisis explain middle-class *female* delinquency? Third, it is questionable whether the absence of the father from the middle-class home, because of occupational necessity, leads to a breakdown in the transmission of male roles between father and son or in the lack of visibility of male roles in middle-class communities and neighborhoods. Altogether, it would seem that the masculine identity theory of middle-class delinquency is unsupported.

Of the final two explanations of middle-class delinquency, the value diffusion theory (offered by Kvaraceus and Miller) and the new bourgeoisie approach (proposed by Bohlke), the former is the least supported, and in fact has little basis for acceptance. The connection between delinquency and lower-class values, enunciated by Miller, is not automatic. In addition, the suggestion that middle-class delinquents have adopted all or part of these values, if only temporarily, has not been established; more than that, it has not even been tested. Although Kvaraceus and Miller demonstrate that popular lower-class based music styles are accepted among middle-class youth, this is a far cry from documenting the acceptance of lower-class values as a daily guide to behavior.

Furthermore, the implications of this theory clash with the values of a democratic ethos, although this does not prove the theory wrong. In the absence of strong supporting evidence, one ought to tread lightly before suggesting that the problem with middle-class delinquents is that they have adopted too many "lower-class values." It is not farfetched to assume that this position could be used to thwart such democratic principles as public, mass education, for example. If such diffusion does exist, why is it not also suggested that *downward* diffusion can occur in mixed social class settings?

The explanation that is based on status inconsistency and mobility is plausible, but it has not been empirically demonstrated. The assumption that the marginal person must contend with competing factions and make decisions concerning morals and values has been accepted for some time by social psychologists (Shibutani, 1961). The connection between social and geographical mobility and normative conflict is also implicit in the anomie and social disorganization explanations of criminality (see Chapter 4; also see Friday and Hage, 1976; Sutherland and Cressey, 1978).

A direct link between geographical mobility, or relocation, and delinquency, however, has not been clearly established. A few studies conducted in the first half of this century did find that more mobile youth had higher rates of delinquency (Sutherland and Cressey, 1978), but a more recent study among black migrants to Philadlephia failed to confirm the earlier research findings (Savitz, 1967). In fact, the findings of this study indicated that youthful migrants were *less* delinquent (as measured by court records) than native residents.

Again, we are presented with a relatively small and inconsistent set of findings with which to evaluate a proposition. With respect to the delinquency-producing effects of social, or occupational, mobility of parents, the data are virtually nonexistent. Despite a rather respectable theoretical and logical foundation, therefore, the status inconsistency explanation has not yet been supported empirically (although Bohlke, 1967, offered a number of research strategies to test the theory). Because the basic assumptions of this theory coincide with accepted theoretical ideas concerning criminality, it is one that demonstrates potential in its ability to explain such behavior and thus its empirical investigation should be encouraged.

On a concluding note, it should be stressed that some have contended that students should strive to find factors that explain delinquency among all types of delinquents, lower or middle class (Linden, 1978).[1] This theme has been raised before, with respect to female delinquency, for example, but it will probably be impossible to find a single theoretical component that adequately explains so complex a phenomenon as juvenile delinquency. Some variables, however, seem to have more explanatory power than others. In particular, those factors associated with social control theory (see Chapter 7) appear also to be associated with middle-class delinquency. Hirschi's (1969) research, for example, was based on a partially middle-class sample. Nye's (1958) study of the relationship between family conditions and delinquency, discussed earlier in this book, also included a middle-

class sample (although *broken homes* and middle-class delinquency are probably not related; Grinnell and Chambers, 1979).

Several commentators, starting with Vaz as early as 1967, have
suggested that the middle-class youth culture (or subcultures) can
probably be connected with such elements as family stability,
school ties, and peer group associations. Therefore, whether separate paths to middle-class and lower-class delinquency do exist,
these avenues seem to be associated with social control variables.

SUMMARY

The explanation of middle-class delinquency has progressed beyond the facile propositions offered in the period following World
War II, but the subject remains in substantial need of continued
investigation. It would appear that for decades sociologists concentrated on the explanation of lower-class delinquency. When it
became apparent that a considerable amount of middle-class delinquency existed, many scholars sought to develop interpretations of this behavior in terms that would not compromise theories
of lower-class delinquency.

The most discussed explanation of middle-class delinquency
has been the youth culture hypothesis. Perhaps this theory has
been so popular because it has been used to understand rebellious
behavior among college students as well as delinquency among
their younger brothers and sisters. In retrospect, it seems the
youth culture argument was unsystematically developed, utilizing
concepts which were generally insightful but too vague to accommodate empirical assessment. As a result, social scientists have
been left with a partial explanation of middle-class delinquency
at best, with little prospect for further rigorous development.

Much the same state of affairs exists with other explanations of
middle-class delinquency. One theory, that of status inconsistency
and social mobility, is internally logical and potentially testable,
and deserves further serious investigation.

Overall, the state of knowledge concerning middle-class delinquency is relatively weak. At this point, it might be better to start

afresh, probably from the perspective of social control theory. Whatever theoretical or research approach may be taken, the investigation of middle-class delinquency presents one of the most significant challenges facing students in this field.

NOTE

1. In this chapter middle class and upper class are used synonymously. Delinquency among the children of upper-class people has been virtually ignored. A few studies have attempted to compare delinquency (using self-report questionnaires) among youth from several social class levels (Clark and Wenninger, 1962; Empey and Erickson, 1966). The results indicate little difference between middle-class and upper-class youngsters in the extent or nature of their delinquent acts. Until contrary data are consistently provided, therefore, the content of upper-class and middle-class delinquency may be equated.

REFERENCES

Ariès, Philippe, 1962, Centuries of Childhood. New York: Knopf.

Bohlke, Robert H., 1967, "Social Mobility, Stratification Inconsistency and Middle Class Delinquency." Pp. 222–232 in Edmund W. Vaz (ed.), 1967a, q.v.

Clark, John P. and Eugene P. Wenninger, 1962, "Socio-economic Class and Area as Correlates of Illegal Behavior Among Juveniles." American Sociological Review 27:826–834.

Cohen, Albert K., 1955, Delinquent Boys. New York: Free Press.

———, 1967, "Middle-Class Delinquency and the Social Structure." Pp. 203–207 in Edmund W. Vaz (ed.), 1967a, q.v.

———, 1972, "Social Control and Subcultural Change." Youth and Society 3:259–276.

Empey, Lamar T., 1982, American Delinquency, second edition. Homewood, Ill.: Dorsey.

Empey, Lamar T. and Maynard L. Erickson, 1966, "Hidden Delinquency and Social Status." Social Forces 44:546–554.

England, Ralph W., Jr., 1967, "A Theory of Middle Class Juvenile Delinquency." Pp. 242–251 in Edmund W. Vaz (ed.), 1967a, q.v.

Fannin, Leon F. and Marshall B. Clinard, 1967, "Differences in the

Conception of Self as a Male among Lower and Middle Class Delinquents." Pp. 101–112 in Edmund W. Vaz (ed.), 1967a, q.v.

Flacks, Richard, 1971, Youth and Social Change. Chicago: Markham.

Friday, Paul C. and Jerald Hage, 1976, "Youth Crime in Postindustrial Societies: An Integrated Perspective." Criminology 14:347–368.

Gibbons, Don C., 1981, Delinquent Behavior, third edition. Englewood Cliffs, N.J.: Prentice-Hall.

Grinnell, Richard M., Jr. and Cheryl A. Chambers, 1979, "Broken Homes and Middle-Class Delinquency: A Comparison." Criminology 17:395–400.

Hirschi, Travis, 1969, Causes of Delinquency. Berkeley, Calif.: University of California Press.

Kvaraceus, William and Walter B. Miller, 1967, "Norm-Violating Behavior in Middle-Class Culture." Pp. 233–241 in Edmund W. Vaz (ed.), 1967a, q.v.

Linden, Rick, 1978, "Myths of Middle-Class Delinquency: A Test of the Generalizability of Social Control Theory." Youth and Society 9:407–432.

Nye, F. Ivan, 1958, Family Relationships and Delinquent Behavior. New York: Wiley.

Parsons, Talcott, 1942, "Age and Sex in the Structure of the United States." American Sociological Review 7:604–616.

———, 1954, "Certain Primary Sources and Patterns of Aggression in the Social Structure of the Western World." Pp. 298–322 in Talcott Parsons (ed.), Essays in Sociological Theory, revised edition. New York: Free Press. First published in 1947.

Savitz, Leonard, 1967, Dilemmas in Criminology. New York: McGraw-Hill.

Shanley, Fred J., 1967, "Middle Class Delinquency as a Social Problem." Sociology and Social Research 51:185–198.

Shibutani, Tamotsu, 1961, Society and Personality. Englewood Cliffs, N.J.: Prentice-Hall.

Silverman, Ira J. and Simon Dinitz, 1974, "Compulsive Masculinity and Delinquency: An Empirical Investigation." Criminology 11:498–515.

Sutherland, Edwin H. and Donald R. Cressey, 1978, Criminology, tenth edition. Philadelphia: Lippincott.

Tanner, Julian, 1978, "New Directions for Subcultural Theory: An Analysis of British Working-Class Youth Culture." Youth and Society 9:343–372.

Vaz, Edmund W. (ed.), 1967a, Middle-Class Juvenile Delinquency. New York: Harper & Row.

———, 1967b, "Juvenile Delinquency in the Middle-Class Youth Culture." Pp. 131–147 in Edmund W. Vaz (ed.), 1967a, q.v.

12

DELINQUENCY THEORY: ANALYSIS AND SYNTHESIS

The explanations of delinquency vary widely in substance and empirical verification. Certainly, no one theory can be used to explain all delinquency, or even certain types of delinquency. Furthermore, there is no unifying trait that can be used to connect the diverse and often competing theories. Each explanation has its own strengths and weaknesses, and some theories are, overall, more persuasive than others. Yet, it remains for those who are examining the state of knowledge not only to analyze what has been offered but also to attempt a synthesis of approaches that may be complementary because each explanation seems to focus on a different aspect of the same problem. First, a few words of summary with emphasis on the limitations of applicability; then the discussion of synthesis.

INDIVIDUALISTIC EXPLANATIONS: BIOLOGICAL AND PSYCHOLOGICAL

The biological and psychological approach to delinquency is probably best applied to delinquents who have repeatedly committed offenses or those who are engaged in such violent offenses as murder and forcible rape. This is not meant to suggest that individualistic explanations offer the only means of understanding murder and rape by juveniles, or that they are even the best explanations of this behavior, but only that, to the extent that such theories are useful, they are most applicable to this form of deviance.

Individualistic theories best explain repetitive and violent acts of delinquency. These behaviors represent a minority of all delinquent acts and are committed by a minority of all delinquent juveniles. If the focus is on individual differences, one can emphasize how some people differ markedly from the general population, and why such people are probably the ones who have committed unusual and sometimes bizarre acts. In other words, individual differences are not likely to be useful in explaining common patterns of behavior.

The biological and psychological theories of delinquency have been rejected by sociologists because these theories were, in the past, characterized by faulty methodological procedures and moralistic conceptions of crime and delinquency, and because they tended to exculpate society's established and official procedures for the treatment of criminals and deviants. There was also a tendency for such views of criminality to focus on individual changes, rather than on social reforms, in their implications for delinquency prevention, and such implications were resisted by social scientists. Modern individualistic explanations of delinquency, however, particularly biological theories, are associated with more valid research designs than those witnessed in the past. In addition, while such theories tend to view juvenile delinquents as different from other youths and their behavior as offensive, such conceptualizations are far from the themes of degeneracy and moral imbecility, which characterized many of the individualistic theories of criminality in the nineteenth and early twentieth centuries.

As the methodology becomes more rigorous and as more sophisticated conceptualizations of the contributions of internal factors to delinquency are developed, which include interaction with environmental influences, individualistic explanations will probably be accorded more attention in future research.

SOCIAL DISORGANIZATION AND ANOMIE

Explanations of delinquency rooted in the concepts of social disorganization and anomie were proposed, in part, in opposition to the perceived inadequacies of the individualistic approaches which were so popular at the turn of the century. The view of delinquency, and deviant behavior in general, as a product or factor that exists outside of the individual may no longer appear to be a great innovation, but at the time these ideas were proposed such a view was quite challenging. Both social disorganization and anomie offered explanations of delinquency that addressed the issue of large numbers of juveniles committing offenses, often in group contexts and in accordance with their positions in the community and in society. Both theories sought to explain delinquency with factors that attributed disorganization or "abnormality" not to the individual but, instead, to his environmental circumstances. These conceptualizations influenced the thinking of sociologists for several decades.

Disorganization and anomie, however, have never been easy to define, certainly not to measure and thus to test empirically. Nor have these concepts been easy to explain to laypersons. Both terms, furthermore, connote a sense of devaluation and degradation of the living conditions of those who are most often caught up in the official stages of the juvenile justice system. In addition, the early development of these theories relied almost exclusively on official records, thus limiting the applicability of the explanations.

Attempts to test the assumptions of these theories have generally been successful, although difficulties in constructing universal measures of anomie and disorganization have hindered such efforts. The more important function these ideas provide is an interpretation of delinquency that is in keeping with a major line of thought concerning the nature of societies and of human behavior within societies. In particular, the term anomie is rich with conceptual possibilities for a better understanding of delinquency. For example, the connection between anomie and de-

linquency committed in various groups and organizational settings, among all social classes, is an important subject for future
research.

SUBCULTURAL EXPLANATIONS

Partly as an attempt to explain delinquency in terms of social
organization rather than disorganization and partly in response
to impressions of ever-increasing violence among juvenile gangs,
several theories of lower-class gang delinquency were proposed in
the 1950s and continued to appear in the decades that followed.
Each of these theories posited that gang delinquency is, in one way
or another, connected with cultural patterns of behavior that are
embodied in the class structure of society. One theory suggested that
exposure in school to conflicts between lower-class and middle-
class values precipitates delinquency (Cohen); another argued
that strains between aspirations of ideal economic success goals
and the actual opportunity for achieving success fall most heavily
on lower-class youth, and thus delinquent behavior is encouraged
(Cloward and Ohlin); a third maintained that delinquency is a
result not of class conflicts but, instead, of general adherence to
lower-class cultural values, expressed as focal concerns (Miller).

While these explanations focused on gang behavior, their contribution to an understanding of delinquency may be considered
from a general point of view. The key issue is whether class values
or conflicts influence behavior to the extent suggested by adherents
of these theories. According to many social scientists, class values
do exist and they do influence behavior. The difficulty has always
been in measuring key concepts, and this is particularly true with
respect to the concept of focal concerns. In this regard, Cohen's
view of the middle-class measuring rod, as expressed primarily in
the school system, is particularly attractive. Not only is such a concept testable, but it also places importance on socialization factors
and school experiences in the etiology of delinquency, and these
concepts help to forge an identifiable link between class values
and behavior.

Cohen's theory of delinquency is also appealing because it applies to behavior that is more typical of juveniles than adults. By contrast, the economic opportunity explanation proposed by Cloward and Ohlin conceptualizes juveniles as calculating, rational, and strongly economically oriented. Perhaps this image of youth is more accurate in the 1980s than it was in the 1950s. Some contend that "childhood" is in fact disappearing in the United States (Postman, 1982). If so, Cloward and Ohlin's theory should be given additional attention. The important point, of course, is the continued investigation of delinquency to monitor such potential changes and to adapt or adjust relevant theories accordingly.

INTERPERSONAL AND SITUATIONAL EXPLANATIONS

First, with the development of Sutherland's concept of differential association, and then later, with Sykes and Matza's theory of neutralization and Matza's idea of drift, students of delinquency were expressing concern over conceptualizations of delinquency that were too deterministic, either from an individualistic point of view or from a societal perspective. These interpersonal and situational explanations placed the crux of the matter on individual perceptions of existing situations—perceptions, to be sure, which are heavily influenced by peer group associations.

There are distinctions, however, that separate Sutherland from those who were to come later. Sutherland's presentation is quite formal, consisting of nine propositions. To some extent, this degree of explicitness has encouraged several efforts to test the theory. By and large these studies have confirmed that delinquency is often committed in groups or social settings. The existence of a ratio of law-abiding versus delinquent attitudes in a particular person, however, as differential association would suggest, has been extremely difficult to demonstrate empirically. The theory is essentially stated in terms too broad to quantify and thus to test.

Matza's theory of drift and neutralization largely expands and even exaggerates the theory of differential association. Basically, this theory maintains that adolescents lack deep commitments and are likely to be influenced by the choices and opportunities available to them at any given time. While this image of juveniles resembles what Cohen had been describing earlier (as opposed to rational, calculating decision makers), it is quite vague and has been even more difficult than Sutherland's work to test in any standardized fashion.

Added to the difficulty of loose definitions is the problem of identifying attitudinal states in previous situations, particularly as these preceded given acts of delinquency. In fact, attitudes are often deliberately presented in an effort to dissemble and mislead, as Erving Goffman (1963) has shown and as Matza himself contends.

Overall, interpersonal and situational theories of delinquency conceptualize behavior in terms that are so vague and that depict delinquent behavior in such an ephemeral manner that they compromise the utility of these explanations in studies of delinquency.

CONTROL THEORIES

Control theories of delinquency assume that juveniles will gravitate to nonconformist behavior in the absence of barriers to those factors that make delinquency attractive. These barriers have assumed many forms, depending on particular variations of control theory. The psychoanalytic version, for example, stresses personality features, such as the superego, as a major inhibitor of deviant behavior. Reckless' containment theory stresses a positive self-concept as the most important insulator against pressures toward delinquency, especially in large, urban areas.

Although containment theory has received some support in the literature, the control perspective has tended to evolve toward the social bond as an explanation of delinquency. In this form, the argument posits that the major impediments to juvenile misbehavior rest with attachments and commitments to basic institutions of socialization in society, and thus the theory encompasses the relationship between delinquency and family, school, religious, and peer variables. Research into these factors has consistently indicated relatively strong connections with delinquent behavior. The focus in social control theory on socilization, commitment, and attachment reduces the moralistic judgments connected with some of the earlier research on delinquency, family conditions, and school experiences. The relatively amoralistic orientation of social control theory, together with continuing significant research results, suggest that this explanation will attract considerable interest from scholars in the future.

Despite the optimism associated with social control theory, it cannot answer some important questions that must be addressed if a more complete understanding of delinquency is to be developed. How are commitment and attachment produced, and what factors may destroy those social bonds that have been created? What determines the associations one has to choose from, within the framework of the physical environment? Are juveniles more likely to be pulled into delinquent activity or pushed from conventional attachments and commitments? Answers to these questions must come from perspectives outside of social control theories, again illustrating the need for complementary and synthesizing approaches.

SOCIETAL REACTION: THE LABELING APPROACH

For several decades in the twentieth century, criminologists have considered the effects of reactions to delinquency on the future behavior of delinquents. The central issue from this perspective is not what causes delinquency in the first place, but how the identification of one as a delinquent might contribute further to nonconformist activity.

The approach to delinquency that has become known as labeling became most popular, as judged by theoretical works and research efforts, during the 1960s. Some of the comments by those writing in behalf of labeling clearly indicate that part of the appeal of this view lay in its deemphasis on the causes of criminality in the first place. Some criminologists had apparently become so disenchanted with the search for the causes of criminality that they wished to concentrate on something else thought to be more easily identifiable—the consequences of tagging someone as a criminal or a delinquent.

A presumed consequence of identifying someone as a delinquent, especially if the identification is public or formal, is an alteration of the individual's self-concept to correspond with the image of him projected by the label. In other words, if a juvenile is thought to be a delinquent, it is contended, he will think of himself in that way and act accordingly.

The position that self-concept can affect behavior not only has a long tradition in social science, but its application to delinquency had been explicitly developed and researched by Reckless and his associates in the 1950s and 1960s. It is logical to assume, therefore, that certain major events in a juvenile's life alter his self-concept and subsequent behavior.

Anecdotal and observational data suggest that juveniles are influenced by the reactions of others to their behavior. Attempts to specify the nature and degree of attitudinal change from particular formal identification procedures, however, have not supported this contention of labeling theory. Research has simply not demonstrated that tagging one a delinquent, through arrest, court appearance, or commitment to an institution, consistently affects self-concept in the direction of greater identification with delinquent attitudes. Neither has identification been significantly associated with an increase in delinquent behavior. Clearly, some changes in self-concept are produced by the labeling process, but the magnitude of such changes has been overestimated. However, if the focus of societal reactions emphasizes general expectations of behavior by others, rather than the effects on self-concept per se, then the explanatory power of labeling may be increased.

Another aspect of labeling is the contention that biased, discriminatory factors operate in the juvenile justice system, especially in terms of such variables as the race, sex, and social class of juvenile suspects or defendants. This view has been fairly heavily researched. During the 1970s, the charge of bias within the juvenile justice system was transformed by neo-Marxist criminologists (radical theorists) from minority discrimination to lower-class oppression.

The numerous studies conducted on this topic have demonstrated the existence of patterns of discrimination against minorities, although the discrimination has been more pronounced in some periods and locations (pre-1970s in the South, for example) than others. The evidence for specific class-based decisions, either in making laws that affect juveniles or in enforcing them, however, is controversial, and division among scholars in the interpretation of research is influenced by ideological and political orientations that lead to a difference more in emphasis than in acceptance or rejection of the fact of social class in America.

While the data provide some evidence of discriminatory practices in the juvenile justice system, the evidence is not one-sided. Numerous factors are related to decision making among the police and juvenile court officials, factors which may have little to do with racial and class discrimination. Included among significant variables, in addition to race and class, are type of offense, offense history, demeanor of subject, interest group pressure, and police and court organization.

INEQUALITY AND OPPRESSION AS CAUSES OF DELINQUENCY: CONFLICT AND RADICAL THEORY

Conflict theory proposes that delinquency is in part a type of accommodation to the efforts of those in power (or who have access to power) to control others. Radical criminologists have modified this view to maintain that crime results from upper-class oppression of the lower class, although radical theory has actually had little to say on this subject with respect to juveniles. While several theorists have posited class-oriented conflicts in the explanation of delinquency (Cohen as well as Merton, and Cloward and Ohlin, for example), these theories were not specifically based on the notion of ruling-class domination and oppression. The appeal of these theories has been their efforts to identify why *juveniles* commit crime. Cohen's thesis comes closer to identifying specific adolescent responses to class-generated frustrations, while the theory of Cloward and Ohlin has a slightly greater affinity to Marxism in that it relies on economic motivations for delinquency. The depiction of modern adolescents as economically oriented may be more accurate in the 1980s than 20 or 30 years earlier. If it is true that there is enhanced economic motivation, then radical theory will gain additional support, although the contention that economic decisions are deliberately made by those in the ruling class to control the lower class will still be challenged by some, and despite evidence for such a view, this notion will continue to elude verification.

Overall, it would appear that the major contribution to the field of delinquency made by conflict and radical theories (and labeling theory) is in the awareness of prejudice and discrimination in the enforcement of laws and in some of the negative consequences felt by juveniles in this process. Certainly, these are major accomplishments, and they help to construct a more meaningful understanding of delinquency. As facilitators in the understanding of primary causes of delinquency, however, these theories are deficient and their usefulness in that quest is limited.

WHERE DO WE STAND? A SYNTHESIS

The search for the causes of delinquency has covered several centuries and numerous viewpoints. While we should despair of ever finding *the* answer, it is possible to point to promising theoretical positions that should provide valuable information on the understanding of delinquency. Most notable of these perspectives is social control theory.

Actually, any theory of delinquency that incorporates the learning and appreciation of social rules is worthy of consideration in the investigation of delinquency. For this reason, no explanation should be totally rejected outright. The strong points of any perspective and the interconnections between theories should be noted if the phenomeonon under observation is to be fully understood.

The ideas discussed in this volume are not necessarily mutually exclusive. There are points of convergence or complementarity among the various theoretical approaches to delinquency. Each of the theories presented in this text has at least one thing in common, the explanation of juvenile delinquency.

Although it is possible to single out some interpretations as potentially more fruitful than others in the explanation of delinquency among males and females, of any social class, such as social control theory, the most productive path to an understanding of youthful offenses may well lie in the synthesis of theories.[1] Social control factors, for example, may be combined with the concepts of social disorganization and anomie to explain not only the consequences of lack of attachment to basic social institutions, but also the ways in which such disaffiliations are produced.

It has already been mentioned that modern individualistic approaches to delinquency incorporate environmental influences. The time is ripe for a true synthesis of individualistic and social perspectives on delinquency—one that attempts to incorporate major points from both positions. Some attempts in this direction have already been made. The utilization of IQ and learning disabilities in the explanation of poor school performance, negative self-image, dissatisfaction with school experiences, and delinquency is a good example of the synthesis presently advocated. Numerous other possibilities exist, and these should be encouraged.

Certainly future research cannot profitably ignore the possibilities of integrating societal reaction views with other sociological perspectives. The notion of self-concept has emerged in this study as a central element in the explanation of delinquency. Since the assumptions of labeling theory incorporate self-concept, it would seem logical to modify the views of this perspective to incorporate the importance of self-concept in other explanations. In other words, self-image could be used as a bridge, a central unifying construct by which labeling and other views could be merged. Calls for an interactionist perspective (see Chapter 8), which would analyze the *mutual* effects of social experiences on self-concept, are a move in this direction.

Theories of delinquency that stress the importance of cultural or structural variables (whether or not these are conceptualized in terms of social class values) may be difficult to assess, but their importance cannot be denied. The potential value of these perspectives lies in the extent to which they can be incorporated with theories that focus on the more immediate environmental or personal experience of juveniles. Numerous theorists from different perspectives, such as Cohen, Cloward and Ohlin, Matza, and Quinney, have suggested that social status positions (social class and ethnic status, for example) influence the experiences juveniles receive in the community and at the hands of juvenile justice personnel. It would be beneficial to a better understanding of delinquency if such views could be incorporated with social control and interpersonal explanations. The combined approach would be able to explain some of the sources of attachments and associations (whether to conformist or delinquent values and behavior), as well as their consequences.

Synthesis of Theories: An Example

An integrated theory of delinquency should incorporate several levels of explanation, such as societal or cultural, institutional and interpersonal. Social control theory offers a promising explanation of delinquency at this time. This approach, however, cannot explain how disaffections from institutions may occur, nor can it adequately predict what specific attitudes and behaviors an unattached juvenile will develop. The answers to these issues lay outside of social control theory. A useful avenue of investigation, in conjunction with social control theory, is anomie theory. Anomie offers an explanation of why juveniles become disappointed with and uncommitted to schools. It can also provide an understanding of why families or communities are unable to exert much control or influence over juveniles, particularly during the troublesome years of adolescence.

Neither social control nor anomie theory can independently explain why a juvenile selects delinquency once disaffections with school, family, and community occur. To "round out" this synthesis, some accounting for particular reactions needs to be developed. To some, the assumptions of labeling might be beneficial at this point. That is, a juvenile selects companions or engages in behavior according to the reactions he receives from others. This position, however, accounts for behavior *subsequent* to societal reaction. There is still a need to explain delinquent behavior before an official (or unofficial) label has been applied.

The theories of differential association and drift might be better connected with social control theory in an effort to develop a more comprehensive understanding of delinquency. These explanations enable one to explain the *choices* of juveniles who are relatively unguided by adults in their families, schools, and neighborhoods. In this synthesis, juveniles are hypothesized as more likely to seek peer companionships, in the absence of adult guidance and control. Peers, in turn, are now considered more influential on a juvenile's behavior than are adults.

Figure 15 illustrates this integrated explanation of delinquency.

| Anomie or social disorganization | → | Lack of social control by adults in the family, school, and community | → | Increased influence of peers on adolescent behavior | → | Delinquency |

FIGURE 15

Of course, this synthesis does not explain all delinquency, nor is it the only one which could be developed. Delinquency may occur as a result of loosened ties with traditional institutions, whether or not peer influences are established. As indicated in Chapter 7, some studies have concluded that peer influences are either unrelated or negatively related to delinquency. However, the proposed view is generally compatible with available evidence and is worthy of continued research.

Of course, biological and psychological factors cannot be ignored in the explanation of certain types of aberrant behavior.

In addition, any synthesis would have to incorporate the special conditions and experiences of particular categories of juveniles, such as females and those from the middle class (and the integration discussed above is able to account for delinquency among these youth). While it may be necessary to develop theories specifically addressed to the socialization experiences of females or to the life-styles of middle-class youngsters, the utilization of the ideas and themes of those explanations already discussed will most likely serve as the basis for such theoretical developments. In this regard, some have suggested that the labeling and radical perspectives should be particularly useful in future investigations of female criminality (Leonard, 1982), while others have advocated the study of the effects of opportunity structures on female delinquency (Figueira-McDonough and Sela, 1980).

What is needed in delinquency theory and research is a better understanding of how delinquency develops and is either maintained or discontinued, whether for a short period of time or more permanently. At this point it would seem that the way to approach this goal is to amalgamate existing theories, building on the relative strengths of each and increasing their explanatory power.

We should not pretend to be so knowledgeable of human behavior as to unequivocally cast aside any effort to explain it. The informed student of delinquency should know what various theories offer, their strengths, their weaknesses, and their interconnections. If this is accomplished, more sophisticated interpretations of juvenile delinquency become possible, and the eventual management of such behavior comes more within our reach.

NOTE

1. This conclusion is similar to that advocated by Lamar Empey (1982).

REFERENCES

Empey, Lamar T., 1982, American Delinquency, revised edition. Homewood, Ill.: Dorsey.

Figueira-McDonough, Josefina and Elaine Selo, 1980, "A Reformulation of the 'Equal Opportunity' Explanation of Female Delinquency." Crime and Delinquency 26:333–343.

Goffman, Erving, 1963, Stigma. Englewood Cliffs, N.J.: Prentice-Hall.

Leonard, Eileen B., 1982, Women, Crime, and Society. New York: Longman.

Postman, Neil, 1982, The Disappearance of Childhood. New York: Delacorte Press.

AUTHOR INDEX

Abrahamsen, David, 66
Adams, Reed, 139, 149
Adams, Stuart N., 61–62, 64, 66
Adler, Freda, 101, 128, 218, 225–226, 230, 234, 236
Ageton, Suzanne S., 47, 67, 189, 190, 193, 195, 206, 214
Aichhorn, August, 51–52, 54, 66
Akers, Ronald L., 138–139, 150, 205, 206, 213, 215
Albrecht, Gary L., 165–166, 177
Alexander, Franz, 51–52, 66
Ariès, Philippe, 209, 213, 242, 253
Arnold, William R., 210, 213
Austin, James, 41, 68, 153, 178, 208, 209, 215, 234
Austin, Roy L., 45, 64, 66

Ball, Richard, 147, 150
Banfield, Edward C., 122–123, 128
Barton, William H., 228, 234
Beccaria, Cesare, 4
Becker, Howard S., 181, 184–186, 194–195
Beker, Jerome, 61–63, 66
Bentham, Jeremy, 4
Berger, Alan S., 125, 128
Bernard, Thomas J., 12, 39, 69, 217

Binet, Alfred, 43
Black, Donald J., 210, 213
Block, N. J., 43, 66
Bohlke, Robert H., 247, 250–251, 253
Bonger, Willem, 201, 213, 225, 234
Bonnet, Phillip, 27, 36
Bordua, David J., 94, 97, 108, 128
Bottomore, T. B., 212–213
Braithwaite, John, 206, 213
Briar, Scott, 147–148, 150, 210, 216
Broder, Paul K., 37
Bromberg, Walter, 57, 66
Bronner, Augusta F., 52, 57, 62, 68
Burgess, Ernest W., 74–75, 79, 97–98
Burgess, Robert L., 138–139, 150
Burkett, Steven R., 165–166, 177
Bursik, Robert J., Jr., 118, 128
Butler, Edgar W., 61–62, 64, 66

Canter, Rachelle J., 228, 234
Carter, Timothy J., 206, 210, 214
Cavan, Ruth S., 223–224, 226, 235
Cernkovich, Steven A., 174, 177, 228, 231, 232, 235
Chambers, Cheryl A., 252, 254
Chambliss, William J., 82, 97, 187, 195, 200, 203, 212, 214
Chilton, Roland J., 94–95, 97

272 AUTHOR INDEX

Christiansen, Karl O., 22–23, 25,
36–38
Cicourel, Aaron, 186, 195
Clark, John P., 215, 253
Cleckley, Hervey, 60, 66
Clelland, Donald, 206, 210, 214
Clinard, Marshall B., 54, 67, 97, 98,
125, 129–130, 249, 253
Cloward, Richard A., 102, 109, 110–
120, 127–128, 207, 258, 259, 263–
264, 266
Coates, Robert B., 197
Cohen, Albert, 6, 54–56, 67, 100–110,
113, 120, 126–128, 146, 150, 172,
177, 244–245, 247, 253, 258–260,
263, 266
Cohen, Lawrence E., 210, 214
Cole, Stephen, 91, 97
Conger, John Janeway, 66, 67
Connor, Walter D., 212, 214
Cortès, Juan B., 18–19, 22, 36
Cott, Allan, 28–30, 36
Cowie, John, 221, 235
Cowie, Valerie, 235
Cressey, Donald R., 23, 45, 57–59, 67,
69–70, 82, 84–85, 99, 136, 140–
141, 150–151, 218, 237, 251, 254
Cullen, Francis T., 229, 235
Cullen, John B., 235
Cunningham, Orville, 216

Dalgard, Odd S., 23–24, 36
Datesman, Susan K., 226, 232, 235
DeFleur, Lois B., 81, 84, 97
DeFleur, Melvin, 138, 150
Dinitz, Simon, 54, 58, 62–63, 69, 125,
130, 159–160, 176–179, 196, 249,
254
Doerner, William G., 197
Dugdale, Richard L., 21, 36
Duke, Daniel L., 232, 235
Duke, Paula M., 232, 235
Dunham, H. W., 79, 97
Durkheim, Emile, 71, 87–88, 91–93,
152
Dworkin, Gerald, 43, 66

Ehrhardt, Anke A., 233, 236
Elliott, Delbert S., 47, 67, 106–107,
115, 128, 189–190, 193, 195, 206,
213
Emerson, Robert M., 186, 195
Empey, Lamar T., 4, 11, 118, 128, 152,
173–175, 177, 192, 196, 200–201,
209, 213, 215, 228, 230, 235, 238,
240, 253, 268–269
Engels, Frederick, 202, 212, 215
England, Ralph W., Jr., 240–241, 249,
253
Erickson, Maynard L., 118, 130, 166,
178, 253
Eve, Raymond A., 174, 177, 232, 236
Eynon, Thomas G., 191, 196
Eysenck, Hans J., 31–34, 36, 43, 60, 67
Eysenck, Sybil B. G., 32, 33, 36, 60, 67

Fabrikant, Richard, 84, 97
Fannin, Leon F., 125, 129, 249, 253
Farnworth, Margaret, 206, 216
Farris, R. E. L., 79, 97
Feldman, David, 49, 67
Ferdinand, Theodore N., 223–224,
226, 235
Ferracuti, Franco, 123, 131
Ferrero, Guglielmo, 218–219, 220, 236
Figlio, Robert, 131, 198
Figueira-McDonough, Josefina, 268–
269
Finestone, Harold, 79–81, 97
Fink, Arthur E., 13–14, 16, 21, 36, 40,
43–44, 59, 67
Finnegan, Terrence, 197
Flacks, Richard, 238, 243–244, 254
Foggitt, Roger H., 38
Forrest, A. R., 33, 37
Foster, Jack D., 188, 196
Freud, Anna, 51, 67
Freud, Sigmund, 41, 49–51, 54, 65, 67,
220–221, 224, 235
Friday, Paul C., 251, 254
Friedlander, Kate, 52–53, 67
Friedrichs, David O., 203, 205, 213

Gabrielli, William F., Jr., 38
Gagnon, John, 127–129
Garabedian, Peter G., 198
Gatti, Florence M., 18–19, 22, 36
Gibbons, Don C., 6, 11, 63, 67, 176–
177, 191, 193, 196, 198, 224,
227–228, 235, 238–240, 248, 254
Gibbs, Jack P., 184, 196
Gibbs, Leonard E., 188, 196
Gintis, Herbert, 202, 213
Giordano, Peggy C., 147, 188, 196,
228, 231–232, 235
Glaser, Barney G., 8, 11
Glaser, Daniel, 38, 138, 150, 236
Glueck, Eleanor, 17–18, 36–37, 56, 62–
64, 67, 163–164, 168, 170, 177, 218,
227, 235
Glueck, Sheldon, 17–18, 36–37, 56,
62–64, 67, 140, 150, 163–164, 168,
170, 177, 218, 227, 235
Goddard, Henry H., 21, 37, 44–45
Goffman, Erving, 54, 67, 260, 269
Gold, Martin, 193, 198
Golden, Kathryn M., 235
Goodman, Paul, 146, 150
Gordon, David M., 204–205, 212–213
Gordon, Robert A., 45–48, 67, 94, 97,
128–129
Goring, Charles B., 16, 37
Gough, Harrison G., 65, 68
Gould, Leroy C., 189, 196
Gove, Walter R., 183, 186, 196
Grant, J. Douglas, 69
Grant, Marguerite Q., 69
Greenberg, David F., 207–208, 213
Grinnell, Richard M., 252, 254
Griswold, Manser, 227, 235
Grosser, George, 224
Guerry, A. M., 70

Hackler, James C., 174, 178
Hagan, John, 209, 213
Hage, Jerald, 251, 254
Hakeem, Michael, 54, 68
Halbasch, Keith, 139, 150
Halleck, Seymour L., 66, 68

Han, Wan Sang, 114, 129
Handy, Leva M., 38
Hare, R. D., 34, 36–38, 61, 67–68
Harris, Anthony R., 233, 235
Harvey, Dale G., 106, 129
Haskell, Martin R., 138, 150, 168, 172,
177
Hathaway, Starke R., 58, 63, 68
Hayner, Norman S., 81, 97
Healy, William, 51–52, 57, 62, 66, 68,
221, 235
Hepburn, John R., 142, 150, 174, 177,
189, 196
Hewitt, Lester E., 52–53, 68
Heyman, Doris S., 61–63, 66
Higgins, Paul C., 165–166, 177
Hindelang, Michael J., 47–48, 68, 147,
150, 172, 174, 177, 193, 196, 206,
210, 213, 228, 235
Hinners, James E., 212, 215
Hippchen, Leonard J., 26–27, 36–39
Hirschi, Travis, 6–7, 12, 47–48, 68,
106, 116, 129, 143, 147, 150, 152,
161–162, 164–166, 169, 171, 173–
175, 178, 184, 186, 189, 196, 213,
232, 251, 254
Hirst, Paul Q., 202, 215
Hoffer, Abram, 26, 37
Hoghughi, M. S., 33, 37
Hollingshead, August E., 105, 129
Holzman, Harold R., 29–30, 37
Hooton, Earnest A., 16, 37
Horwitz, Allan, 210, 215
Hunt, J. McV., 38
Hutchings, Barry, 25, 37, 38

Ianni, Francis A. J., 82, 97
Inciardi, James A., 4, 12, 213
Inkeles, Alex, 55, 68
Itil, Turan, 38

Jacklin, Cary N., 233, 236
James, Jennifer A., 197, 229, 232, 236–
237
Jeffery, Clarence R., 37, 138, 150

274   AUTHOR INDEX

Jenkins, Richard L., 52–53, 68
Jensen, A. R., 43, 68
Jensen, Gary F., 106, 108, 129, 142–143, 150, 160, 163, 166, 172, 174, 178, 189–193, 196, 211, 213, 215, 232, 236
Jesness, Carl F., 61, 63, 68
Johnston, Norman, 12, 37, 129, 150, 179, 237
Jonassen, Christen T., 81, 97

Kamin, Leon, 43, 67
Kay, Barbara, 179
Keilitz, Ingo, 30, 37
Kelly, Delos H., 106, 129, 174, 178
Kelly, Henry E., 26, 28, 37
Kirkegaard-Sorensen, Lis, 38
Kish, Rhea, 234
Kitsuse, John I., 186, 196
Klein, Dorie, 223, 225, 236
Klein, Malcolm W., 68, 108, 129, 194, 196
Klemke, Lloyd W., 185, 197
Klockars, Carl B., 206, 215
Kluegal, James R., 210, 213
Knop, Joachim, 38
Knox, George W., 174, 178
Kobrin, Solomon, 81, 83, 98, 111, 129
Konopka, Gisela, 221, 227, 236
Kornhauser, Ruth R., 174, 178
Kraus, Jonathon, 211, 215
Kress, June, 225, 236
Kretschmer, Ernest, 16, 37
Kringlen, Einar, 23–24, 36
Krisberg, Barry, 41, 68, 146, 150, 153, 178, 208–209, 215
Krohn, Marvin D., 206, 213, 215
Kvaraceus, William, 245–247, 250, 254

Lander, Bernard, 91, 94–95, 98
Lanza-Kaduce, Lonn, 213, 215
Lemert, Edwin M., 96, 98, 180–183, 185, 194, 197
Leon, Jeffrey, 209, 213
Leonard, Eileen B., 230, 236, 268–269
Lewis, Oscar, 122, 129

Liazos, Alexander, 106, 107, 129, 207, 212, 215
Liebow, Elliot, 109, 116, 123, 129
Linden, Eric, 174, 178
Linden, Rick, 249, 251, 254
Lindesmith, Alfred R., 127–129
Lindner, Robert, 66, 68
Lipsitt, Paul, 191, 197
Little, Craig B., 215
Loeb, Janice, 33, 37
Lombroso, Cesare, 15–16, 21, 37, 218–221, 236
Lombroso-Ferrero, Gina, 16, 37
Lubeck, Steven G., 173–174, 177
Lundman, Richard J., 210, 215
Lyerly, Robert R., 175, 178

MacCoby, Eleanor E., 233, 236
MacIver, R. M., 6, 12
Mahoney, Anne B., 191, 197
Marx, Karl, 200, 202, 203, 206, 212, 215
Matza, David, 133, 143–151, 259–260, 266
McCord, Joan, 60, 68, 151
McCord, William, 60, 68, 147, 151
McDonald, James F., 98
McEachern, A. W., 192, 197
McKay, Henry D., 71, 74–83, 85, 89, 91, 97–99, 111, 130, 132, 167, 169, 179, 199
McKenzie, Roderick D., 97–98
Meade, Anthony C., 193, 197
Mednick, Sarnoff A., 25, 32–34, 36–38
Meier, Robert F., 54, 200–201, 215
Mennel, Robert M., 215
Merton, Robert K., 89–93, 95, 98, 102, 110–111, 129, 137, 199, 264
Miller, Alden D., 197
Miller, Walter B., 92, 98, 102, 119–125, 129–230, 236, 245–247, 250, 254, 258
Miller, Wilbur C., 66–67
Monachesi, Elio D., 58, 63, 68
Monahan, Thomas P., 169, 178, 227, 236
Money, John, 233, 236
Montanino, Fred, 183, 197

Morris, Ruth R., 229, 236
Morris, Terence, 70, 81, 84, 98
Morrison, Helen L., 29, 38
Moynihan, Daniel P., 124–125, 129
Murchison, Carl, 45, 68
Murphy, Patrick T., 5, 12
Murray, Charles A., 28–30, 38
Murray, Ellen, 179

Neilson, Kathleen, 168–169, 179
Newcomb, Theodore, M., 234
Nicol, A. R., 38
Norland, Stephen, 228, 236
Nye, F. Ivan, 163–164, 169–171, 178, 228, 236, 251, 254

Oates, Joyce C., 116, 129
O'Connor, Gerald G., 191, 197
Offord, D. R., 106, 129
Ohlin, Lloyd E., 102, 109–120, 127–128, 193, 197, 207, 258–259, 264, 266
Olexa, Carol, 130
Orcutt, James D., 159–160, 178

Palmer, Ted, 59, 63, 68
Park, Robert, 75, 97–98
Parsons, Talcott, 54–55, 68, 128, 130, 241, 244, 254
Perrow, Charles, 197
Petersen, David M., 70, 79–80, 98–99
Pfeiffer, Carl C., 27, 36
Phillips, John C., 174, 178
Philpott, William H., 27, 38
Piliavin, Irving, 147–148, 150, 210, 216
Platt, Anthony, 167, 178, 208–209, 216
Polk, Kenneth, 106–107, 130
Pollak, Otto, 218, 221–224, 226, 234, 236
Postman, Neil, 259, 269
Poushinsky, Mary F., 129

Quetelet, Adolphe, 70
Quicker, John C., 115, 130

Quinney, Richard, 138, 150, 200, 203–206, 212, 216, 266

Radosevich, Marcia, 215
Radzinowicz, Leon, 5–6, 12, 140, 151, 213
Rahav, Giora, 174, 178
Rankin, Joseph H., 160, 174, 178
Rathus, Spencer A., 63, 68
Reckless, Walter C., 84, 152, 155–160, 175–176, 178–179, 181, 196, 260
Redl, Fritz, 66, 69
Reid, Sue T., 22–23, 38
Reid, William H., 34, 38
Reiss, Albert J., Jr., 142, 151, 210, 213, 224–225, 236
Rhodes, A. Lewis, 142, 151
Richards, Pamela, 228, 236
Richardson, Ken, 43, 69
Rivera, Ramon, 130
Riviere, Joan, 67
Robins, Lee N., 60–62, 69
Robison, Sophia M., 83, 98
Rodman, Hyman, 109, 116, 130
Rojek, Dean G., 106, 108, 118, 129–130, 142–143, 150, 163, 166, 172, 178, 191–193, 196
Roman, Paul M., 185, 198
Rosanoff, Aaron J., 22, 38
Rosanoff, Isabel A., 38
Rosen, Lawrence, 84, 95, 98, 124–125, 130, 168–169, 179
Rosenberg, Raben, 38
Roth, Loren H., 24–27, 29, 38, 234, 236
Rothman, David J., 209, 216

Sagarin, Edward, 46–47, 69, 128, 130, 134, 151, 183, 185, 197
Sanders, Wiley B., 3, 12, 153, 179
Satterfield, James H., 29, 38
Savitz, Leonard, 12, 37, 129, 150, 179, 237, 251, 254
Scarpitti, Frank R., 159–160, 177, 179, 210, 216, 228, 235
Schafer, Walter E., 106–107, 130
Schalling, D., 34, 36–38, 67

Schauss, Alexander, 26, 38
Schlapp, Max G., 26, 38
Schuessler, Karl, 58, 69, 132, 151
Schulsinger, Fini, 38
Schur, Edwin M., 147–148, 151, 186, 197
Schwartz, Michael, 159–160, 179
Schwendinger, Herman, 206–208, 216
Schwendinger, Julia R., 206–208, 216
Sela, Elaine, 268–269
Sellin, Thorsten, 82, 98, 131, 198–199
Selvin, Hanan C., 6–7, 12
Senna, Carl, 43, 69
Senna, Joseph J., 3, 12, 192, 197
Shah, Saleem A., 24–27, 29, 38, 234, 236
Shanley, Fred J., 238, 254
Shaw, Clifford R., 71, 74–83, 85, 89, 91, 97–99, 111, 130, 132, 167, 169, 179, 199
Sheldon, William, 15–17, 38
Shibutani, Tamotsu, 250, 254
Shoemaker, Donald J., 216
Short, James F., Jr., 108, 115–116, 118, 130, 141–142, 146, 151
Shover, Neal, 230, 236
Siddle, David A., 33, 38
Siegel, Larry J., 3, 12, 63, 68, 192, 197
Sieverdes, Christopher M., 210, 216
Silverman, Ira J., 125, 130, 249, 254
Simon, Rita J., 101, 130, 218, 222, 225, 230–231, 236–237
Simon, William, 125, 128
Simpson, George, 97
Simpson, Jon E., 191, 196
Skipper, James K., Jr., 93, 175, 178
Slater, Eliot, 235
Slatin, Gerald T., 106, 129
Slavin, Sidney H., 30, 39
Smart, Carol, 223, 225–226, 231, 237
Smith, Daniel D., 192, 197
Smith, Douglas A., 216, 233, 237
Smith, Edward H., 26, 38
Smith, William Carlson, 82, 99
Snyder, Eloise, C., 191, 197
Snyder, Howard W., 197
Somerville, Dora B., 227, 237
Spaulding, John A., 97

Spears, David, 43, 69
Spergel, Irving, 116–117, 130
Spitzer, Steven, 204–105, 212, 216
Stanfield, Robert E., 141, 151
Stark, Richard, 164–166
Steffensmeier, Darrell J., 101, 130, 230–231, 237
Steffensmeier, Renee H., 101, 130, 230–231, 237
Stephenson, Richard M., 210, 216, 235
Strachey, James, 67, 235
Strauss, Anselm L., 8, 11
Street, David, 191, 197
Strodtbeck, Fred L., 108, 118, 130, 146, 151
Stryker, Sheldon, 160, 179
Sullivan, Clyde, 59, 69
Sullivan, Kathryn, 129
Sutherland, Edwin H., 23, 39, 45, 57, 59, 69–70, 79, 82–85, 99, 110, 130, 132–133, 135–137, 139–141, 148, 151, 155, 189, 199, 218, 237, 251, 254, 259
Sykes, Gresham M., 145, 150–151, 216, 259
Sykes, Richard E., 201, 215

Tangri, Sandra S., 159, 179
Tannenbaum, Frank, 180–181, 187, 197
Tanner, Julian, 249, 254
Taylor, Ian, 88, 99, 206, 216
Tennyson, Ray A., 130
Terman, Theodore S., 43
Thomas, Charles, 210, 216
Thomas, William I., 74, 99, 218, 220–221, 224–225
Thornberry, Terence P., 210, 216
Thornton, William E., Jr., 194, 197, 229, 232, 236–237
Thorsell, Bernard A., 185, 197
Thrasher, Frederick M., 105, 108, 111, 131, 180–181, 187, 197
Timasheff, Nicholas S., 8, 12
Tittle, Charles R., 216
Toby, Jackson, 152, 179, 227, 237
Traub, Stuart H., 215

Trice, Harrison M., 185, 198
Tulchin, Simon H., 45, 69
Turk, Austin T., 200, 217
Turner, Stanley H., 95, 98

Vaz, Edmund W., 101, 129, 131, 237, 239, 252-254
Vedder, Clyde B., 227, 237
Villemez, Wayne J., 216
Vinter, Robert D., 197, 234
Vold, George, 4, 12, 17, 22, 39, 45, 63-64, 69, 199, 217
Voluvka, Jan, 38
von Hentig, Hans, 14, 39
Voss, Harwin L., 69-70, 79-80, 98-99, 106-107, 115, 128, 142, 151, 160, 179, 190

Waldo, Gordon, 54, 58, 62-63, 69
Walton, Paul, 99, 215-216
Ward, David A., 67
Ware, M. Ellis, 27, 39
Warner, Jerry T., 211, 217
Warren, Marquerite Q., 59, 69
Wasserman, Michael, 210, 215
Weiner, Norman L., 210, 217
Weis, Joseph G., 142, 151, 196, 213, 228, 237
Wells, L. Edward, 161, 179
Wenninger, Eugene P., 253

Werthman, Carl, 187, 198
Whimbey, Arthur, 43, 69
Whimbey, Linda S., 43, 69
White, Mervin, 165-166, 177
Whyte, William F., 111, 131
Wilkinson, Karen, 153, 167, 179
Wilks, Judith A., 80, 99
Williams, Jay R., 193, 198
Willie, Charles V., 210, 217
Wineman, David, 66, 69
Wise, Nancy B., 228, 237
Wolfgang, Marvin E., 118, 123, 131, 150, 192, 198
Wooden, Kenneth, 5, 12
Wunderlich, Roy C., 27, 39
Wuthnow, Robert, 178

Yablonsky, Lewis, 60, 69, 108, 131, 168, 172, 177
Yaryura-Tobias, Jose A., 27, 39
Young, Jock, 99, 215-216
Young, Pauline V., 82, 99

Zaremba, Barbara A., 37
Zeleny, L. D., 44-45, 69
Zetterberg, Hans L., 8, 12
Znaniecki, Florian, 74
Zola, Irving K., 151
Zorbaugh, Frederick M., 99
Zuckerman, Harriet, 91, 97

SUBJECT INDEX

Anomie, 71–72, 86–96, 132, 174, 250, 257, 265–267
  adaptations to, 89–90
Atavists (born criminality), 15–16, 219
Autonomic nervous system (ANS), 32–35

Biochemical imbalances (see also diet and delinquency), 25–28
Biological (biosocial) explanations, 13–14, 149, 219, 221–222, 224, 227, 233–234, 255–256, 267
Bodytype (somatotype), 14–20
Bourgeoisie, 201, 203, 207

Capitalism (capitalists), 200–201, 203–206, 208–209, 213
Cartographic school, 70
Castration complex (penis envy), 220–222
Causality, issue of, 6
Chicago Area Projects, 80–81, 85
Childhood, concept of, 209, 259
Child-Saving Movement, 167, 209
Chromosomal configuration (xyy), 25
Class conflict, 201–202
Classical school of criminology, 4

Concordance rates, 20–22, 24, 46
Conflict theory (perspective), 186, 199–200, 263–264
Containment theory, 152, 155–161, 176, 181, 260
Control theory (see also social control theory), 149, 152–155, 175–176, 239, 260
Core personality, 56, 61–62
Crimes
  of accommodation and resistance, 201–204, 263
  of control, 203
  of domination and repression, 203–204
  of economic domination, 204
Cultural factors, 81–83
Cultural transmission, 83–85
Culture of poverty, 122

Deferred gratification, 244
Delinquency and
  academic performance (school performance), 7, 14, 29–30, 93–94, 102, 106–107, 127, 173, 265
  broken homes, 6–7, 167–173, 177, 227, 252
  capitalism, 206–209

conditionability (see also ANS), 25, 31–35
diet, 26–28
differential opportunity structures, 102, 109–119, 258–259
drift, 133, 143–149, 259–260, 267
family factors (relationships), 7, 14, 47, 128, 142, 152–155, 160, 163–164, 167–168, 170–175, 177, 207, 227, 232, 234, 244, 251–252, 260
feeblemindedness, 21, 44, 45
growth (concentric) zones (of a city), 74–80, 91
inheritance (see also family tree studies and twins studies), 14, 20–25
intelligence (general), 42–49, 128, 172, 265
learning disabilities, 25, 28–31, 172, 265
lower-class culture (values), 102, 119–126, 174, 258
middle-class measuring rod, 6, 102–109, 126, 172, 258
organized crime, 82, 112, 117
religion, 153–154, 163–167, 175, 260
school system (factors), 102–107, 115–116, 127, 152–155, 172–173, 175, 207–208, 232, 244, 252, 260
self-concept (image), 84, 152, 154–161, 176, 181, 186–191, 260, 262, 265
sex roles, 219, 221–222, 224–225, 227, 229–231, 233, 244–245
Delinquency, type of,
female, 11, 22, 101, 218–234, 250–251, 268
gang (also subculture), 52, 100, 105, 107–122, 146–147, 180, 187, 200, 226
conflict (violent), 108, 110–114, 116–117
criminal, 110–114, 116–117
racket, 117
retreatist (drug), 110–114, 116–117, 127–128
theft, 117–118
latent, 52
lower-class, 100–128, 180, 187, 201, 203–204, 206, 221, 223–224, 238, 245–246, 249, 251–252, 258
manifest, 52
middle-class, 11, 122, 128, 180, 184, 187, 206, 208, 212, 223, 226, 238–253, 268
Delinquency areas, 74–85
Demonology, 4
Differential
association (see also peer group associations), 84, 132, 134–143, 155, 160, 171, 174, 259–260, 267
identification, 138
social organization, 135
Division of labor, 87–88
Dramatization of evil, 180

Ecological approach (studies), 73–80, 91, 94–95, 132
Empirical/inductive method, 9, 211

Family tree studies, 21, 44
Jukes, the, 21
Kallikaks, the, 44
Female
emancipation (women's movement)
emancipation (women's movement), 219, 225–227, 230–231, 233–234
dominated households, 123–125
personality, 220
Femininity (female behavior), 223–224, 226, 230–231, 233
Focal concerns (lower-class), 119–122, 258
Four wishes, the, 221

Interest groups, 263
Interpersonal maturity (I-level), 59–61, 63–64

Juvenile court (justice system), 5, 140, 143, 145–147, 166, 169, 172, 181, 186–194, 200, 208–212, 223, 228, 262–263, 266

Labeling (theory/perspective), 11, 180–195, 261–262, 264, 267
Learning theory, 138–139
Lower-class value diffusion, 239, 245–246, 250
Lumpenproletarians, 202

Marginal youth, 247–248
Marxist (Marxian) theory (see also neo-Marxism), 200–201, 204, 206, 264
Masculine anxiety (identity), 120, 125, 239, 244–245, 249–250
Masculinity (masculine behavior), 223–224, 226, 229, 233
  complex, 220
  hypothesis, 229–230
Michigan Child Guidance Institute, 52
Minnesota Multiphasic Personality Inventory (MMPI), 58, 63
Mobilization for Youth Program, 118
Moral insanity (see also psychopathy), 40

Near group, 108
Neighborhood integration, 109–114, 116, 119
Neo-Marxism, 186, 203, 210–211, 262
Neutralization (techniques of), 144–147, 174, 260
New Jersey School for the Feeble-Minded, 44

One-sex peer unit, 120–122
Opportunity structure, 87, 89–90, 232

Peer group (associations), 14, 142–143, 145–146, 160–161, 174, 207, 223–225, 232, 234, 252, 259, 261, 267
Personality
  and bodytype, 16–18
  characteristics, 31–34, 55–64
  Type I, 53
  Type II, 53
  Type III, 53
Petty bourgeoisie, 205
Positive school of criminology, 5–6
Primary deviance, 180–181, 183
Proletariat, 201, 203
Psychoanalytic (psychiatric) approach, 5, 10, 49–55, 65, 149, 152, 155, 167, 260
Psychoanalysis (psychoanalytic) concepts
  id, 50, 53–54, 155
  ego, 50, 54
  Oedipus Complex (oedipal conflict), 51–52
  superego, 50, 52–54, 155, 260
  unconscious, 50, 52–54
Psychological theories (see also intelligence, personality, and psychoanalysis), 41–42, 65, 219, 221–222, 224, 227, 233, 255–256, 267
Psychopathic deviation (Pd), 58, 63
Psychopathy (also sociopathy), 31–32, 59–62, 183

Radical theory (perspective), 186, 199–213, 263–264
Reaction formation, 102, 104
Reference groups, 138
Relative deprivation, 92–93
Rorschach tests, 53, 62

Secondary deviance, 180–181, 183
Self-fulfilling prophecy, 193
Significant others, 148–149, 159–160

Situation of company, 146
Social bond (see also social control
    theory), 84, 161
  attachment, 161–162, 171–174, 176,
      260–261, 265–266
  belief, 161–162, 176
  commitment, 171–172, 174–176,
      259–262, 266
  involvement, 161–162
Social class, 14, 47, 103, 106, 123,
      126–127, 149, 167–168, 171, 181,
      186, 189–190, 203, 206–213, 223,
      243, 245, 253, 258, 263, 265–266
Social control theory, 148–149, 152–
      154, 162–163, 171–176, 183, 232,
      251, 253, 260–261, 264–267
Social disorganization, 70–86, 94–96,
      132, 167, 251, 257–258, 265, 267
Social mobility (status inconsistency),
      239, 246–248, 250–252
Social surround, 92

Solidarity
  mechanical, 87
  organic, 88
Spurious relationship, 7
Subculture of violence, 123
Subterranean value systems, 145, 239
Surplus labor, 202, 204

Theory, 8
  verification of, 9, 10
Twins studies, 21–25, 46

Wayward girl syndrome (unadjusted
    girl), 221, 224–225, 227–229

Youth culture (subculture), 239–244,
    248–249, 252